Personal
KABBALAH

2 Paths to Inner Peace and Life Purpose

Penny Cohen, LCSW

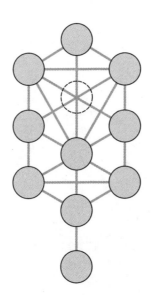

Credits

Lightning flash (page 16), Cordovero Tree of Life with Hebrew letters (page 25), Cordovero Tree of Life with patriarchs (page 29), Cordovero Tree of Life showing the functions of the psyche (page 30), and Cordovero Tree of Life showing the functions of the body (page 31) from *Adam and the Kabbalistic Tree*, by Z'ev ben Shimon Halevi, © 1974 by Z'ev ben Shimon Halevi. Used by permission of Red Wheel/Weiser.

Tzimtzum (page 13), Cordovero Tree of Life with Divine names (page 26), and Cordovero Tree of Life with archangels (page 28) from *A Kabbalistic Universe*, by Z'ev ben Shimon Halevi, © 1977 by Warren Kenton. Used by permission of Red Wheel/Weiser.

Lurianic Tree of Life with Divine names (page 26) adapted from *Meditation and Kabbalah*, by Aryeh Kaplan, © 1982 by Aryeh Kaplan. Used by permission of Red Wheel/Weiser.

Lurianic Tree of Life with Hebrew letters (page 24) adapted from *Sefer Yetzirah: The book of Creation*, by Aryeh Kaplan, © 1997 by The Estate of Aryeh Kaplan. Used by permission of Red Wheel/Weiser.

Tetragrammaton (page 19), *Sefirot* symbollically pertaining to the body (page 19), Overall Tree of Life showing the correspondences with the four worlds (page 32), and Jacob's Ladder: the interlocking of the four worlds (page 33), from *Kabbalah: Tradition of Hidden Knowledge*, by Z'ev ben Shimon Halevi, © 1979 by Warren Kenton. Used by permission of Thames and Hudson.

Illustrations by Robert Steimle

Library of Congress Cataloging-in-Publication Data

Cohen, Penny, LCSW.
  Personal kabbalah : 32 paths to inner peace and life purpose / Penny Cohen.
     p. cm.
  Includes index.
  ISBN 0-8069-5898-7
  1. Cabala--History. 2. Sefirot (Cabala) 3. Hebrew language--Alphabet--Religious aspects--Judaism. I. Title.

BM526.C63 2005
296.1'6--dc22

2005003792

10 9 8 7 6 5 4 3 2 1

Published by Sterling Publishing Co., Inc.
387 Park Avenue South, New York, NY 10016
© 2005 by Penny Cohen
Distributed in Canada by Sterling Publishing
c/o Canadian Manda Group, 165 Dufferin Street
Toronto, Ontario, Canada M6K 3H6
Distributed in Great Britain by Chrysalis Books Group PLC
The Chrysalis Building, Bramley Road, London W10 6SP, England
Distributed in Australia by Capricorn Link (Australia) Pty. Ltd.
P.O. Box 704, Windsor, NSW 2756, Australia

Printed in China

Sterling ISBN: 0-8069-5898-7

For information about custom editions, special sales, premium and corporate purchases, please contact Sterling Special Sales Department at 800-805-5489 or specialsales@sterlingpub.com.

THIS BOOK IS DEDICATED, WITH LOVE,

To my mother and father,
Mollie and Sam Lotto,
Who gave me life and love;
To my children,
David and Jessica,
Who gave me a reason to live and love;
To my husband,
Karl,
Who gives me the love and support to be who I am;
To God,
The source of my blessings.

Acknowledgments

This book was not written alone. I had the help of many people to whom I am forever grateful. First and foremost, the late Sheila Barry, who whispered in my ear, "Write me a proposal for a book on Kabbalah."

Hannah Reich, my editor at Sterling, challenged me every step of the way. Your questions, patience, and encouragement were an inspiration.

My thanks to psychologist Edward Hoffman, Ph.D., author of *The Kabbalah Deck, The Heavenly Ladder,* and many other books on Kabbalah and psychology, for his kabbalistic and psychological expertise and advice. Thanks also to Rabbi Israel Daren, for the debates, discussions, and classes on Kabbalah and Hasidism.

Many people gave me additional advice: Marcy Bernstein, Roberta Duban, Judy Henderson, Alma Rutgers, Dick Silverman, Claudette Stark, Rona Weinstein, Hans Wilhelm. Thank you so much for the time and effort you put into reading the manuscript. And an additional thanks to Paul Robinson for the overall support, time, and effort put into gathering and designing diagrams and charts for me.

There are also the people in the five-plus years of the "Kakkabaly" Kabbalah Study Group, who constantly challenged and continue to challenge me to explain abstract concepts more concretely. I learned so much from you.

I am indeed blessed with an incredible support group: my family, friends, children, and extended family: David, Meryl, Jessica, Paul, Steven, Susan, Lisa, and their offspring—the greatest gifts of my life and the people who assigned me the time for rest, relaxation, love, and joy—my grandchildren Jack, Alex, Melissa, Aliya, Zachary, Caleigh, and Cade. Thank you for being the light and love in my life.

And, of course, my heartfelt love and thanks to my husband, Karl, whose unending patience, support, and love empowered me with the time, effort, and courage to write this book.

Contents

ONE

How I Became Involved
in Kabbalah

Kabbalah is the mystical tradition that underlies the Judeo-Greco-Christian philosophies of the West and parallels those of the East. It is the gateway to understanding the mysteries of God and the universe, life and death, reincarnation, love, destiny, and service and their interrelationships.

As a practice, Kabbalah can be studied from two perspectives: the "Work of Creation" and the "Work of the Chariot." The Work of Creation involves the macro-structure—pondering creation and the beginning of time; the structure, function, and dynamics of the universe; space and time; the elements and their effects on humankind.

The Work of the Chariot, or the personal path, on the other hand, explores the micro-structure—our individual relationship to the Divine and our own purpose for being on earth. It provides the basis for happiness and fulfillment by guiding us to find meaning and purpose in life. We get answers to the questions: *Who am I? Why am I here? What is my purpose? How can I fulfill it?* This book is based on the Work of the Chariot, or the personal path of Kabbalah.

The personal path of Kabbalah teaches us how to communicate directly and personally with the Divine and embrace its essence. In doing so we align with the passions of the soul, access our true nature—our source of unconditional internal love and creativity—uncover and live our purpose, reach a state of peace and harmony within ourselves, and help facilitate peace and harmony in the world.

The personal path of Kabbalah is a way to enter into a state of mind of knowing and expressing ourselves openly and completely, understanding our relationship to the Divine, recognizing signs of guidance, and following those signs to reach our highest potential and make a difference in the world. Following the personal path of Kabbalah is enlightenment in action.

It is taught that when we embrace the Divine, we connect to the sacred powers of the universe, the "flow," in life. By directing these powers, we partner with the Divine. We begin to attract what we want, and life becomes easier and more joyful. The end result is the mystical experience of being in communion with the Divine on an ongoing basis and living in the "flow"—the current of Divine energies that are filled with revelation, inspiration, wisdom, and awe. With this partnership it is easier to reach our highest potential in all areas of our lives, including personal fitness, family and interpersonal relationships, career, and spiritual fulfillment. We experience peace, love, joy, and harmony within ourselves and live in a way that brings these same attributes to others and the world. It's constantly being open to Divine light and love and living in the flow of life where we feel divinely guided, supported, and blessed.

Perhaps the best way to describe this sense of being divinely guided and in the flow is to explain how I was guided to study and teach Kabbalah and write this book.

It began more than twenty years ago while I was going through a divorce. I was an atheist at the time; then I had a mystical experience (described in detail in Chapter Twelve) that changed my life. It was similar to a near-death experience. I was surrounded by light and a love that was indescribable. During this experience also came an insight and inspiration: I would write at least two books and do research. On what, I had no idea.

For more than twenty years I've been trying to figure out this mystical experience—what happened to me, how it happened, what it meant, and how to maintain that state of love and find my purpose. Since it happened spontaneously, I also kept asking if there was a specific key or systematic approach to spiritual awareness and enlightenment so that I could reach this state intentionally, step by step.

To get answers I reviewed my journal, my dreams leading up to the mystical experience, and what was happening to me. I delved into Transactional Analysis, communication and relationship workshops, and then parapsychology, Hinduism, Buddhism, Shamanism. Kabbalah came last, and it came by accident. Looking for something to do one Friday evening with friends, I came across a brochure from Wainwright House (a New Age institute in Rye, New York) describing a workshop on Kabbalah. Since none of us knew anything about it, we decided to attend. As I walked into the room, I spotted the diagrams of the Tree of Life and Jacob's Ladder hanging on the wall. My body immediately started to tingle. I was mystified. As the instructor began to explain the symbols in these diagrams, I realized that everything I had learned in the other traditions fit into these paradigms. Awed, I wanted to learn more. At the end of the evening, they announced a six-day workshop the following week. I just "happened" to be on vacation with no plans that week, so I registered for it.

During the week there were many discussions of oneness, cause and effect, life, death, reincarnation, the soul's journey, and mystical experiences. Many of my questions were resolved. The answer to the final question on the systematic approach to enlightenment came to me during one of the long meditations. It was a vision of the kabbalistic Tree of Life with a key opening the gate into the middle point (*sefirah*) of the diagram.

At the end of the week I bought several books on Kabbalah, hoping to study and learn more about the Tree of Life and how to uncover my purpose. I began meditating regularly and praying to find my purpose.

The following week, while teaching the second week of a twelve-week course on creativity at a local senior center, I mentioned to the participants that I had just taken a workshop on Kabbalah. They tried convincing me to teach it next. I laughed, telling them that kabbalists were traditionally male, over forty years old, married, and steeped in the study of Torah (the Five Books of Moses). By the end of the creativity course three months later, however, the participants were still urging me to teach Kabbalah. I acquiesced—with qualifications. I explained that I was not an authority on Kabbalah, but I'd be happy to facilitate a study group with the understanding that I was a student along with them and we would learn together. If any questions came up, we would all do the research to try to get answers. I facilitated this group for three years.

Then skimming through the newspaper one day, I noticed an advertisement for a weekend conference on Kabbalah and Jewish mysticism. While waiting to register, I ended up talking to the rabbi who had arranged the conference. I mentioned that I'd gotten into Kabbalah through the back door, first having a mystical experience and then trying to understand it. I explained that I understood the spiritual aspects and how to use the Tree of Life for a systematic approach to enlightenment, but I wasn't very knowledgeable in traditional Jewish practice. She told me that she had the traditional knowledge, and we ended up teaching a class together for twenty-four weeks. A group of people from this class who wanted to continue studying convinced me to facilitate an ongoing group in my home. Again, I was driven to go deeper and began studying with Orthodox rabbis as well as other secular Kabbalah teachers to understand it from different perspectives. I continued praying, pleading to be shown my purpose.

Although Kabbalah was a relatively new subject for me as a teacher, I had been leading workshops for more than ten years in many different areas, including relationships, communication, stress management, creativity, and the sixth sense. I decided it was time to specialize. So in 1995 I offered workshops and lectures in all my areas of expertise and resolved that the one that drew the most people would be my specialty.

Kabbalah won, with more than a hundred people attending a lecture. I began teaching workshops and study groups on Kabbalah and the Tree of Life at local colleges, synagogues, and a variety of organizations and alternative health groups.

Participants began asking to work with me privately. I was forty-eight years old and had no "official" credentials, not even a college degree! So I returned to school for both my bachelor's and master's degrees. Four years following graduation and after receiving a license in social work, I opened a private psychotherapy practice and—at national conferences, in front of professional groups, and for organizations—I began offering workshops integrating spirituality and psychotherapy.

Many people who came to me for individual therapy did so after attending a workshop. Some had mystical experiences and wanted to understand them better. Others just wanted to delve more deeply into their spiritual roots, to understand their relationship to the Divine and find their purpose. Still others wanted to work on developing more confidence and self-esteem or more fulfilling relationships. I was already using prayer and meditation techniques in my clinical work with individuals, and I began including the psychological and practical steps on the Tree of Life. This helped people see where they were, determine where they wanted to be, and understand the steps they needed to take.

In order to find purpose, they had to work through physical addictions and personality issues (such as doubt, fear, anxiety, regret, resentment, hurt, and vengeance), unleash their intellectual and creative passions, and discover ways to fulfill them. This involved both internal and external processes, including ways to meditate and pray effectively, as well as practical means to change their ways of processing thoughts, feelings, speech, and behavior.

These techniques open us so we perceive things from a different perspective, a higher level of consciousness—from truth rather than the unconscious illusions we carry from our past (commonly known as conditioning). When we are in truth, we feel spiritually guided. Feeling spiritual guidance makes it possible to deal with painful experiences differently and learn from them.

My clients used these techniques and began reporting that they felt better, they had more energy, their relationships were more satisfying, and they'd begun to identify their passion. Working on their purpose, they reported being grounded, focused, directed, spiritually guided, and much more joyful.

While I expanded my practice, I also attended a spiritual book club that met weekly. Every so often I'd share how a concept could be interpreted kabbalistically and applied in daily life. As several of us left the meeting together one week, I was approached and asked to write a proposal for a book on Kabbalah. I wrote a sixty-page outline—for this book! This is how I was guided to Kabbalah, teaching, and writing this book—or, more accurately, how Kabbalah and this book proposal came to me.

When I reflect on the progression of events, I realize that none of it was an accident. The meditating and praying I began doing was my way of communicating with God. And God answered me through a progression of dreams and by opening paths and opportunities in all parts of my life.

Kabbalah has afforded me tremendous growth personally and professionally. Spiritual guidance and support have helped me deal with the pain and loss of divorce without anger or vindictiveness, and have even led to forgiveness.

Studying Kabbalah has given me the courage and faith to express my true self, take risks, and move into areas I would never have dared otherwise. I've truly become a different person—a person who lives with faith and passion, a person who feels totally guided and blessed, a person who loves life and the people in it. By transforming my life, my views, and my perception of reality, Kabbalah has changed the world I live in. It is different because I am different. I pray that as I recognize and embody my purpose in life, this work gives meaning, joy, and blessing to others in theirs.

· TWO ·

Origin of the Tree of Life
and Jacob's Ladder

———◆———

Kabbalah is the mystical interpretation of the Torah (Five Books of Moses), detailed in the *Sefer Yetzirah* (the Book of Creation), the *Bahir* (the Book of Brilliance), and the *Zohar* (the Book of Splendor), the most widely followed text of the Kabbalah as we know it today. To kabbalists the stories in the Torah are seen as metaphors for varying levels of consciousness and different measures of vibration and light. For example, the expeditions of Abraham, Jacob, and Moses through the lands of Canaan and Egypt are metaphors for the journeys of the soul. References to the ocean and the sea are interpreted as symbolic representations of flows of light and energy.

The word *Kabbalah* means "to receive" or "that which is constantly being received." What is being received? The flow of energy in the universe—of waves, particles, photons, sounds, and vibrations—all in different frequencies, levels, and proportions. Along with this energy are impulses, insights, or impressions in thoughts, images, feelings, prophecies, and revelations. The ultimate reception is Divine illumination: the experience of being in communion with all that is, the Absolute, the Creator, receiving the "Way of God," and unleashing the passions of the soul.

These experiences of communing with the Divine are often referred to as mystical or peak experiences. They unfold from the inside out and emerge as different levels of inspiration, revelation, awe, and grace. The patriarchs of the Bible had many peak experiences that involved prophecy and revelation.

The dream of Jacob's Ladder represents such a peak experience and is thought to have influenced the main concepts of Kabbalah.

In the Bible, Jacob lied to his father, accepting a birthright in his brother Esau's place. Jacob's mother, fearing Esau's anger toward her favorite son, sent Jacob to another land to find a wife from her brother Laban's family. Alone in the desert one night while lying on a rock, Jacob fell asleep and had a dream. It was of a ladder with steps reaching up to heaven.

Angels were ascending and descending the steps. Jacob heard God speaking to him, promising to take care of him and bring him home. Upon awakening, Jacob said, "Surely God is in this place—and this is the gate of heaven." This ladder is considered the ladder of existence by kabbalists.

Through deep study and contemplation of the Torah (the Five Books of Moses), astrology, dreams, and revelations, kabbalists discovered a pattern to existence. Using the number of times certain words were repeated in the Bible, and the numbers that appeared in it, kabbalists developed formulas, qualities, and essences expressing the makeup of the universe and man's relationship to the Divine. Kabbalists discerned patterns in everything: patterns of energy that are stronger at various times of the year than others (such as on specific holidays and the Sabbath); patterns of energy that correspond to the shape, sound, and meaning of the letters of the Hebrew alphabet and to vibrations in the universe; patterns of energy coming from the zodiac, planets, stars, and universe that affect nature and humankind; patterns of energy that correlate with the patriarchs of the Bible and represent different stages of humanity's inner life; patterns of energy in humans and different aspects of human nature; patterns of energy that correspond to the human body, emotions, and the nature of the soul. These patterns of energy are all depicted in the paradigm known as the Tree of Life.

The Tree of Life is a ladder or map of existence. It shows the functions, structure, and dynamics of the universe. It also shows the evolution of human consciousness.

On a personal level the Tree of Life not only shows us where we are in our level of existence, but also offers ways of overcoming obstacles by bringing the unconscious to consciousness, opening to higher states of awareness, connecting with different levels of energy in the universe, and harnessing and directing them to achieve enlightenment and fulfillment. In more traditional terms this might be explained as ascending to heaven, cleaving to the Divine, bringing heaven down to earth, and living divinely.

Contemporary kabbalists teach that when we open to these universal energies and harness and direct or channel them in our daily lives, we begin to live life in the flow. We begin to experience inner peace, joy, and the passion to fulfill our Divine purpose.

Kabbalah can be studied from a Jewish perspective, from a Western esoteric and Christian perspective, or from an eclectic, universal perspective. The traditional Jewish perspective focuses on the hidden mystical teachings derived from the Torah (the Five Books of Moses), the *Sefer Yetzirah* (the Book of Creation), the *Bahir* (the Book of Brilliance), and the *Zohar* (the Book of Splendor). The Jewish approach to Kabbalah involves following philosophical, moral, and ethical laws of the Torah as well as rituals that are based on the cycles of Jewish festivals and major life milestones. For Orthodox Jews, it involves following the 613 *mitzvot* (literally "commandments," but loosely translated to mean good deeds). Praying, dancing, singing, and meditating are also used.

Western and Christian kabbalists concentrate more on the ecstatic experiences drawn through prayer and meditation. These are geared to our personal connection with the Divine. An eclectic, universal perspective combines a variety of traditional techniques as well as those borrowed from other spiritual traditions and psychological practices that fit into the Tree of Life.

This workbook is written from an eclectic, universal perspective, and its approach can be used by people of all faiths. The meditations, psychological exercises, and practical steps foster the ability to open to, apply, and integrate the sacred into daily living and experience the miraculous in the seemingly mundane.

The history and various schools of Kabbalah, for those interested in learning more, are discussed in the Appendix.

The study of Kabbalah is divided into three basic areas: wisdom, devotion, and action—the theoretical, meditative, and practical approaches. The theoretical involves studying the Torah to understand the Tree of Life, the *sefirotic* system and the paths, and the way they all relate to us personally. The meditative provides a systematic progression of meditations, prayers, and psychological exercises with which we can open to higher energies, effect changes in our bodies and our lives, and gain wisdom. As for the practical, studying and performing *mitzvot* play a major role—it's living divinely. Here, too, we can follow a progression of steps on the Tree of Life.

BASIC PRINCIPLES AND SYMBOLS OF THE TREE OF LIFE

This chapter contains many Hebrew names, words, and concepts and may feel a bit technical or overwhelming. If that happens, you may wish to skim over it lightly to get an idea of the principles and symbols without trying to memorize them. As you read on or reread the material, you will begin to grasp the ideas quite painlessly and find yourself absorbing it easily.

ALL IS ONE

"Shema Israel Adonai Eloheinu, Adonai Echad." "Hear, O Israel, the Lord our God, the Lord is One."

It is often said that God is in this world but not of it, and that God is both immanent and transcendent. God fills creation and at the same time is separate from it. God without end is known as *Ein Sof*—endless, infinite, everything. At the same time God, the transcendent, is "no-thing," *ein*—beyond existence as well as within. Since God is everything, then everything comes from the One. Therefore, the absolute *Ein Sof* is present in everything. The spark of light that is present in everything is called the *Ein Sof Or:* the endless light or Divine energy.

This concept might be likened to a lit candle radiating a strong, bright flame. This flame then lights other candles. The light and flame from the first candle remain just as full and glowing as they were before igniting the next candles. If the wicks of these candles are shorter or longer, the flames may be of different sizes even though their essence and makeup are the same. Nevertheless, part of the first candle flame is still burning in all the others, and all the other flames come from and are part of the first. Furthermore, the first flame, like the other flames, is still whole in itself.

In humankind a spark of the endless light, the *Ein Sof Or*, burns within all of us, making us all one—all connected. Yet we are also unique unto ourselves. Kabbalists believe everything is made up of light and energy, all condensed in different sizes and packages. This includes inanimate objects, such as rocks and wood. At the same time everything has a different concentration, shape, and vibration of energy, making it unique.

To better understand this, picture yourself as you are now. If you were to take a microscopic look beneath your skin, you would find parts of yourselves that are very old life-forms, such as the chemical components of amino acids that make up the DNA and RNA shared by all life-forms on earth. These atoms—broken down into quarks, particles, and waves—go back to a time before the earth, sun, moon, and stars were created. They were part of a gaseous cloud made up of heat and energy that contracted so much, it became the solar furnace that exploded in the Big Bang and created the cosmos. These particles, generated at the beginning of time, come from the ecosystem of the earth. We are as old as creation—in existence since the beginning of time. We have lived more than fifteen billion years.

CAUSE AND EFFECT

To take the concept "all is one" a step farther, kabbalists believe that whatever happens anywhere affects the whole. And, in turn, the whole has an impact on all its parts.

A candle flame glows from an internal wick. The wick at the center gives off light and heat to the surrounding environment. A candle that is larger than others around it may melt one of them. If one candle flame goes out, it affects the light and heat in the environment. Similarly, according to Kabbalah, every thought, feeling, word, or deed has an impact on our own bodies as well as on the universe. If you change your thoughts, feelings, or actions, it will affect everyone and everything else, in both the material and the spiritual worlds.

The Kabbalah often uses the expression "As above, so below; as below, so above." What we do on earth affects the spiritual worlds, just as the worlds above affect us here on earth. What we think, feel, and do has an effect on universal energies and the heavens—and the reverse is true as well. Taking this even farther, what we do in one life will have an impact on another, as in the concept of Karma.

Watch what happens when we throw a pebble into a pond. We can see the ripples of water expanding into ever-larger circles. If we were to watch for an indefinite length of time, eventually we would see a wave forming and coming back to us. This is the same pattern found in all things. What we put out comes back to us. Energy doesn't die. It just changes form.

In Kabbalah reward and punishment are the consequences of our thoughts, speech, and actions; they are cause and effect.

THE CREATION STORY

> Ten *sefirot* out of Nothingness.
>
> ten and not nine,
>
> ten and not eleven
>
> Understand with Wisdom
>
> Be wise with Understanding.
>
> Examine them
>
> And probe from them
>
> Make [each] thing stand on its essence
>
> And make the Creator sit on His base.
>
> —*Sefer Yetzirah* 1:4

God is the artist and designer of creation. Everything was formed by Him—the Hebrew letters, the *sefirot* or vessels to contain his light and energy, the elements fire, air, water, and earth, the planets, stars, and constellations, and all creatures, including archangels, angels, demons, souls, animals, and humans, all of which are represented on the Tree of Life. As mentioned earlier, the stories of the patriarchs are interpreted as different levels of consciousness. In the same way, Creation stories are described in metaphor. The sea, for example, is symbolic of the oneness of light and energy. From this, water—or sparks of light or energy—separate from the sea.

The sea is the source of oneness in *Keter* that flows into *Chokhmah* and is called a "stream sprouting wisdom." The spring flows into another vessel that is called *Binah*, understanding. Here the sea separates into vessels filled from the source. These vessels take their names from Chronicles 29:11: "Thine, O Lord, is the greatness, and the power, and the glory, and the victory, and the majesty; for all that is in the heaven and in the earth is Thine; Thine is the Kingdom, O Lord, and Thou art exalted as head above all."

Prior to creation, God had an image of humankind in mind—an archetypal blueprint. This image is known as primordial man, *Adam Kadmon*, which is in the form of ten *sefirot*, points of light. Think of the concept of "primordial man" as the template for the creation of humankind, rather than an actual human being. *Adam Kadmon* does not refer to Adam of the biblical account of Adam and Eve.

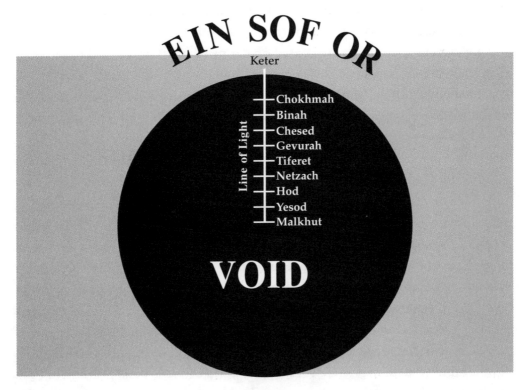

Tzimtzum

TZIMTZUM

The *Ein Sof Or*, the endless light, the Absolute Everything, was all there before Creation. In the sixteenth century Rabbi Isaac Luria stated that when God willed to behold God, a vacuum or void needed to be created. After God provided this vacated space (which some people say is a black hole), a beam of light penetrated the space. This took place over millennia, perhaps even beyond time, during a series of trial-and-error expansions and contractions, before the current world manifested. Prior to the world as we know it, God created several other worlds and destroyed them because they were either too imbued with light and too forceful—and therefore could not be tolerated by humans—or too dark, restricted, and rigid. The world as we know it was created through a lightning flash of expansions and constrictions.

The contraction and expansion process is known as the theory of *tzimtzum*. See page 13.

When God willed to see God, he said, "Let there be light." Kabbalists interpret this utterance from God as the first emanation after the contraction or void. It brought about the first separation from the Absolute.

This vacated-space concept is based on the principle that for God to see God, there had to be a separation. When there is all light or all energy, there is no space for reflection. A droplet of water isn't a droplet until it separates from the ocean. To be visible, it must be separated from the whole, which means there must be a space between the two.

In the separation or void, a beam of light revealed God's image in the form of a lightning flash that manifested as the ten points of light known as *sefirot*—sapphires or vessels—represented as circles on the Tree of Life. These each represent different levels of light and energies in the universe, qualities of God, and levels of consciousness in humankind. Some kabbalists see the *sefirot* as powers or vessels; others consider them instruments or tools. This exact replica of *Adam Kadmon*, primordial man, that manifested in God's mind prior to creation did so in spurts of expansions and contractions.

The first expansion brought about the first three points of light. Formed out of the element of fire, these *sefirot* are considered the world of emanation or *Atzilut*—Divine Mind—the realm of spirit. *Atzilut* is the world of eternity and nearness to God.

The following page shows the contractions and expansions. The fourth circle in the first emanation is *Daat*. *Daat* is not considered one of the ten *sefirot*, but it is often included on the Tree of Life as a dotted circle. It represents knowledge.

Supernal Trinity
God said, "Let there be light."

The first expansion brought about the first three points of light. Formed out of the elements of fire, these *sefirot* are considered the world of emanation, or *Atzilut*—Divine Mind, the realm of spirit—the world of eternity and nearness to God.

Keter: Crown, Will
Column of Equilibrium
◯

Binah: Understanding
Column of severity, or form
◯

Chokhmah: Wisdom
Column of mercy, or force
◯

Daat: Knowledge
◌

Law of Sequence
And God said, "Let there be air."

Following the expansion of the Supernal Trinity, or Divine Spirit, there were two more contractions and expansions. The second group is represented by *Chesed* (loving-kindness) on the right, *Gevurah* (strength, judgment, or justice) on the left, and *Tiferet* (beauty) in the center. This triad was formed by the element of air, and is known as the world of creation, the world of *Beriah*.

Gevurah: Strength
Justice or Judgment
◯

Chesed: Love
Loving-Kindness, Mercy, Grace
◯

Tiferet: Beauty
◯

And God said, "Let there be water."

The next contraction and expansion formed the third triad. *Netzach* (victory) is on the right, *Hod* (splendor) on the left, and *Yesod* (foundation) in the middle. These were formed from the element of water and are symbolic of the world of formation, *Yetzirah*.

Hod: Splendor
◯

Netzach: Victory
◯

Yesod: Foundation
◯

And God said, "Let there be earth."

The last contraction is the element of earth and is symbolic of the world of *Asiyah*. It is the world of making—the world as we know it today. It is represented by *Malkhut* (kingship) and is known as the world of action and actualization.

Malkhut: Kingship
◯

The sphere at the top center is the crown that represents the oneness of us all. It is called *Keter*. Divine Wisdom, on the top right, is known as *Chokhmah;* and Divine Understanding, top left, is *Binah*. These three are commonly called the Supernal Trinity, or Divine Spirit, and they are at a level that is generally unknown to us.

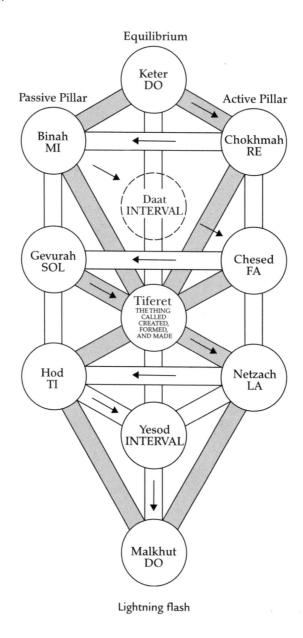

Lightning flash

These three *sefirot* also head up the vertical columns on the Tree of Life: force on the right, form on the left, and equilibrium in the middle. The right column is expansive, the left is restrictive, and the center is balance.

Each *sefirah* (the singular of *sefirot*) in the lightning flash pertains to a different musical note of the octave, a different color, a different Hebrew vowel, a different energy vibration in the universe, and, most important, a different objective quality of God and of humankind. In the diagram on page 16, the arrows show the line of descent (the lightning flash) on the tree equivalent to the octave.

Keter (will) represents do; *Chokhmah* (wisdom) is re; *Binah* (understanding) is mi. *Daat* (knowledge) is considered a non-*sefirah*. It is the chasm or void before creation and is shown on the tree as an interval. *Chesed* (loving-kindness, mercy) is fa; *Gevurah* (judgment) sol. *Tiferet* (beauty) is equilibrium—another interval with no sound. *Netzach* (victory) is la, and *Hod* (splendor) is ti. *Yesod* (foundation) is another interval, and *Malkhut* (kingship) is do.

These sounds are often used in meditation to center and energize the body. The correlations of the *sefirot* to the body are depicted on pages 19 and 20, and the colors pertaining to the *sefirot* are on page 21.

HUMAN MIND AND CREATION

Kabbalists believe that a person's mind works similarly to the creative process, emulating the work of creation. For instance, in class I ask my students to draw their own creative process. One night an artist was amazed at the results. She said when she first decides to do a new painting, she stands in front of the blank canvas. Her mind floods with many thoughts, images, and ideas. "Sometimes it's chaotic," she said. Then she paces back and forth in front of the canvas. An idea comes to her. She ponders it, and a plan evolves. She draws the picture. Then she applies paint in varying amount of colors, shapes, and textures. Ultimately she has a finished product. She added, "It's just like the creation process, like the mind of God. Will—the desire to paint a picture. Emanation—an idea emerges. Creation—a plan percolates. Formation—drawing the picture and painting it. Materialization or actualization—having a finished project. Man's mind works just like that of the creation of the universe." As to her first remark about chaos, many kabbalists compare the process of emanation to chaos.

An architect in the class described a similar process: "I get an idea for a building, develop a plan, draw up the blueprints, and finally the building is built. Emanation, creation, formation, materialization or making."

TETRAGRAMMATON

> Even every one that is called by My Name; for I have created him
> for My Glory, I have formed him: yea, I have made him.
>
> —Isaiah 43:7

The ten *sefirot* were organized in a specific archetypal pattern—the image of God. It is said that when God made himself known to Moses, he spewed forth the four letters of his name: *Yud, heh, vav, heh*. These letters represent the four levels of creation; the four worlds of fire, air, water, and earth in creation; or the four worlds of Divine, spirit, psyche, and physical in humans. Written vertically and depicted as black fire overlaid on white fire, the letters look like a stick figure of a man. It is said that God made man in his image. This image is called the Tetragrammaton. In the diagram on the facing page, the Tetragrammaton is compared to the figure of man seen on the right, which also reveals how the *sefirot* correspond to different parts of the body—in the order of the lightning flash. Here, man is known as *Adam Kadmon*, the Divine, primordial man.

Yud, heh, vav, heh: The top letter in the diagram, which looks like an apostrophe with a little twist at the top, is the Hebrew letter *yud*. It is followed by the *heh* that frames the letter *vav* in the middle. The bottom letter is another *heh*.

In the Lurianic tradition the Tetragrammaton is broken down so the top of the *yud* represents *Keter*. The body of the *yud* represents *Chokhmah*. The first *heh* represents *Binah*. The *vav* represents the next six *sefirot* (*Chesed, Gevurah, Tiferet, Netzach, Hod, Yesod*) going down the tree. The final *heh* represents *Malkhut*.

The four worlds represented by the different letters in the Tetragrammaton mirror different levels of consciousness and varying types of experiences, while the *sefirot* in the diagram relate symbolically to different body parts. As shown on page 20, the varying realms are:

Tetragrammaton

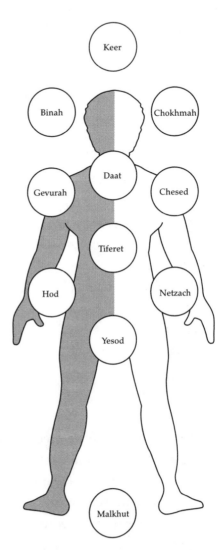

Sefirot symbolically pertaining to the body

Consciousness and Experience Relating to the Four Worlds

World	Consciousness	Experience
Atzilut	spiritual being	being, essence
Beriah	intellect, creativity	knowledge, morality, ethics
Yetzirah	the psychological	feelings, thoughts, speech
Asiyah	the physical	action

The *Sefirot* Related to the Body Parts

Sefirah	Body Part
Keter, the crown	head
Binah	left brain
Chokhmah	right brain
Daat, the non-*sefirah*	neck, voice box (sometimes considered the third brain or third eye)
Chesed	right shoulder
Gevurah	left shoulder
Tiferet	heart
Netzach	right hip
Hod	left hip
Yesod	genital area
Malkhut	legs

The key to following the Tree of Life is the harmonizing of opposites, the balancing of dualities. Think of the yin and yang in Eastern philosophy, male and female energies, positive and negative forces, active and passive qualities, form and force structures. Working on the Tree of Life means seeing both sides of the tree, the two sides to everything that can be neutralized or collapsed and brought into balance or equilibrium. For example, if we're too critical or judgmental, we may feel and act superior to others. Or, if we think too much and tend to suppress feelings, we can become stressed and out of balance. Kabbalists teach that when these opposite forces are brought into balance, we can reach a state of equanimity, harmony, and balance within ourselves. Meditating on the colors of the *sefirot* can help keep us in balance.

· Meditation/Visualization: Colors ·

To get a sense of this lightning flash as it pertains to the colors and the body, here are the colors:

Sefirah	Attribute	Color
Keter	crown	blinding, invisible white
Chokhmah	wisdom	color that includes all colors
Binah	understanding	yellow and green
Chesed	loving-kindness	white and silver
Gevurah	strength	red and gold
Tiferet	beauty	yellow and purple
Netzach	victory	light pink
Hod	splendor	dark pink
Yesod	foundation	orange
Malkhut	kingship	blue

> Note on meditations: To get the most from this meditation and the subsequent ones, read through it completely until you understand it, then close your eyes and imagine yourself going through the steps. Alternatively, tape-record it in your own voice and play it back whenever you want to meditate.

· Meditation: Colors ·

Close your eyes. Relax by breathing into your diaphragm. Expand your breath into your abdomen, lungs, and chest, then exhale very slowly. Do this three times. When you are relaxed, imagine each color in its place on the chart one at a time. *Keter* is a clear, crystal radiance. See it above your head like a crown. Experience yourself resonating with the radiance. Take your time. Notice how you feel.

When you are ready, move down horizontally to the right, to *Chokhmah*. The color is a white that includes all colors. Again, take your time. Notice what you are experiencing. Then slowly move horizontally to the left, to

Binah, which is green. Take as long as you need. Then move diagonally down to the next *sefirah,* to *Chesed,* silver. Experience yourself resonating with the vibrations of the color. Move horizontally across to the left to *Gevurah,* which is red. Then move horizontally down and to the center to *Tiferet,* purple. Take as much time as you need.

Move horizontally to the right to *Netzach,* light pink. Stay as long as you need. Now move horizontally across to the left to *Hod,* dark pink. When you are ready, move diagonally down to the right to *Yesod,* which is orange, and then vertically down to *Malkhut,* blue. When you are finished, stay a few minutes to experience all the color vibrations resonating at once. Notice how you feel. When you are ready, open your eyes and write about your experiences.

TWENTY-TWO HEBREW LETTERS AND TEN *SEFIROT:* THIRTY-TWO PATHS TO WISDOM

A legend says that 975 generations before the creation of heaven and earth God created the Torah (Five Books of Moses). It was first in the mind of God as a blueprint of creation. Then creation manifested as the light and energy from *Ein Sof* was channeled through the vehicle of letters of the Hebrew alphabet. These patterns of energies created spiritual forces that rule the zodiac, constellations, planets, and stars, which have an impact on earth and human beings. They can affect the chemistry in our bodies and the electromagnetic waves in our brains, which, in turn, affect the way we think, speak, and act. In reverse, it is taught that by meditating on and reciting the Hebrew letters, we can influence creation and the worlds above.

As explained on page 16, the *sefirot* were formed by the sounds of the lightning flash and are the vowel sounds in the Hebrew alphabet. The twenty-two Hebrew consonants are the letters that form the paths connecting the ten *sefirot.* Together they form what is known as the thirty-two paths to wisdom. They are the thirty-two steps we need to learn in order to reach the Divine.

Twenty-two Foundation letters:

He engraved them, He carved them,

He permuted them, He weighed them,

He transformed them,

And with them, He depicted all that was formed

And all that would be formed.

—*Sefer Yetzirah* 2:2

In the *Zohar* it is taught that the letters from *alef* to *tav* were the twenty-two Hebrew letters with which God created the heavens and the earth.

It is important to note that you don't have to know Hebrew or be Jewish to meditate on or embrace the Hebrew letters. The Hebrew language in not just connected to Judaism. Like the Aramaic languages, Hebrew is a universal ancient language. It is considered to be the oldest, most continuously used, unchanged language there is. In Kabbalah the Hebrew letters represent different forces of energy in the universe. Kabbalists see them as conduits of God's energy. By meditating on the sounds, shapes, and mystical meanings it is possible to bring on power for healing, wisdom, and love. You don't have to memorize the Hebrew or even know it to meditate on the letters.

The twenty-two letters of the Hebrew alphabet are consonants. There are also ten vowels, but these are represented by dots, commas, and lines, below, above, or in the middle of the consonants. The twenty-two consonants represent the paths connecting the *sefirot*. The *sefirot* themselves are represented by the vowels or by the numbers 1 through 10.

In human beings, each path corresponds to one of the paths of the nervous system, which consists of thirty-one nerves branching out away from the spinal cord and returning to it plus the twelve cranial nerves as one center, making up the thirty-two paths. These paths also represent the flow of quantum energy that forms the zodiac.

It's important to note that the placement of the Hebrew letters as well as the actual diagrams of the Tree of Life may vary depending on the kabbalistic school. The Cordovero school places the letters according to the lightning flash, starting from the top down. The Lurianic chart places them according to the zodiac. In this system, the three horizontal paths correspond to the elements of fire, air, and water; the twelve diagonal paths correspond to the signs of the zodiac; and the seven vertical paths correspond to the sun and moon and five originally known planets—Mercury, Venus, Mars, Jupiter, and Saturn. Since we will be using the Lurianic chart in the following chapters, these correspondences will be elaborated as we negotiate each path.

Following are the Lurianic and Cordovero charts.

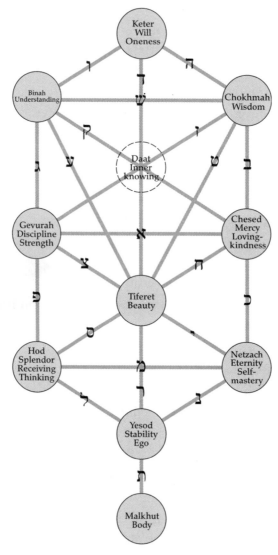

Lurianic Tree of Life with Hebrew Letters

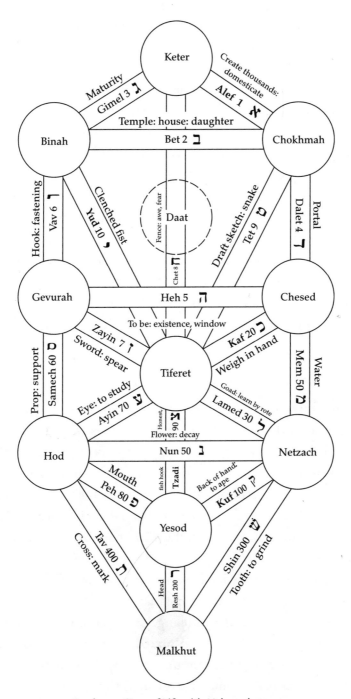

Cordovero Tree of Life with Hebrew letters

JACOB'S LADDER: THE SECONDARY TREES WITHIN THE PRIMARY TREE OF LIFE

The primary Tree of Life represents the ten *sefirot* or sources of different waves of light and energies. As these energies penetrate the parallel worlds of emanation, creation, formation, and action, they take on different forms.

As a microcosm of the macrocosm, humans made in the image of God are in the world of *Asiyah* and, therefore, part of the four worlds. Also, the four worlds of fire, air, water, and earth in the form of heat, breath, liquid, and solid are within human beings. The four worlds are represented in a full tree unto itself, each consisting of ten *sefirot* and twenty-two paths.

What follows is a detailed account of how the four worlds overlap. It shows the integration of body, psyche, soul, and spirit, as well as representations of Divine names, archangels, and patriarchs. It also shows the physical and psychological functions and their placement on the Tree of Life.

Atzilut

The first emanation and the root from which the other trees grow is *Atzilut*, the Divine world, the world of spirit. This world carries with it an image of God. Based on Ezekiel's vision, where the prophet saw the appearance of a vast man seated upon a likeness of a throne surrounded by a fiery radiance, it is represented as *Adam Kadmon*, primordial, androgynous man, and is likened to the glory of God. *Atzilut* represents closeness to God. *Atzilut* is the world of unchanging unity and eternity that was brought into being by ten utterances—the ten aspects of divinity—and is represented by the Divine names of God. It's important to note that the various kabbalistic schools use different names for the Divine, although the essence is the same for the *sefirot* they represent. Since the diagrams showing the patriarchs, archangels, psyche, and body are depicted on the Cordovero diagrams and are incorporated in the diagram of Jacob's Ladder, the Cordovero chart as well as the Lurianic chart are included. The Divine names on the Lurianic chart are the same as those in *Sha'are Orah* (Gates of Light), written by Rabbi Joseph Gikatilla, a Castillian kabbalist of the thirteenth century.

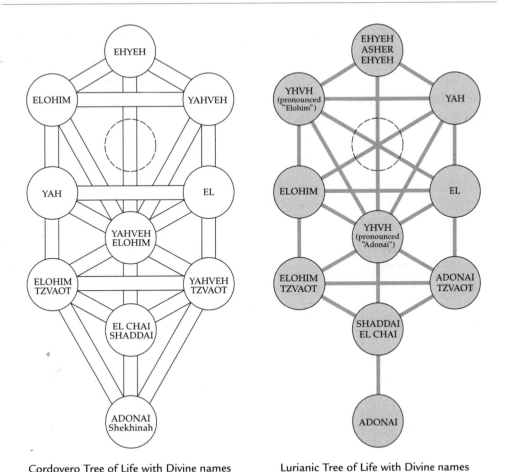

Cordovero Tree of Life with Divine names   Lurianic Tree of Life with Divine names

This source is considered the most comprehensive on the Divine names, explaining the essence of each *sefirah*.

Beriah

From *Atzilut* we descend to the lower world, separated from the eternal world, into *Beriah*—the world of creation. In this world we have cosmic cycles, day and night manifesting in time, light and dark, and birth and decay. More specifically *Beriah* represents separation from the Absolute and the creation of the universe in six days. (Of course, one day in the Bible could be equivalent to a thousand years or more.) Again, the placement of the days of creation varies in different kabbalistic schools.

Beriah is the spiritual world where archangels were created. Archangels and angels, which are created in *Yetzirah,* are made from fire. They rule the planets. They have no free will, act as messengers of God, and represent morality and ethics. They also help facilitate intellect and creativity. Different species and levels of archangels and angels help us along our path of life.

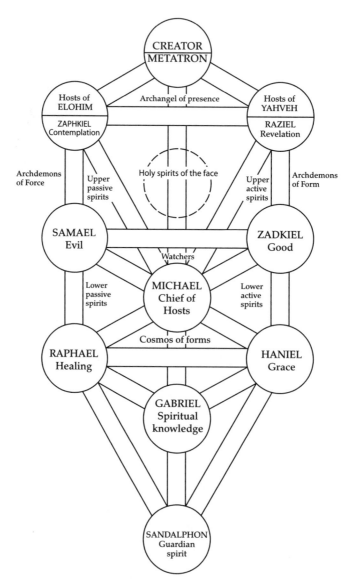

Cordovero Tree of Life with archangels

Yetzirah

Next is the world of *Yetzirah,* the watery world of formation and the creation of angels in the spiritual world. It is represented on the Tree of Life by a variety of angels, the zodiac, patriarchs of the Bible, or different aspects of the psyche, including thought (both rational and intuitive), speech, feelings, and action. In humans *Yetzirah* is the psyche.

Following is a chart of the patriarchs of the Bible. A second chart shows the different aspects of the psyche.

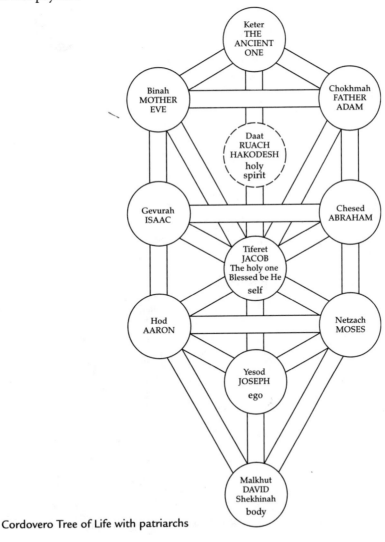

Cordovero Tree of Life with patriarchs

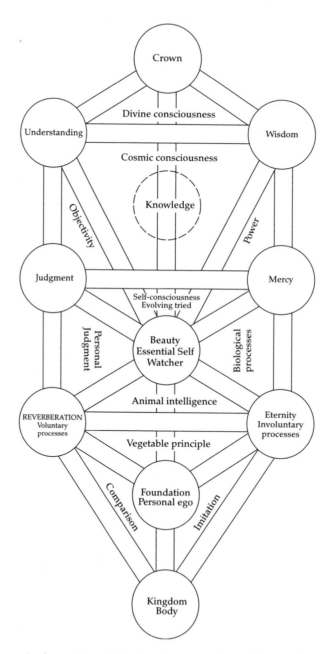

Cordovero Tree of Life showing the functions of the psyche

Asiyah

The world of *Asiyah* is the physical, material world. It is the world of action as we know it today: the terrestrial world and all the creatures on the earth, as well as the celestial world of the zodiac, including planets, stars, and constellations. In humans it is the world of the body. It is depicted here as different physical functions of the body.

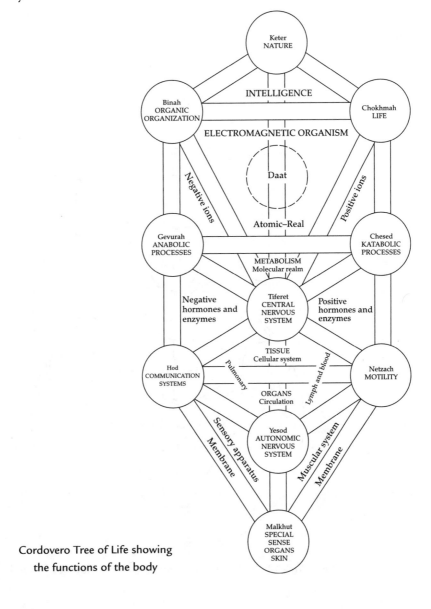

Cordovero Tree of Life showing
the functions of the body

Lined up in a row, overlapping at *Tiferet,* these four worlds—emanation, creation, formation, and action—are referred to from below to above as earth, paradise, heaven, and the Divine glory of God. In humankind these four trees overlap each other at *Tiferet* and depict the integration of the body, psyche, soul, and spirit.

This is known as Jacob's Ladder. Superimposing one large Tree of Life (see below) over the four worlds of Jacob's Ladder (page 33) gives a replica of the human being with the four worlds: physical, psychological, intellectual, and spiritual..

Here is a diagram of Jacob's Ladder and the Tree of Life representing humankind.

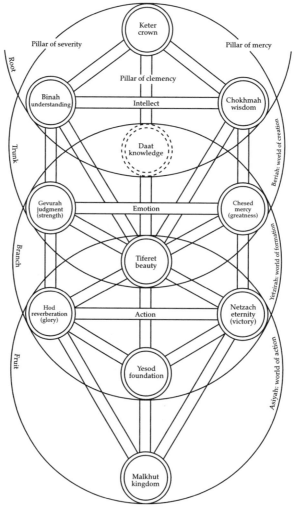

Overall Tree of Life showing the correspondences with the four worlds

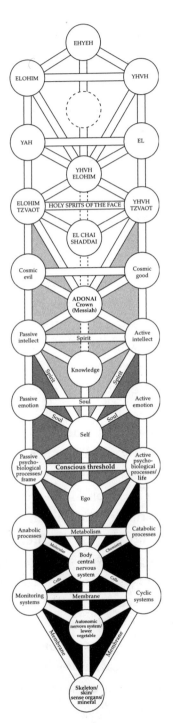

Jacob's Ladder: The interlocking of the four worlds

HUMANITY'S FALL FROM GRACE AND THE GARDEN OF EDEN

As the Bible recounts in Genesis, God created Adam and, from Adam's rib, Eve. In the Garden of Eden, God showed Adam and Eve fruitfulness. God then commanded: "Of every tree thou mayest eat freely . . . but of the tree of knowledge of good and evil thou mayest not eat, for in the day that thou eatest of it, thou shalt surely die." The serpent persuaded Eve to eat the fruit from the forbidden tree by telling her it would make her wise. She convinced Adam to eat the fruit as well. Knowing they had disobeyed God, Adam and Eve both tried to hide. When God confronted them, Adam blamed Eve, and Eve blamed the serpent. Because Adam and Eve ate the fruit believing the serpent, not from any intention to go against God's commandment, God permitted them to live, but because of their shame He clothed them with animal skin (flesh) and banished them from the beautiful Garden of Eden. They now had to adhere to the demands of the flesh and corporeal nature, the aging process, and physical urges. They moved from the world of creation (*Beriah*) down to the physical world (*Asiyah*). They had to work to restore in themselves the rightful place of pure consciousness and unity that was freely given in the Garden of Eden.

Like Adam and Eve in exile, we all sense other realms of existence. The goal of the kabbalist is to regain Divine consciousness and recover the primordial state of grace without renouncing this world. The Work of the Chariot, therefore, is to cleave to the Divine and return to the Garden of Eden—in other words, to get in touch with our Divine nature and live our life's purpose.

The *Zohar* illustrates this point with a story. The *Zohar,* also known as the Book of Splendor, is the primary text on Kabbalah. It was published in Spain in 1280 and is believed to have been written by Moses de Leon, who considered himself merely a scribe recounting the work of Rabbi Shimon Bar Yochai, who lived during the first century C.E. After denouncing the Romans, both Shimon Bar Yochai and his son, Rabbi Eleazar, were sentenced to death. They hid in a cave for thirteen years and had many conversations regarding the makeup of the universe and man's relationship to it.

In one such conversation Rabbi Eleazar asked his father, "Why does God send men's souls to earth knowing that they have to die?" Rabbi Shimon answered that man's purpose is to know the glory of God and manifest the Divine in this world to bring about its transformation.

EVOLUTION OF THE SOUL AND REINCARNATION

The overlapping trees on Jacob's Ladder show not only the creation process in its entirety, but also the interrelatedness of body, psyche, soul, and spirit and the process of birth, death, and rebirth that we undergo until we unite with the Divine. Kabbalists teach that we are reincarnated and experience many lifetimes until we perfect ourselves to the point of becoming Godlike and return to oneness.

To sum up a very complex process, Kabbalah teaches that after a person's death, the soul goes through a progression of events, observations, and lessons. This process includes a life review, and the soul experiences the impact of its actions on others. It is then determined what the soul still needs to overcome or create on its way to perfection. The soul waits for the right life situation to appear so that it can come back into the world in order to evolve further.

There is a kabbalistic tale that before birth we are taught the entire Torah by the Angel Gabriel. After the teaching is completed, Gabriel kisses us above the upper lip (hence the indentation) so we forget what we have learned. The reason for this forgetting is to give us free will in life—it is up to us to choose whether to live by universal laws and precepts or not.

Kabbalists believe that there are different levels of the soul that reside in the four worlds.

- *Nefesh* is the lowest level. It is related to the body and the material world of *Asiyah*. This is the level of connection to the plant and animal kingdoms and to nature. It's also the physical level of action and pleasure. The *nefesh* is the part of the animal soul with an endless appetite; it always wants to receive for itself. It manipulates because it is needy and dependent. Its behavior is often conditional.

- *Ruach,* the next level of the soul, is connected to the world of emotion, the psychological level of *Yetzirah.* This is the human spirit. Here we still have desires and wants, but we are less self-centered and more concerned about and sensitive to others. Working through this level, we open to kindness and the expression of unconditional love.

- *Neshamah* is the Divine Soul, the intellectual level in *Beriah.* It is pure intellect and connected with the absolute all, the Endless Light, the *Ein Sof Or.* As we elevate to this level of soul we begin questioning the meaning of our life and we begin uncovering and living our life purpose and being of service. We become egoless. It takes a great deal of practice, discipline, and commitment to achieve this level of consciousness.

Lurianic kabbalists add two other souls, *Chayah* and *Yechidah,* which are usually grouped together and often defined as Divine spirit. These two levels are transpersonal, beyond the body, and can be reached through higher intuition. Only truly evolved human beings experience these levels of awareness.

- *Chayah* is the vitality of spirit, the life force—the ability to derive pleasure totally from within ourselves, without physical influences. It is the total life experience, that of being alive and enlightened with Divine spirit.

- *Yechidah* is unity of spirit and represents oneness and uniqueness, the merging of the soul of the individual with the soul of God. We lose our sense of separateness.

Kabbalists teach that the soul can evolve through different lifetimes—during which we are given many lessons and keep incarnating until we reach perfection—or within one lifetime. Sometimes it happens spontaneously—often through trauma, a near-death or out-of-body experience, or reaching rock bottom and finding God—and sometimes it happens after years of devotional study and good deeds. Our task in each lifetime is to work toward reaching perfection in order to unite with the Divine and live righteously. Living righteously, according to kabbalists, means doing what is right for all, not being self-righteous. It's living responsibly.

In order to reach the level of *neshamah*, we need to purify our bodies, minds, and hearts and refine our character. This means breaking through physical addictions, maladaptive behaviors, personality flaws, and psychological blocks; it also means pursuing our intellectual interests, discovering our Divine purpose, and fulfilling it—by sharing our knowledge, hearts, and souls with others. In this way we can reach our highest potential.

AS ABOVE, SO BELOW: HUMAN RELATIONSHIP TO THE DIVINE

There are two different levels of creation: the physical and spiritual. The spiritual world consists of souls and transcendental spiritual entities—angels and forces. Souls are entities that enter and leave physical bodies to help the body perform specific functions and help the soul evolve. Transcendental beings (angels and forces) are entities without free will and are ruled by God. Their actions are regulated by a unique set of laws. Angels are the souls of stars.

The physical level consists of the terrestrial plane, including everything on earth, as well as the astronomical plane, consisting of the zodiac, constellations, stars, and planets.

The spiritual world is considered the "world above," while the physical is the "world below." The world below is an earthly manifestation of the world above.

Kabbalists believe every breath we inhale and exhale, every thought that we have, every word that we use, every action we take gives off different measures of energies that are recorded in the *sefirot* and affect the upper worlds, as indicated by the expression, "What goes around comes around." In turn, the worlds above reflect back to us and give us what we need to learn or overcome—the cause and effect of our own actions. This can come in the form of cosmic or cataclysmic events or personal challenges. For every question we ask, an answer manifests.

Insights often come through angels, though we may not be aware of it. Ministering angels and archangels bring messages from God to man and from man to God. Ministering angels have specific tasks to perform, but cannot do them unless given permission by God.

Angels may appear for many reasons: to rescue us from danger, support us with a difficult task or project, help us make the right decision, or simply bestow on us peace and serenity. Some survive for short periods of time. In the *Zohar* it is stated, "Every day ministering angels are created from a river of fire and they utter a song and die. They are new every morning."

Some kabbalists speculate that angels are formed by human thought, speech, action, and prayer. It has been said that prayers are angels rising up to heaven. Anytime a positive thought or good deed is performed, we create another angel.

Kabbalists believe that demons exist in the world and that we create demons by negative thoughts and evil actions. Demons reside between the two worlds, undetectable entities ruled by their own laws. There are different classes of demons, just as there are different classes of angels. As we will discuss in more detail later, demons often trick people into destructive behavior.

COMMUNING WITH THE DIVINE: ARE YOU PUSHING PEOPLE'S BUTTONS OR SACRED BUTTONS?

God's energy, like the Big Bang, is incredibly powerful. None of us is capable of knowing the Absolute, the *Ein Sof,* in its entirety. Because we are here on earth, we are limited. We can receive only what our minds and bodies are capable of comprehending based on our own vibrations and how open and capable we are of channeling the information. Channeling here means sharing what we receive. Kabbalists teach that when we ask to receive, it should always be with the intention of sharing. If what we receive is for our own use only, then it becomes self-absorbing rather than spiritually expanding. What comes in needs to go out. This creates flow.

When we ask to receive, God's power and words can be so intense that energies come in fast—too fast for us to integrate and share. If we're not totally open, what we ask for can come back at too high a frequency for us, or so much can come at one time that we can't distinguish what we are being told or shown—or even that we are being answered at all. It can actually be destructive, burning us out or making us sick. If so much comes in that we can't channel it, the energy stagnates. Because of this, many of us fear opening to God or can't comprehend the answers and therefore decide there is no God.

There's a tale of four rabbis trying to reach Paradise. They practiced a highly concentrated form of meditating on Divine names, invocations, and mandala-like images—similar to the visions of Ezekiel and Jacob's Ladder—in order to achieve direct experience with the Divine. One lost his mind, another became a heretic, and the third rabbi died. Only one came out unharmed: Rabbi Akiva, a second-century sage who received a vision of the Divine and became a great teacher. He was the only one who was "worthy of God's glory." He was the only one who was prepared by living righteously whose body and mind were prepared enough to resonate with the higher frequencies of spiritual energy.

To reach Paradise in our world, we must go step by step so we reach the higher levels in a balanced way. Rather than reaching for the Absolute all at once, it is important to determine the specific energies we want to reach. In other words, we need to know what gates to open or buttons to push. The brain and body can only grasp and handle so much at one time. We each resonate only at a certain frequency. Reaching silence first helps us become an open vessel, and then by focusing and meditating on specific areas of the Tree of Life, we can channel the appropriate type and amount of energy needed. Using the ten *sefirot* as different channels helps us distinguish among the varying qualities. The way to do this is through knowing the essence of each *sefirah*. It's also important to note that although the essence of each *sefirah* is constant, it takes on a slightly different character depending on whether we're ascending or descending the Tree of Life.

Below is a basic layout of the *sefirot* on the Tree of Life. You can use it as a mandala. Just picturing it in meditation can help generate a state of holiness—or wholeness, if you will—creating a connection to the oneness of all. So it's a good idea to memorize the placement of the *sefirot* and their general essences. One of the best ways is to draw your own Tree of Life. This process can help draw you closer to higher energies.

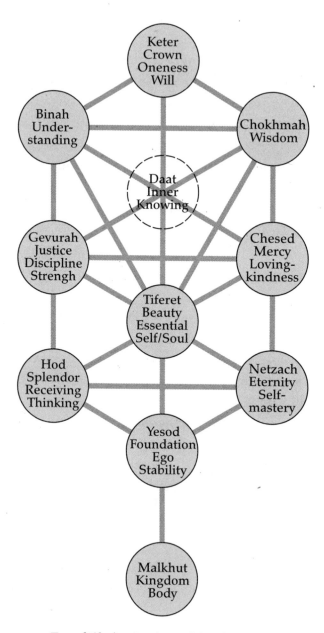

Tree of Life showing the qualities of the *sefirot*

· Meditation: The *Sefirot* ·

Another way to experience the *sefirot* is through visualization.

Hold the picture the Tree of Life in your mind. Think of either sitting or standing in the circle of *Keter. Keter* represents oneness. Think and meditate on the concept of oneness or "the Endless Light." Pause. Notice what you experience in your body. Pay attention to colors or images that may come to mind, if any. Notice what thoughts come up for you, if any. Pause and simply experience the essence of the *sefirah*.

Then move to *Chokhmah* (wisdom). Think about or contemplate wisdom. Pause. Notice what you experience in your body. Pay attention to colors or images that may come to mind, if any. Notice what impressions come to you. Pause and just be with the essence of *Chokhmah*. Move to *Binah* (understanding from God's point of view) and do the same. Continue to each *sefirah,* including the non-*sefirah* of *Daat* (inner knowing), then *Chesed* (mercy, love, greatness), *Gevurah* (judgment, justice, strength), *Tiferet* (beauty), *Netzach* (victory, eternity), *Hod* (glory, reverberation, receptivity), *Yesod* (foundation, ego, stability), and *Malkhut* (kingdom, body).

Now picture the entire Tree of Life in your mind. Notice what it feels like as the universal flow of energy moves from *Keter* to *Malkhut* and back up again from *Malkhut* to *Keter*. When you are ready, open your eyes. Write about your experience.

KABBALISTIC TREE OF LIFE

There are many different ways to gain insight, inspiration, and guidance using the kabbalistic Tree of Life. As explained earlier, each *sefirah* on the Tree of Life is represented by the attributes of God, the Divine Hebrew names of God, the patriarchs of the Bible, archangels, emotional elements, physical attributes, the zodiac, sounds, colors, plants, and aromas, among other things.

Kabbalists believe that meditating on a symbol or reciting a name for a specific *sefirah* activates the energy flow through that *sefirah*.

The way we can use these symbols is if we have an issue we've been pondering, we can focus on the Divine name, ask the question, and sit until insights come. Sometimes, however, we may receive very high energy by focusing on the Divine name. The energy comes at such a high frequency that we can't determine what it is. That's when we can call on archangels and angels. Alternatively, we can focus on the essence of the patriarch representing a specific *sefirah* or the actual attribute of the *sefirah* to get more specific or slightly different insights.

If something requires an answer, make a question about it. Make it as specific and concise as possible. If the question pertains to a physical ailment or involves action, focus on the *sefirah* of *Malkhut*. The Divine name for *Malkhut* is *Adonai*.

· Meditation ·

Write your question and then put the pen down. Do a basic relaxation (see pages 54–57), then focus on the Divine name: *Adonai*. Think the name, say it to yourself, and then just sit with it. Ask your proposed question to yourself. Make a mental note of any thoughts, images, feelings, or sensations.

After a minute or so, focus on the name of the archangel, for that *sefirah*. In the case of *Malkhut* it's Sandolphon. Call on Sandolphon by repeating the name, thinking it, feeling it, and then just being with it. Again, ask the same question. Sit with it. Make a mental note of any thoughts, images, feelings, or sensations.

Then focus on the patriarch representing *Malkhut*, King David. Think about the attributes of King David—cleaving to the Divine and having hope and faith. (See page 47). Keep repeating the essence of hope and faith, thinking it, feeling it, and then just being with it. Then ask the same question again. Sit with it and make a mental note of any thoughts, images, feelings, or sensations. Then concentrate on the attribute of *Malkhut*, which is Kingdom. This is a process of cleansing your body to become a channel for the Divine. (See page 47). Think of your body as a clear channel for Divine love, wisdom, and understanding. Again, ask the same question. Sit with it. Make a mental note of any thoughts, images, feelings or sensations.

When you come out of the meditation, write down your experiences.

In each of the following chapters outlining the *sefirot* I have included the esoteric symbols of the Divine name, the archangel, the patriarch, and the attribute of the *sefirah* at the beginning of the chapter. For those readers who are interested in this aspect of Kabbalah, this information will prove useful.

It is important to realize that, along with meditation, kabbalists believe that to accomplish anything, psychological well-being and action are necessary because good deeds stimulate God's blessings.

This book uses some of the esoteric symbols listed above. It also concentrates on psychological introspection and on practical steps that can be used to examine each *sefirah* in order to understand ourselves more fully and awaken to the Divine.

As we climb the ladder of the Tree of Life we elevate the mundane by purifying our thoughts, feelings, and actions. We begin to work through our physical addictions and conditioning and free ourselves of attachment to the past. This is when we become truer to ourselves and begin to connect with our soul. That's often when we gain a glimpse of something more—some sense of cause and effect, a grand scheme at work, a cosmic awakening, and sometimes a sense of being guided or touched by universal forces. We open to a sense of immortality and the Divine.

· Exercise: Divine Questions to Ponder ·

At this point, it's helpful to think about where we stand in our relationship to the Divine. Keep in mind that answers can change at any time based on new experiences, education, and our own evolution. The understanding of the Divine and of creation is an ongoing process. Write the answers to the following questions:

1. Do you believe in God?

2. Just what is it you believe about God? Do you determine God to be absolute, immanent, transcendent, nothing—or something altogether different?

3. Do you experience God as an authority figure, friend, foe, or yourself?

4. What is your image of God, and how did you acquire it?

5. Has your image of God changed since childhood?

6. Do you believe in a God that is outside you, within you, or both? Why?

7. Who are you in relation to God?

8. How do you normally address God?

9. Do you experience God as your master?

10. What experiences have you had that led to your belief or nonbelief in God?

11. How does your image of God affect your behavior?

12. How does your image of God stifle or promote your spiritual growth?

13. How comfortable are you regarding your attitude toward God?

14. Do you perceive God as loving or punishing?

15. Are you still searching for God?

16. If you don't believe in God, would you like to?

17. If so, how would you perceive God?

18. What does it mean to you to cleave to the Divine?

19. What do you currently do, if anything, that allows you to feel a connection to the Divine?

20. Can you recall an experience that left you feeling deeply grateful? When was it and what happened?

21. Along with the sights, sounds, aromas, can you recall an awareness of a warm, loving presence that permeated your being? What did you think of it?

22. Can you recall ever having experiences with or visits by angels?

23. What are your beliefs about angels?

24. What is your relationship to God? Do you negate God? Do you fear God? Do you love God? Are you in awe of God?

25. What does it mean to you to surrender to God?

26. Do you pray to God? If so, how?

Kabbalists teach that man's spiritual quest is finding our Divine purpose, living our highest potential, and sharing with others in service. Spiritual evolution in Kabbalah is concerned with finding answers to questions such as *Who am I? Why am I here? What is my purpose? How can I serve?* Using the Tree of Life and Jacob's Ladder as flow charts and visual representations, we will now journey into the body, psyche, soul, and spirit.

THREE

Malkhut: Kingdom
Body and Sense Perception

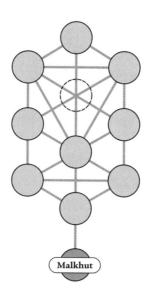

Malkhut

Divine Name: *Adonai*—The Lord

Malkhut is the lowest *sefirah* on the Tree of Life. As the receiver of all that is, the energies are drawn down through all the *sefirot* and end in *Eretz Hachaim*, the Land of Life, the earth, which contains everything. Everything includes the life force of all the souls that move and crawl on earth, as well as those in the heavens: angels, hosts of heaven, celestial armies, and beings. *Malkhut* is represented in the Divine world by the Divine name *Adonai*, the Lord. The essence of *Malkhut* is sovereignty, nobility, and kingship. This includes reverence for life and faith in the Absolute.

Archangel: Sandalphon

Sandalphon, the archangel representing *Malkhut*, is the transformed prophet Elijah who was transported to heaven without the intermediary of death. He was immortal. He is the archangel who brings the prayers of humans before God and helps people develop faith. Sandalphon helps lift the veil for us to have a glimpse of oneness with the Divine.

Patriarch: King David

King David, the patriarch representing *Malkhut*, was a warrior sent by God to save the people of Israel. He became the first king officially appointed by God. He slew the giant Goliath and, later, fighting an army, pursued his enemies and destroyed them. King David's constant cleaving to the Divine gave him hope. David's music and poetry gave him a direct link to God. His psalms, the Songs of David, offered inspiration for his people. He became a symbol of autonomy, hope, and faith. It was from his lineage the Messiah was expected to come.

Attribute: King—Kingdom

The essence of *Malkhut* is king or kingdom. On a personal level this is the process of cleansing our bodies and our environment to become sanctuaries for Divine presence. We have a reverence for life, faith in the Absolute, and hope for the future. To emulate the essences of *Malkhut*, you can meditate on that *sefirah* and on any of the above representations. The essence is experiencing your body and environment as sanctuaries for God to reside. You are living regally. At the end of the meditation state the affirmation: *I am a temple for God and the physical manifestation of living the attributes of the Divine.* Give thanks for the ability to connect in this way.

MALKHUT: KINGDOM (BODY)

Malkhut is the lowest *sefirah* on the Tree of Life. It is both the beginning and the ending. As the receiver of all that has gone before, it is the last step in the creation or materialization of the world as we know it today. It is also the first step in our return to the Garden of Eden and oneness.

The Hebrew word *melech,* from which the word *Malkhut* is derived, means "king." The Divine essence of *Malkhut* is sovereignty, nobility, and kingship. In the physical world it's experiencing the Kingdom of God within us. It starts with making our bodies and environments sanctuaries in which God, the *Shekhinah*, can reside. That means ridding ourselves of all tensions, negativity, or physical obstacles in order to experience Divine light, love, and creativity.

GOD IN EXILE: THE *SHEKHINAH*

Malkhut, in the Divine world, is represented by the *Shekhinah*. The *Shekhinah* is the feminine side of God, the part of God that is in exile here on earth. As the story goes in the *Zohar,* in order for the *Shekhinah* to unite with the Divine there has to be a marriage between *Malkhut* and *Tiferet* or a marriage between the body and the soul. God is often compared to a king in the Bible. Rabbi Joseph Gelberman, in *Pearls of Wisdom,* observes that reuniting with the Divine might be likened to a king and queen who have two children. The king's children disobey him, and he expels them from the kingdom. The queen, distraught over her children leaving, cries out. She sees the punishment as too great. The king tells the queen to go with the children. As the queen leaves the kingdom, a part of the king goes with her. In loneliness and despair the king calls them home and they strive to unite. Kabbalists believe that the return home to the Kingdom of Heaven can only take place when each person comes out of the wilderness, liberates him- or herself from old habits and ego slavery, and opens to the Divine soul, the source of higher awareness, and the connection with all that is. Kabbalists interpret the term *wilderness* as a metaphor for the wilderness of the mind. *Slavery* is often viewed as a metaphor for being slaves to our past.

KING AND KINGDOM

Malkhut represents our body and environment, our king and kingdom. It is the world of *Asiyah,* the material, physical world—the world that connects us with the plant and animal kingdoms. In the body it is experienced as skin and flesh. It is also the part of ourselves in direct contact with the environment, the world we relate to and from which we receive external impulses through sensory perception of sight, hearing, touch, taste, smell.

Like all of creation, the body is composed of the elements of fire, air, water, and earth. These transpose into solids, liquids, gases, and heat, which transform into minerals, chemicals, electromagnetic forces, and thought. These are transmitted by arteries, veins, vessels, organs, tissues, muscles, tendons, pumps, and chambers, all of which influence the respiratory, muscular, chemical, and electrical functioning of the body. In turn, the body is influenced by the way we breathe, what we eat, how we move, what we think, how we speak, and the environment surrounding us. All these cells, molecules, chemicals, mechanisms, and electromagnetic forces are enclosed in tissues and flesh, the skin that separates us from the outside world.

A kabbalistic principle states, "If you wish to perceive the invisible, observe the visible." Our body is the first step. Observing, knowing, and caring for our body is of the utmost importance. Just as the cosmos must consist of the perfect balance of the elements of fire, air, water, and earth to function properly, we need to balance breath, nutrition, movement, and thought for the body to function properly.

Balance Within the Body

Balance is a primary concept in Kabbalah, as we will see as we look into the dualities while moving up the Tree of Life. Here it involves the balance within the body. Balancing our intake of food and nutrients, air, exercise, and thought is crucial not only to ourselves but also to the universe. If we eat in excess, we are not only hurting our own bodies, but also robbing the universe and others of food and energy. If we don't eat enough nutritionally balanced meals, we won't have enough energy to keep us going. We may feel tired and weak and maybe even sick, and then need other people to take care of us. The same goes for exercise and thought. Too much exercise can make us tired, while not enough exercise may make us lethargic.

The body without awareness is a vegetable. It breathes, digests, and excretes without consciousness. It's like being in a coma. The body without thought doesn't move. It needs thought to function. It needs thought to take care of itself. Furthermore, it needs thought that is truth, thought that is reality-based, that is balanced. If thought is not reality-centered, it can turn to negativity, which often shows up as physical ailments or in fantasy that manifests in irrational behavior. Without balance in what we consume and thoughts that are true, we become a weak link in the global scheme of things.

Maimonides, who wrote *The Guide for the Perplexed*, was a renowned physician, philosopher, and rabbi of the twelfth century. He was also probably one of the earliest holistic healers. Maimonides insisted that the keys to good health were diet, exercise, and a clear mental outlook. Without this balance, he explained, specific emotional imbalances could occur, such as chronic anxiety, anger, and depression, which often manifest in physical ailments. He emphasized that with proper care, we can awaken our higher mental capabilities and even attain prophetic states of consciousness. In *The Guide for the Perplexed* he declared, "If a person, perfect in his intellectual and moral faculties, and also perfect, as far as possible, in his imaginative faculty, prepared himself (properly) . . . he must become a prophet, for prophecy is a natural state of man." When we're balanced and in flow, everything seems to run smoothly, and we tap into our creativity with ease.

Flow

Flow is another important concept in Kabbalah. What comes in must go out, even if it isn't in the same form. This involves the importance of exhaling as much as inhaling; excreting as much as ingesting. If the flow isn't balanced in the body, we lose steam and feel tired or weak, become hyper and out of control, or become sick. We may even die. In any case, we rob ourselves of vital energy.

The *Sefer Yetzirah* states that the thirty-two paths to wisdom on the Tree of Life parallel the human nervous system. Both the paths and the nervous system have a dual purpose. The nerves transmit messages from the brain to all parts of the body, and they also deliver information from the senses to the brain. Our thoughts affect our feelings, and what we perceive through the senses influences our thoughts. The paths of wisdom on the Tree of Life link the Divine mind (the world above) and the physical universe (the world below) and involve the mind's control over creation; they are also a way to reach the higher mind. Navigating these paths is how we experience the mystical.

The *Sefer Yetzirah* also states that everything in the body parallels the forces of nature and is influenced by the zodiac—the formation of the planets, constellations, moon, sun, and stars. The subject of kabbalistic astrology is vast; suffice it to say that just as tides and seasons are affected by the rotation of the earth and the position of the moon and planets, so are the biorhythms in humans. These in turn influence body fluids and their chemical reactions. Kabbalists contend that some planets affect specific parts of the body such as the endocrine, pituitary, and pineal glands. Other planets regulate the adrenals, gonads, thymus, and pancreas. Some interact with positive and negative ions that regulate the electromagnetic flow within our bodies.

Kabbalists believe that our date of birth dictates our basic character traits, the lessons we need to learn, and what we need to overcome in order to live by our own free will within the cosmic framework. Kabbalists also believe that although we are influenced by planetary movement, we don't have to be ruled by it if we respond rationally and proactively rather than emotionally or reactively. We have the ability to affect what's above, which in turn reflects what's below.

Although it helps to know the correlation of the zodiac to the body, it is not necessary to know astrology to study and benefit from the Kabbalah. The goal is to get to know ourselves so well that we create what we want rather than reacting emotionally to what comes. It means knowing our bodies, clearing our minds, opening our hearts, having direction, and taking action.

Body Awareness

The eighteenth-century Hasidic Rabbi Nachman of Breslov (1772–1810), the great-grandson of the Baal Shem Tov (the founder of Hasidism), said, "Strengthen your body before you strengthen your soul." Many other spiritual traditions believe the same thing. Gautama Buddha said, "The true ascetic does not gratify the body, but he cares well for the body, that he may advance the spiritual life. Cared for, it is a better vessel for truth." Feeling balanced physically helps us feel better about ourselves and helps us think more clearly.

The Divine quality relating to *Malkhut* is kingship. Emulating the *sefirah* of *Malkhut*, we want to experience being master of our own universe. That means taking care of our body and being in charge of our environment.

Awareness is the first step. We need to balance fire, air, water, and earth. That means we need to eat nutritious meals in appropriate portions and get sufficient amounts of sleep, exercise, and fresh air. The following self-care inventory will help you assess how well you are taking care of yourself.

· Exercise: Self-Care Inventory ·

1. Is my diet a healthy one?

2. Do I eat nutritionally balanced meals?

3. Do I eat in suitable portions?

4. Do I exercise regularly?

5. How long do I exercise for?

6. Do I wake up feeling rested?

7. How much sleep do I get?

8. How much sleep do I need?

9. When did I have my last medical checkup?

10. Do I meditate regularly?

11. Do I feel good about my appearance? If not, what am I doing about it?

12. What incomplete dental conditions do I have going on?

13. When did I have my teeth cleaned last?

14. (For a woman:) When did I have my last pelvic exam, Pap test, breast exam? (For a man:) When did I have my last prostate exam?

15. What nonprescription drugs or medications do I use?

16. What personal habits do I have that need changing?

17. What are my physical strengths?

18. What are my physical limitations?

19. How do I deal with my physical strengths and limitations?

CONNECTING TO THE DIVINE

Connection to the Divine is a primary concept in Kabbalah and another attribute of *Malkhut.* When we lack this connection to wholeness and oneness, we feel disconnected from ourselves. With this disconnection, we often experience being out of control. We don't take care of ourselves and develop physical addictions, such as overeating, undereating, bulimia, and anorexia; we may become alcoholics, workaholics, shopaholics, or sex addicts. Gluttony and greed may take over. Or we may look to others to take care of us and fill our needs.

There are many ways kabbalists connect with the Divine and with the plant and animal kingdoms. These include: meditation and prayer, connecting with nature, taking a day of rest by observing the Sabbath, and blessing our food.

Meditation and Prayer

Kabbalists meditate and pray regularly. Orthodox Jewish men pray three times a day. Many people think they are relaxed when they really aren't. A client came to me after jogging ten miles and said he was relaxed. When I asked how relaxed he was mentally, he said his mind was filled with nonstop thought. Meditation helps not only with physical relaxation, but also clears the mind. Choose a time to be with yourself and relax.

The first step is silence. The need for silence is based on the concept that wisdom comes into being out of nothingness—the *ein,* the silence, that no one knows anything about. When we reach silence, we enter the silent pulse of the universe, the source of all knowledge, wisdom, and joy, the absolute *Ein Sof.* This is the state of mind in which prayers are heard and insights received. Without silence, there is static, and we don't have a clear transmission.

It takes a lot of practice to reach a total state of silence. Until we reach that state, we can practice relaxation. Here are some basic relaxation techniques. Remember, it helps to read through these techniques and the other meditations slowly to gain full comprehension. You will get more from the technique if you understand it as you read it or listen to it.

· Basic Relaxation: Sensory Awareness ·

Since *Malkhut* is the area of sensory awareness, it helps to do a relaxation exercise to get in touch with internal sight, sound, taste, smell, and touch.

Sit for a few minutes and set an intention to relax. Pay attention to your breath. Notice the way it comes in and out through your nostrils. Breathe evenly and deeply. Are your breaths short or long, deep or shallow? Notice how your breath spreads through your body before you exhale. Keep paying attention to your breathing. Begin to notice the sounds in the room. Practice being with them without reacting. Notice what happens in your body. Pay attention to the air temperature and to fragrances in the room. Again, just be with them without reacting. Notice what images come to mind. Do you see things in black and white or in color?

Now go through your body very slowly, paying attention to each part. If any part is tense, mentally relax it. Notice what you're experiencing in your forehead, and stay with it for a minute or so. Then pay attention to your eyes, staying with them for a minute or so. Move slowly to your temples, sinus passages, nose, jaw, tongue, lips, chin, and neck. Continue down through the top of your spine, shoulders, chest, heart, and lungs. Progress through your rib cage, the middle of your spine, the bottom of your spine, your stomach, and your waistline. Notice your buttocks, genital area, thighs, knees, calves, ankles, and feet. Be present with what you are experiencing internally.

Pay attention to your skin sensations. When you become very relaxed, you may begin to sense even more vibrations within and around yourself. You may experience a tingly sensation on your skin—like soft pins or needles or else a change of temperature. Internally you might sense vibrations—like energy bouncing off the inner walls of the skin. Just be with your energy.

Notice what you are experiencing. Take an inventory of your body and determine on a scale of 1 through 10, with 10 being the highest, how relaxed you really are.

· Visualization: Connecting with Nature ·

In *Malkhut* we have a strong connection to nature, to the earth, and to the plant and animal kingdoms. Kabbalists teach that connecting to nature and observing the greater scheme at work helps elicit awe. And from awe, we develop faith in and connection to the Divine. After the first session, I gave a client a homework assignment to connect with nature by taking a walk on the beach, a hike in the woods, or just to think about the patterns in nature. She said that while walking on the beach, she stepped down on the sand and watched how the movement of the sand affected everything else around it. She realized she affected nature. She also compared the ebb and flow of tides to the cycle of life; birth and death, expansion and contraction. From this she understood that just as nature is affected by the moon and stars, so are we. She said it made her feel she was receiving messages from nature about life and that she was part of a greater whole.

For those who are more visual, imagine yourself taking a walk on the beach. Visualize the changes of the tides, the ebb and flow of the water, and see the power of the waves. As you look down, notice the seashells and other treasures in the sand. Visualize the fish moving through the water at different speeds, taking up space in the water. What happens to the water as the fish move through it? See yourself moving air as you move through space. Imagine how your movement affects the air. As you breathe in the warm air, a message comes to you. Notice what it is. Pause and reflect.

Imagine yourself taking a long walk in the woods. The leaves are starting to turn colors in the autumn breeze. They are bright red, orange, and yellow. You see a huge tree trunk and notice the ripples in the bark, and it reminds you of the ripples in the water. You walk over to hug the tree and feel its energy. As you let go of the tree, you notice a leaf on the ground.

Pick it up. There's a message for you. Notice what it says. Pause and reflect.

It's winter and you decide to take a walk outside. The trees are barren and the chill keeps you bundled up in a jacket, hat, and gloves. Notice how you feel in this type of weather. How does it affect your thinking? As you look out at a field covered in snow, you see many animals. One stands out more than the others. You have a connection with this animal. It calls to you. Notice in detail what it looks like. You can feel the animal's feelings. Notice the sensations you're having. The animal has a message for you. Listen closely. What is it saying?

Now see yourself taking a long walk in a park in the spring. As you look up at one of the trees, notice small buds beginning to burst open. Think about your connection to the plant kingdom. Vegetation absorbs water, grows, and eventually feeds animals and humans. Plants are connected to the elements; they all need light, air, water, and earth to be nourished, just as we need light, air, water, and earth. As you pick up a petal and breathe in the aroma, a message comes to mind. What is it? Pause and reflect.

It's nighttime now, and you're looking up at the dark sky. It's a clear night, and the stars are glistening with brilliant radiance. You're in awe of the makeup of the universe. Each star seems to be talking to you as you wonder about life, nature, the change of seasons, birth, growth, and decay. You realize there is a pattern to all this, an awesome serenity. Who or what created the pattern? Reflect for a long time. Then, when you are ready, open your eyes. Write about your experiences.

The connection with nature and with the animal and vegetable kingdoms is recommended in most spiritual traditions. Notice the way nature exists, the ebb and flow of tides, the change of seasons, the weather. These are all messages on how to live life.

To bathe in the essence of *Malkhut,* get out in nature on a regular basis. Garden, play with animals, do anything that connects you to the plant and animal kingdoms. Take long walks on the beach, go hiking in the woods, fish in lakes, streams, or the ocean. Connect with the elements, the sun, air, water, and earth. Smell the flowers.

· Basic Mantra Meditation ·

For those who are more auditory, you can listen to music or else say a mantra repeating a word or phrase until you relax totally. Kabbalists often hum a *niggun,* a wordless melody repeated over and over again. Or you can chant a word or phrase, such as *peace* or something similar, or even a number, over and over until the noise in your head stops and you begin to experience silence. Keep repeating the word or phrase again and again. If thoughts come up, acknowledge them and then let them go as you continue to repeat the word or phrase.

Blessing Our Food

Kabbalists teach that blessing our food connects us with everything in the universe and energizes us even more. By paying attention to food and absorbing it mentally while we eat, we are more open to the energy and nutrients in the food. Furthermore, blessing our food shows our awareness of God's greatness and universal sustenance. We can honor this by constantly acknowledging where food comes from. For instance, if you're eating corn on the cob, think about everything that preceded biting into the ear of corn. The corn was placed in the earth as a seed. The seedling was nurtured by earth, water, air, and sun. The tiny seedling grew into a small plant. Absorbing more of the nutrients provided by nature, the plant grew taller and flourished. The husk started growing. When the corn matured, it was cut down, taken to market, and sold to you. You cooked it and ate it. By honoring the food on your plate, you are constantly honoring the heart of the universe, the Divine life force. The more you honor this force, the more you experience and are energized by it.

Take a Day of Rest: Observe the Sabbath

Malkhut, as the seventh day of creation, is also considered the day of rest. This involves taking one day a week, twenty-four hours, not to think, not to "have to" do, but just to be, to rest, to contemplate. A day of contemplation gives you the space and time to appreciate God's sustenance in the world and in your life.

Caring for the Environment

The Bible states that the *Shekhinah* (the feminine side of God) in exile had no dwelling and roamed from place to place. Exodus 25:8 says, "And let them make Me a sanctuary that I may dwell among them."

King David was given instructions from God to draw up plans for a house in which the *Shekhinah* could dwell. David gave these instructions to his son Solomon, who eventually built Solomon's Temple. The blueprints gave specifications for every room, down to the minutest detail, including the weight of each object.

In order to experience being in charge of our kingdom here on earth and to be the sovereign ruler and live with the Divine presence within us, we need to be concerned with our environment, our home, a place in which the *Shekhinah* can dwell here on earth.

The condition of our home and how energy flows through our surroundings affects our health, our wealth, our relationships, and our lives. Similar to the Taoist concept of Feng Shui, kabbalists believe our energies are affected by the environment in which we live.

In practical terms, dirt and clutter are transgressions. Seeing and sensing a cluttered environment contributes to a visual and sensory overload that is constantly working on our nervous systems and brains. Like an air-conditioner motor humming continually in the background, these annoyances are always present. Thoughts about them keep going around in our heads. We may not even realize it, but the thoughts clutter our minds, taking up time and space and sapping our energy. Our homes, cars, and physical surroundings are reflections of what is going on inside us.

To fill our homes with love and godliness—mirroring the emanation process of expansion and contraction—a space or void needs to be created. That means getting rid of everything we don't want, getting rid of everything we are tolerating, getting rid of everything that is not serving a purpose now.

To clean out the clutter, we need to look at the most minute details. For instance, if there is a nail sticking up from a wooden floor, we might walk by it three times a day and say to ourselves, *I'm going to cut my foot one of these days. I'd better knock it in.* But we don't do it. This causes internal clutter. It might take three minutes to find a hammer and flatten the nail into the wood. Those three minutes would release a lot of extra baggage in our minds.

· Exercise: Cleaning Out the Physical Clutter ·

What do you need to clean up?

Make a list of everything that is not serving a purpose, everything that is just taking up space, everything you are tolerating. The following list offers some starting points; keep adding to it. When you look at cleaning out the clutter and getting rid of things you don't want, it is helpful to ask yourself, *Is this serving a purpose in my life now?* If it isn't, get rid of it.

After making the list, start working on one thing at a time, taking it step by step, doing maybe only one item a week—whatever fits best into your schedule. Trying to do too much at one time can be so overwhelming, you quit altogether. So just take it step by step. The inventory below may help you to think about your environment and life.

· Exercise: Inventory ·

Does your home represent you? Does your home live up to your standards of neatness? Check off the areas you need to clean up.

INDOORS

Garage	Bedrooms	Bathroom
Yard	Closets	Appliances
Kitchen	Drawers	Storage area
Home repairs	Office	Family room
Living room	Attic	Basement
Plants	Floors	Refrigerator

OUTDOORS

Do you have sidewalks or driveways that need repair?

Do you have trees or plants that need pruning?

Is your grass fertilized or cut regularly?

Do any dead shrubs need to be removed?

Does the outside of your house need painting?

PETS

How well do you take care of your pets?

Are their shots up to date?

Are their cages clean?

Do you take time to play with your animals?

· Meditation: Cleansing ·

A traditional cleansing practice is going to a *mikvah*, a ritual bath. We can use any type of water as a visualization for cleansing. Do a basic relaxation.

Imagine yourself in the mountains, where natural hot springs cascade over rocks into deep pools of bubbling, steaming hot water. Alone, you breathe in the fresh air and say a short prayer of gratitude for the sun rising and the beauty of the day. Then you begin to shed your clothes. Walk down a few smooth rocks and find one to sit on in this amazing natural steam bath. All your worries, tensions, and fears are washed away slowly and steadily. As you lay your head back and breathe in the steam, you are embraced in serenity.

Stay here about twenty minutes. Slowly stand up, walk to the other side of the pool, and ascend a few rocks leading out. Wrap yourself in the white towel you left waiting and give thanks for the connection to nature and godliness.

· FOUR ·

Yesod: Foundation
Ego, Self-Image, and Stability

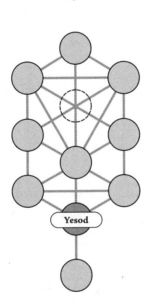

Divine Names: *Shaddai, El Chai*—Almighty Living God

Yesod is the ninth *sefirah* coming down the tree and the second going up. It has two Divine names, *El Chai* and *El Shaddai*. *El Chai,* the Living God, is the receiver of all the energies from above and the mediator of what flows into *Adonai (Malkhut),* the tenth *sefirah,* below. *El Shaddai* is Almighty God. *El Shaddai* means "enough"—enough of the amount of "ever-flow" (the energy that goes into *Adonai,* or *Malkhut*), the creation of the physical world. It was derived from a concept of creation in which the world would continue to expand until burning itself out; the Creator had to say *"Dai"* (enough). This light in the center produces another light that is the foundation of the world. Combined, the names *Shaddai* and *El Chai* represent the Almighty Living God. *Yesod* represents foundation—the foundation for righteousness.

Archangel: Gabriel

Gabriel is the archangel who represents *Yesod*. Some kabbalists see Gabriel as a female—the only female in the higher realms of archangels. Gabriel personifies childbirth and spiritual knowledge. She is a teacher, guiding us into knowledge and support of the Divine.

Patriarch: Joseph

Joseph, the patriarch representing *Yesod*, is the man with a coat of many colors—many facets of the animal soul, or ego. In his youth Joseph had a big ego. Because he retold his dreams of superiority and of his brothers bowing down to him, they threw him into a snake pit—only to retrieve him later, thinking they could make some money if they sold him into slavery.

As a trusted servant, Joseph controlled his sexual urges when his master's wife tried to seduce him. Angered, she accused *him* of making advances. Joseph was thrown into jail, where he interpreted dreams for the inmates. Hearing about this, the pharaoh invited Joseph to the palace to interpret his nightmares. Gaining favor with the pharaoh, Jacob was given a position of great power. Much later, when his brothers came begging for food in a time of famine, rather than being angry and seeking revenge, Joseph helped them. He realized that things happen for a reason, and a greater purpose was at work.

Joseph symbolizes the source of challenge and conflict in man. He dealt with his fate by making the most of every situation. He was a man of dreams who overcame many obstacles: He was thrown into the pit of despair, was forced to inhibit his sexual drive, learned self-control, and came to perceive his life—despite the suffering—as guided by God.

Attribute: Foundation

The essence of *Yesod* is foundation. In *Yesod* we have a firm foundation for connecting to God through study and prayer. We have a positive self-image and confidence; we live responsibly. We feel good about ourselves and our lives and are grateful to the Divine. To emulate the essence of *Yesod*, we experience ourselves with a strong foundation and fulfilled with God. After meditation, state this affirmation: *I am filled with the almightiness of God, which gives me a strong foundation, well-being, confidence, and the will to live responsibly.*

YESOD: FOUNDATION
(EGO, STABILITY)

Yesod, the second *sefirah* from the bottom in the middle on the overall Tree of Life, is the next gate to enter on our ascent on the Tree of Life. The Divine essence of *Yesod* is foundation or stability.

Yesod is also the area of awareness known as the ego. It's our persona, the way we show ourselves to the world, our personality. Our personalities are shaped by impressions from past lives as well as how we experience our lives and ourselves in this life. What is below the surface—hidden thoughts, repressed feelings, and unconscious behavior—is what Carl Jung considered the "shadow" side of ourselves.

This "shadow," or the unconscious, rules us. It often triggers responses in us that are unintentional, irrational, or just mean. The goal is to make the unconscious conscious. When we are aware of our thoughts, feelings, and instinctive behaviors and we choose how to respond to them, we no longer behave irrationally, but intentionally. We can choose to come from truth, beauty, Divine love, and creativity, rather than from meanness and evil.

Yesod, as the ego, deals with the concepts of pleasure, pain, and gratification. It correlates with the sexual organs and, therefore, the procreative or regenerative, creative aspect of life. It represents the channeling of sexual/creative energy. This energy emerges when we unite with God.

SEXUALITY/CREATIVITY

Sexual energy manifesting in creativity, according to kabbalists, is the reflection of Divine unity. As mentioned earlier, this is the marriage of *Malkhut* and *Tiferet,* the union of body and soul. Lust or passion is the longing for unity between the dualities—male and female energies, yin and yang, and even the electrons and protons that make up atoms. Sexual energy brings everything to equanimity and oneness. It is the basis of creation itself. Kabbalah emphasizes that sexual energy is a part of life. It can be expressed through the sexual act or through creativity. When the sexual energy is harnessed and directed spiritually, it can lead to mystical experiences. In the union with the Divine, creation takes place and creative energies flow.

In the Indian system of Tantra, the basic life force is known as kundalini, a bioelectric energy that flows through the body and can be harnessed and directed into sexual and creative energy. In Kabbalah, using this energy consciously in either the sexual act or creative endeavors toward living our purpose is considered the greatest demonstration of love for the Creator.

In the body *Yesod* is located in the pelvic area. It deals with the lower part of the trunk, connecting the limbs with the hips and giving us a firm foundation. *Yesod* also rules the genital area. It represents the creative forces in the universe as well as sexual union between humans.

CONNECTING WITH OUR SOUL MATES

The *Zohar* tells us that an emerging soul comes into being from the Absolute as male and female together. When it descends to this world, however, the soul splits and enters either a male or female body in order to learn its lessons in that body. Finding our soul mate is uniting with the other half of ourselves.

Psychologist Eric Berne devised a method of psychotherapy in the 1970s called Transactional Analysis. Fashioning it after Freud's concept of id, ego, and superego, he called the varying states of consciousness "Parent," "Adult," and "Child." The parent state is the nurturing and critical state. The adult state is the rational, logical state. The child state is the playful, or rebellious, state. When two people interact, they each have the potential to develop all three of these states. Usually, however, one person has developed either one or two of them and looks to the other to fill the gap.

For instance, an accountant might be very rational and logical but might not have developed his parent (nurturing) and child (playful) states. He would look to his mate, who probably has developed the two states in which he is lacking and has not yet developed the logical state. They are now two people dependent on each other in order to feel whole. After a while one begins to criticize the other for what he or she is lacking. The relationship reverts back to the parent/child relationship—how they behaved as children. After a while one partner becomes totally needy and the other begins to feel smothered. The goal is to discover and maintain our own sense of wholeness and be interdependent before finding a mate.

To become whole means to develop our parent, adult, and child states and to develop the ability to think clearly, feel what's going on, and speak truthfully. It means knowing our thoughts, feelings, speech, and actions, and actualizing them to live our own truth. By finding our truth, we elevate ourselves to oneness with the Absolute and connect with the Divine spark of light and wholeness in ourselves. The spark of light emanating from within is what attracts our soul mate to us. Unless we are totally in touch with our truth and fulfilled within ourselves, we might pass our soul mate on the street and not recognize him or her.

To attain unity with the Divine, we open to love and give love, we feel passion and live with passion; we live responsibly and go beyond our bodies to the source. In Genesis 2:21 it is stated, "They shall be one flesh." This is often interpreted to mean that when man and woman come together, they remove all barriers (clothing—all skin) to become as one, just as we, individually, can become one with God by eliminating thoughts and other external influences. To cultivate Divine union in our life, whether single or mated, we need to pray, meditate, do service through acts of loving-kindness, and work toward fulfilling our life purpose.

ANIMAL SOUL: *NEFESH*

Yesod and the surrounding areas, including the *sefirot* of *Hod, Netzach,* and *Malkhut,* are considered in Kabbalah to be the animal level of the soul or animal level of consciousness, known as *nefesh.* It's the survival level of existence and primarily associated with the world of instincts and action, the world of *Asiyah.*

There are two parts of the *nefesh* level of soul: the *nefesh beheimit* and the *nefesh Elohit.* The *nefesh beheimit,* the lower level of the soul, is often associated with *klipot*—shells or peels that veil us from the Divine Soul. This involves our animalistic instincts, tendencies, and acting-out behavior. It's the part of us still fixated on ourselves: the self-indulgent, wanting, greedy, and sinful part. This level of soul, in the world of *Asiyah,* the body, overlaps the lower part of the world of *Yetzirah,* the psyche, and moves us into thought and choice. As we elevate the "dark" side of ourselves to responsible living, we develop *nogah*—the glow or light of the *nefesh Elohit.*

The Divine Soul, the highest level of soul closest to the Absolute, is involved with truth and godliness. We open to this level of soul when we get beyond our animalistic tendencies. We begin the process by developing a healthy *Yesod*—a firm foundation, stability, a healthy ego.

Developing a healthy *Yesod* involves making the unconscious conscious and living responsibly. It's having a strong personal foundation or personal empowerment. Since *Yesod* is the foundation of who we are and how we see ourselves, if that is less than godly, we still have work to do.

> Note: The paths between the *sefirot* are ruled by the Hebrew letters. While the *sefirot* are objective, the paths are subjective. The paths show us the lessons we each need to learn to move into the consciousness and the essence of each *sefirah*. They are ruled by the twenty-two Hebrew letters. At each path, to meditate on the Hebrew letter, psychologist Edward Hoffman, author of *The Hebrew Alphabet*, recommends writing out the letter or visualizing it. Consistent with kabbalistic tradition, keep a journal and write down your experiences.

PATH BETWEEN
MALKHUT AND *YESOD: TAV* ת

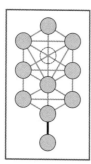

The path between *Malkhut* and *Yesod* is represented by the final letter of the Hebrew alphabet, *tav*, ת. The path of *tav* relates to the planet Jupiter, considered the force of righteousness. The day of the week is Saturday. The direction is center. *Tav* is the first letter in the Hebrew words *Torah* (the Five Books of Moses, the first five books of the Bible), *tefilah* (prayer), *teshuvah* (return to God through repentance), and *tikkun* (repair of the soul). *Tav* also stands for a stamp or seal; an impression. It is primarily the seal or impression of truth. It refers to the kingdom of the Infinite One and exemplifies the secret of faith in Absolute Truth. To us, it can pertain to living our own truth. Meditating on the Hebrew letter *tav*, ת, starts the process internally of talking to God through prayer, returning to truth, and helping ourselves and others in world repair.

TORAH STUDY

Orthodox Jewish kabbalists teach that Torah study is the foundation for living life with godliness, joy, meaning, and purpose.

Students of Torah study it in four different ways, known by the acronym *PaRDeS*. The Hebrew word *pardes* means "orchard" or "garden." It's the way to reach the Garden of Eden. Students of Torah look at each portion of the Torah from four different perspectives:

P = *P'shat:* the simple meaning of the text

R = *Remez:* the meaning hinted at, viewing the text as a series of metaphors, parables, and symbols

D = *Drash:* examining and interpreting the text to apply it as a guide to live by

S = *Sod:* the mystery in the hidden meaning

The four areas of PRDS address the four worlds and the four ways we learn. *P'shat* deals with the simple meaning and a more literal translation—basic concepts. *Remez* addresses emotions and feelings through metaphors, parables, and symbols. *Drash* addresses the more intellectual side, looking for the deeper meaning of how the Torah can be applied in daily life. And *sod* addresses the spiritual or mystical aspect, using *gematria* (Hebrew numerology), astrology, and meditation.

In Kabbalah, community is very important. A recommended practice is to study Torah with at least one other person, brainstorming, questioning, getting feedback, and deciphering the lesson from the four perspectives in order to comprehend it fully. To kabbalists, studying Torah means not only reading and understanding, but also living it. Take a portion of the Torah throughout the week, think about how it pertains to your life, and integrate it into daily living.

PRAYER/MEDITATION

The *tav* is the first letter of the Hebrew word *tefilah,* prayer, which is extremely important in Kabbalah. Prayer is calling on God. We call on God for two reasons: to praise or to petition. This involves using general prayers and personal prayers.

General prayers are blessings acknowledging and praising the attributes of God. This, kabbalists believe, helps bring God's energies down to earth. Personal prayers involve petitioning God and asking for what we want.

To pray effectively, we need to meditate first. Ancient kabbalists were reported to have gone to the Temple an hour earlier to purify the heart and focus the mind before praying. Doing so, they developed profound concentration (*kavanah*) and communion or devotion (*deveikut*) with God with no distractions. *Deveikut* is the cleaving to or communion with the Divine. Maimonides advised, "Prayer without devotion is not prayer."

Kabbalists believe tensions and noises, both internal and external, block us from being in touch with our soul. If we don't remove the blocks by relaxing our bodies, quieting our thoughts, and releasing feelings, the prayers take much longer to be heard. Maimonides said, "Before engaging in prayer, bring yourself into a devotional frame of mind."

Many ancient kabbalists used mantras, chants, and body movements to get into a meditative or altered state of consciousness prior to connecting with God. Then they would pray by focusing on the varying attributes or names of God.

Here are some general affirmations to help us connect with God:

- *May my eyes behold the blessings of the new day.*
- *I place God before me always.*
- *Blessed is the One and Only One.*
- *I believe.*
- *I have faith.*
- *I love.*
- *I see the Divine in everything and everyone.*
- *I accept the Divine in my life.*
- *I am in the likeness of Divine.*
- *I am a radiant channel for Divine light.*

Personal prayers involve petitioning God. To do this we meditate first, then pray to God by focusing on a godly attribute or the energy or light relating to the *sefirah* we are working on. We can say the Divine name, the name of the archangel or patriarch, or the common name or essence.

In order to pray for something we aspire to change about ourselves or wish to attain, we need to know what we want to pray for. In the Garden of Eden, Adam was given trees and plants. In order for the plants to grow, Adam needed to pray for rain. God wants us to ask for what we want and need. He wants us to be conscious, aware. Kabbalists teach that we can pray for materialistic as well as spiritual needs but should do so for the right reason—to experience the connection to the Divine.

Kabbalists also teach that prayers should be said aloud, or that we should at least mouth the phrases. The voice arouses *kavanah,* intention and concentration. We can also visualize what we want to accomplish through pictures, words, or feelings.

Kabbalists use the terms *engrave* and *carve.* Engraving was originally like cuneiform, in which letters were engraved in stone. Material was removed from the stone. *Engrave* means to imprint or visualize; to imagine in your mind through pictures, words, or feelings. *To carve* means to express it—experience it; see it, think it, feel it, hear it, smell it, touch it, taste it. The engraving and carving become more ingrained in the soul when we incorporate all our senses and are totally focused or intent on having what we desire.

TIKKUN OLAM (WORLD REPAIR)
AND TIKKUN NEFESH (SOUL REPAIR)

Tav is the first letter of the word *tikkun. Tikkun olam* is world repair. But before we repair the world, we need to repair our own souls in *tikkun nefesh,* soul repair. We need to become whole. It happens by uniting with God, remembering our soul's purpose and living it here on earth. We begin the process by getting in touch with devout impulses and impressions, as opposed to what kabbalists call animalistic impulses.

IMPRINTS: STAMPS

A *tav* represents a stamp, a mark, an imprint, or an impression. The *Zohar* states that "the *tav* makes an impression on the Ancient of Days." It makes an impression on the will of God. It's the impression of faith, which is the seal of truth.

Kabbalists believe we come into each life with impressions, images, or "stamps" of who we are. Such a "stamp," however, is often veiled by our interpretation of impulses formulated through pictures, words, feelings, and imagination, all of which make imprints on our soul.

As explained in the *Sefer Yetzirah*, we are all influenced by electromagnetic forces created by fire (the radiation of energy), water (the absorption of energy), and the interaction of the two created by air (the transmission of energy). The fourth force is gravity, corresponding to earth. These forces all come about from the will of the Absolute in the form of impulses (vibrations or electromagnetic forces of energies).

Hebrew letters are the vehicles that carry the impulses from the Absolute into the *sefirot* and eventually form into thought waves and patterns in human brains, manifesting in words and ideas.

The sequence of thought may be described as follows: God's will comes as an impulse into *Keter*, known as the "crown of royalty" or "the will of wills." This is known as a "devout impulse." This impulse manifests as Divine thought in *Chokhmah* (wisdom)—the right brain. At this point the energies are so intense, however; too much comes in at once and can't be deciphered. Therefore the thoughts are still hidden from awareness. They are thoughts in potential. In *Binah* consciousness, left-brain consciousness (the breath of the heart of the upper world), it is like a "fire burning within us" until the thought congeals into a sense of understanding, a form or pattern. *Binah* consciousness distinguishes one thing from another; it gives the original idea more direction but is still hidden from consciousness.

Thought descends into *Tiferet*, and it is here that it is made known, but still not actualized. *Tiferet* is the "inner voice that is heard." For it to be realized, however, it needs to be enunciated into speech, which takes place in *Malkhut*. But before the thought is received in *Malkhut* it is filtered through *Tiferet* and through the six *sefirot* of emotions, known as *middot*, which means "measured flows." These *sefirotic* flows are *Chesed* (loving-kindness and mercy), *Gevurah* (judgment, justice, strength, discipline, restraint), *Netzach* (victory, endurance, or mastery over instincts and action), *Hod* (splendor, thinking, communication), *Yesod* (foundation, ego, conditioning), and *Malkhut* (kingdom, body). By the time the original thought is transferred through the brain, heart, nervous system, and liver to culminate in *Malkhut,* materialization or speech, it is hidden or veiled. The original thoughts, the Divine or devout impulses, are filtered through the intellect and emotions and therefore may take on a different meaning or imprint than the original thought when it is expressed or verbalized. The first Divine or devout impulses are now veiled and possibly distorted. This works the same way with knowing who we are.

Devout Impulses: Original Thoughts of Who We Are—Stamp of Truth

Kabbalah teaches that each soul descends into the body with a specific Divine mission. It has within it the Divine spark of God. Comparing it to the sequence of thought, we come into this life with the first impulse of connectedness to God. Then a vague symbolic idea of our purpose germinates in *Chokhmah* (wisdom) consciousness. *Binah* consciousness begins our understanding in words of God's plan or mission for us, and we formulate a plan. In *Daat* consciousness we know and trust in God and have the motivation to fulfill our plan.

In *Chesed* consciousness we may have an overwhelming love of God and begin to work on our purpose. In *Gevurah* that love is tested by evil forces, just like the serpent seducing Eve into eating the fruit of the Tree of Knowledge. If we fail the test, our love of God turns to fear of God. We're now exiled from the Garden of Eden and separated from pure consciousness. We are "clothed in skins." In *Tiferet* we become conscious of who we are. We experience ourselves both joined to and separate from God. We are an individuated self.

In *Netzach*—the area of instincts and actions—if we fear God's wrath, the body releases chemicals that create the desire to either fight or flee (the fight-or-flight response). In *Hod* the thoughts we have are now based on feelings and actions. In *Yesod* we have a new imprint, image, or stamp of ourselves based on how we've behaved or who we think we are in relationship to God and our purpose.

In *Malkhut* we live out that new impression in each lifetime. The farther away we move from this first thought, our spark of divinity and purpose, over a succession of lifetimes, the poorer our self-image becomes, because we no longer know who we are. We have veiled ourselves from the light of God and our Divine purpose.

Physical Imprints

Kabbalists believe that the amount and type of light and energy, the level of consciousness or awareness, with which we come into in each lifetime is attained "according to due"—our merit or worth. It's the amount earned as a result of transforming past evil or frivolous thoughts, speech, and deeds into righteous or responsible living.

As mentioned earlier, Kabbalists believe that we each come into life with a certain body structure and varying stages of psychological and spiritual development. Physically we are imbued with DNA and RNA, as well as a muscular, chemical, and genetic makeup incorporating instincts, patterns, coding, and tendencies from the past. Just as medical conditions can be genetic, so can instinctive behaviors. Spiritually our bodies are imbued with different levels of the soul. The levels carry imprints incorporating hidden cellular memories, experiences, thoughts, feelings, and perceptions within us from the past, going back to the Big Bang and even before (preconsciousness) to *Ein Sof*, the Absolute, prior to *tzimtzum*. The soul is engraved and "stamped" with old impressions, imprints, and essences of who we are and how we lived in our past lives or the past in our current lives.

These imprints emerge in milliseconds based on what we see hear, touch, taste, and smell. They can come as physical sensations, images, or feelings. With each new experience that is reminiscent of something from the past, we react the same way as in the past, often going in circles rather than moving beyond the issue. Until we acknowledge, erase, or revise the old imprints on our soul, or the cellular memories, as well as overcoming instinctive physical reactions that come from our ancestral lineage, we keep repeating old patterns.

The best example I can give of carrying forth an impression of an experience from the past is a personal one. It came when I was reviewing my life about twenty years ago. I was visiting my mother, and we stayed up late into the night discussing my childhood. I told her about a recurring dream I had of either running in front of a tidal wave or trying to climb a pole to get ahead of rising water. Mom shared with me that when I was three months old and she was bathing me, the bassinette broke; water poured all over me, and I went into a screaming rage. After my mother told me this, I released the "stamp" or imprint and never had that dream again.

Evidently, although we may not remember an experience, the essence of it may stay with us and manifest in some other form, such as my fear of water in the dreams and my fear of waves in reality. Until we acknowledge, erase, or revise the old imprints and impulses from past lives as well as this one, we keep repeating similar patterns.

Kabbalists believe that to resolve the past, we need to look at the present and see what we have and where we are. Past issues are carried forth as imprints, so we can change the imprints and see things from a different perspective.

Our self-image, thoughts, and feelings about life are based on these imprints. The goal is to elevate ourselves from the false imprints and past images and get to the truth. In Genesis 12:1 God says to Abraham (then called Abram), "Go forth [*lech lecha*] from your land, your place of birth, your father's house to the land that I will show you." Abraham left the land of his father and let go of the past.

The Hebrew words *lech lecha* are interpreted by kabbalists to mean going into yourself, knowing yourself, fulfilling yourself. When we know ourselves, we know what we need to change to become authentic; our Divine self—our greater spiritual self—has the self-confidence, self-reliance, faith, and vitality to fulfill our purpose.

From a kabbalistic perspective, leaving our homeland is going within and letting go of past false impressions, knowing ourselves, and living righteously and honestly. This begins with the image we have of ourselves. Kabbalists believe that light and love are always available to us. However, a poor self-image—a "false stamp or imprint"—blocks us from experiencing that light, love, and wisdom. To help change old distorted imprints and perceptions of ourselves, we must first see what they are.

· Meditation: Self-Image ·

Do a basic relaxation. Experience yourself taking a long walk in the woods. Experience this through pictures (visually), words (verbally), or sensations (kinesthetically). It's an incredibly vibrant, pleasantly warm day. As you breathe in radiating energy, a feeling of connection with nature engulfs you. Colors and shadows invigorate your soul. The peaceful surroundings connect you to a deeper part of yourself. Walk to a rock overlooking a glistening pond. Warmed by the sun, the rock is shaped like a chair. A small, smooth basin forms the seat and the back. Sit down on the rock. The seat is solid under your body, and nature supports you with strength. Relax in the peaceful setting, and let go.

Glimpse a sparkling pool in front of you. As you look into this body of water, see an image of yourself as you are today, reflected like a clear image in a mirror. Take a good look at yourself and ponder the following:

HOW WILLING AM I TO SEE MYSELF TRULY?

1. What do I see?
2. What do I think of myself?
3. What do I say to myself about myself (self-talk)?
4. How do I experience myself?
5. What do I like about myself?
6. What do I dislike about myself?
7. How lovable and capable am I?
8. How capable am I of loving?
9. How worthy am I of receiving Divine love and wisdom?
10. What would I like to change about myself?
11. What would I be like if I changed?
12. Is it possible for me to change?
13. Do I want to change?
14. How will I know when I have changed?

· Exercise: Impression of My Life ·

Since our environment plays an important role in our existence, we need to look at our perception of our lives. Below are questions to ponder:

1. What do I have in my life? _____.

2. My job is _____.

3. My volunteer work is _____.

4. My environment is _____.

5. My home is _____.

6. My love life is _____.

7. My social life is _____.

8. My leisure time is _____.

9. I am physically _____.

10. In general, my life is _____.

11. When I find my true self, and live the life I want, my life will be _____; I will have _____; and I will feel _____.

Write down the things you would like to change about your life.

REPENTANCE, RETURN TO GOD

Continuing on the first path, the *tav* is the first letter of *teshuvah*, repentance. To return to God we need to do *teshuvah*. Repentance begins with knowing what we need to correct by being aware of and admitting our sins. Biblical examples include Cain admitting to God that he killed Abel and repenting for his sin, and Jacob admitting he deceived his father in asking for the birthright that was due Esau and repenting for it. We admit our sins by admitting our faults and vulnerabilities. We see them by doing a life review.

· Exercise: Life Review ·

Some kabbalists speculate that Yesod is the area in which, upon death, we review our life in reverse. This entails experiencing the impact of our actions on ourselves and others. Ideally we want to come to terms with the effects of our choices and actions. The way we do it is through reflection.

Reflection is an extremely important practice in Kabbalah. Kabbalah originated through reflection and contemplation. Reflection is looking back, remembering, and trying to understand as fully as possible. Reflection helps us gain insight into who we are and why we act the way we do. Over the next few weeks, think back over the personal regrets you have in your life. Moral and ethical regrets will be discussed in detail in *Gevurah*.

PERSONAL REGRETS

Weight	Boundary issues
Health	Overwork
Money	Gossip
Apathy	Laziness
Promiscuity	Greed
Boredom	False pride
Control	Poor memory
Judgment	Knowing my purpose
Criticism	and not following it

· Meditation: Bringing Light to the Darkness ·

To begin the process of relieving ourselves of regret, we can concentrate on each regret in meditation and shine light on it. We do this by surrounding ourselves in light from the various *sefirot*. According to Aryeh Kaplan in *Meditation and Kabbalah,* the light of love pertains to the light of good (*tov*) from *Chesed*. The glow of strength (*nogah*) is from *Gevurah*. The light of glory (*kavod*) is *Tiferet,* beauty. The brilliance (*bahir*) from *Netzach* is victory. The light of radiance (*zohar*) is *Hod,* splendor. And the light of life (*chaim*) is *Yesod,* foundation.

With will and imagination, kabbalists believe we can overcome and achieve what we strive for. Adapted from Kaplan's exercise, these varying lights are considered different thrones. As we visit each throne in meditation, we can bring on the light of that throne. If you are too judgmental, stand between the light of brilliance of *Gevurah* and the light of good of *Chesed* and bring them both in. If you act irresponsibly, bring in the light of life of *Yesod.* Or just in general, as you think of each regret, think of bringing these radiances around you. As each one is brought in, ask if there's a message for you. Wait for insights. Write them down as they come.

FIVE

Hod: Splendor
Communication, Thinking, and Receiving

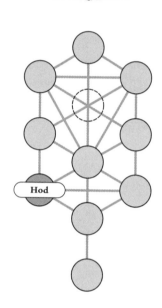

Divine Name: *Elohim Tzvaot*—Creator God of Hosts

The Divine name for *Hod* is *Elohim Tzvaot.* The *sefirah* across from it on the right is *Netzach,* with the Divine name *YHVH Tzvaot.* These two names are often referred to as one, as written in Psalm 94:9: "*YHVH Elohim Tzvaot,* hear my prayer." The reason they are considered one is because they are both ruled by *tzvaot,* the armies or hosts of the Lord. Hosts are celestial beings, angels, and God's helpers in the spirit world; they are sometimes regarded to be the sons and grandsons of God, or forces, powers, or energies. These armies or hosts are responsible for all the wars and miracles in the world. God is the supreme commander over the hosts, and in the Divine world *Hod—YHVH Tzvaot—*is the

"Place of Counsel," in charge of all legal decisions that defend, punish, or reward. There is, however, an angel who has the power to rescind the decrees depending on the force of our repentance and prayers. Kabbalists consider God's armies and hosts to be our thoughts (*Hod*) and actions (*Netzach*). These dictate what we get in life—the miracles and the suffering.

Archangel: Raphael

Raphael, the archangel of healing, represents *Hod.* Raphael's name in Hebrew means "Heal me, O God." Raphael is known to heal all types of ailments and is full of knowledge, including everything having to do with medicine, mathematics, education, books, and legal contracts. He is the personification of health and recreation. Also, as the patron of the dead, he leads souls into judgment and guides them in self-analysis.

Patriarch: Aaron

Aaron is the patriarch representing *Hod.* The older brother of Moses, Aaron was an eloquent speaker and was known as the articulate one. He was chosen to speak for Moses, who stuttered. In order to hear and understand Moses, Aaron also had to be a good listener. Aaron is also known for helping people reach peace. When waiting for Moses to come down from the mountain, the Israelites became restless and anxious looking for an icon to call God. Aaron pacified them by combining their gold into the form of a calf. He would also walk through the camps teaching peace.

Attributes: Splendor, Glory, Reverberation

In *Hod* we experience the splendor of God's glory by co-partnering with God and passing on Divine wisdom. It involves left-brain, cognitive abilities and is the area of receptivity, listening, and communication. To emulate the essence of *Hod,* we can call on any of the above representations or meditate on experiencing Divine splendor and the ability to think and communicate clearly. At the end of the meditation, state the affirmation: *I am in the splendor of God's glory and co-partner with God in passing on wisdom.*

HOD: SPLENDOR
(THINKING, REVERBERATION,
COMMUNICATION)

Hod is the third gate to enter as we ascend the Tree of Life. The primary attributes of *Hod* are splendor, reverberation, and glory. It's seeing the splendor and glory of God's Divine Providence or presence in everything we have and do and reverberating or "echoing" Divine prophecy. It's the area of data processing—of monitoring information and passing it along in the form of listening, learning, teaching, communicating. On the left side of the Tree of Life, *Hod* consciousness involves left-brain cognitive abilities, thinking, and study. Since *Hod* and *Netzach* are the *sefirot* of prophecy, and *Hod* represents thoughts while *Netzach* represents feelings and each influences the other, these *sefirot* are often explored together. In *Hod* and the surrounding paths we work primarily on thoughts.

OBSERVING DIVINE PROVIDENCE:
SEEING GOD AND CO-PARTNERING WITH GOD

In order to see the splendor of God's Divine Providence, it is important to understand what Divine Providence is. Kabbalah teaches that everything is Divine Providence. God is everything. God is around us, within us, everything about us, and our lives. He is the existence of the universe and everything in it. Since the *Ein Sof* is light and energy, and everything consists of light and energy in different sizes, shapes, and forms, then everything is a different shape or form of God—even inanimate objects, which consist of very condensed amounts of energy. Furthermore, we are constantly in communication with this light and energy. We are co-partners with God.

In *Hod*, represented by Aaron, who was Moses' voice, we have the ability to communicate with God in co-partnership to help create peace within ourselves and in the world. Kabbalah teaches that whatever we have, whatever we get, and everything that happens to us is a message from God to help our souls evolve and return to union with the Absolute, the *Ein Sof*. As we begin to awaken to the messages, we begin to understand why things happen the way they do.

Divine Providence can be observed by looking back, seeing and feeling Divine guidance and interventions in our lives at all times. It's often most visible when we look at the synchronicities of thoughts and events.

Many years ago I was working full-time and did some freelance writing on the side. I was working on an article called "Developing the Sixth Sense." During my lunch hour I had planned on interviewing a psychic who had come up from North Carolina and was doing a workshop on the topic in the same building where I worked. When I arrived at the office that morning, however, my boss informed me that he had set up another interview for me, which was to take place during my lunch hour. I was instantly upset, but decided to calm down and recite an affirmation: *I have faith. If it's meant to be, it will be.* I left it up to the Absolute.

At noon I received a call from the man I was to interview at work. "I'm sorry," he said. "There was a bad accident on the parkway. I can't make it to your office and back to mine in time for an important meeting that I have. Can we reschedule my appointment?" "Of course," I said, chuckling to myself, and off I went to interview the psychic.

It's watching the little things that make us aware of the bigger picture and Divine interventions. It's also important to realize that when we ask for something, we do usually get it—but not always in the way we expect.

More recently, while writing, I was struggling with a particular portion and kept thinking I "should" write it out by hand. Sometimes writing by hand helps slow the mind down. Yet the speed of the computer anchored me to the keyboard. Each day that I remained blocked I kept thinking—*Write it out*. Well, I got the help needed. My computer crashed—so I *had* to write it out! I chuckled and cried at the same time. But it worked. I was able to sort out what I was trying to say.

Other little signs of God? Perhaps we're pondering something and the next day open the morning newspaper to a headline giving us the information we wanted. Or walking in a bookstore and having a book fall off the shelf right in front of us—again just what we were looking for. Or else driving behind a truck with a logo that has a message for us.

Another way of seeing Divine Providence is the witnessing of miracles. *Hod* is the area of miracles, both small and large. Miracles happen every day: babies being born, healings taking place, people meeting their soul mates, people recovering from severe illness. Keep acknowledging these signs. Write them down in a journal.

The more we see the relationship between thoughts and happenings, or the miracles in our lives, the easier it is to accept that we are in touch with higher energies and actually communicating and co-partnering with the Absolute in everything we think, say, and do.

Kabbalists believe this communication happens because our thoughts, speech, feelings, and actions are expressed through energy vibrations that are received in the *sefirot*. The *sefirot* reflect back to us what's going on both inside and out—who we think we are, how we behave, and what we have in life. This is mirrored in how we feel, personal challenges, relationships, and opportunities, as well as material things.

The things we don't want in our lives play just as vital a role as those we do want. They show us what we need to work on in order to reach self-perfection. To co-partner with the Divine and consciously begin creating goodness, we have to perfect our ways of communicating—listening, thinking, and speaking.

PATH BETWEEN *YESOD* AND *HOD*: *LAMED* ל

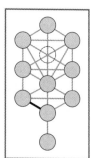

The path between *Yesod* and *Hod* is represented by the Hebrew letter *lamed*, ל. The astrological correlations on the path of *lamed* correspond to the constellation of Libra and the Hebrew month of *Tishrei* (September–October). To Jewish kabbalists, *Tishrei* includes the holidays of Rosh Hashanah and Yom Kippur. This is the time of great reflection, repentance, and revision.

The Hebrew meaning of *lamed* is "to learn" and "to teach." *Lamed* is the first letter of the Hebrew word *lev*, heart. Combining learning and teaching with the heart, Rabbi Akiva saw it as a "heart that understands knowledge." As a path on the left side of the tree, *lamed* involves left-brain cognitive abilities including rational thought, logic, and legal and mathematical activities. The sign of *lamed* is an ox-goad, a curved stick used to prod oxen or cattle. It prods us into action. *Lamed* is also the first letter of *lamed vav,* the number 36. It is taught that the world continues to exist because of thirty-six righteous people, referred to as *lamed-vavnikim.*

To enter into the path of knowledge that comes from the heart, learning and teaching, stimulating healthy cognitive faculties and abilities that prod us into action, we meditate on the letter lamed ל.

REVERBERATION: LEARNING AND TEACHING PROPHECY

The path of *lamed* involves learning and teaching. During the prophecy period, 1312–312 B.C.E., teachings came from God as transmitted through the prophets.

To ancient kabbalists, prophets were people who channeled Divine wisdom and imparted it to others, receiving and sharing. During the "Years of Prophecy" many prophets had visions of seeing the Chariot-Throne of God. These mystics practiced very high levels of meditation. Many had dreams and visions of seven levels of heaven or Paradise with angels standing at each gate protecting it; the last gate was the Throne of Glory. In order to enter, the meditator had to know the code or God name for each gate as well as particular symbols to meditate upon. Some mystics were turned away. Others had terrible misfortunes. As mentioned previously, there is a story of four mystics who tried to reach Paradise; one went crazy, another became a heretic, one died. Only Rabbi Akiva survived, because he was the only one who had learned the lessons of purification before attempting to enter through the higher gates.

While many prophets channeled Divine wisdom, others either channeled evil spirits or interpreted the information in evil ways. It is stated in the Torah that Moses was the only prophet who communicated directly with God. As God told Moses, "I am the Lord. And I appeared to Abraham, to Isaac and to Jacob as God Almighty [*El Shaddai*] but by My name 'the Lord' [YHVH] I did not make Myself known to them" (Exodus 6:3). It is said that Moses was the only one who spoke directly from the heart, and therefore God made himself known to Moses as YHVH. Moses channeled God's voice directly, without intermediaries—God spoke through him. The other prophets received prophecy through angels,

visions, and dreams, which then needed to be interpreted. Although many messages were pure, many also came from the lower spheres of filtered thoughts,
speech, and actions; they were not always accurate.

After the Years of Prophecy, although some mystics still reported having
visions similar to the ancient kabbalists, this means of transmission declined.
Lessons were revealed through Divine Providence, which is absolutely everything
that comes to us as well as what we already have in life. We learn from everyone
and everything, the good and bad, but especially the challenging events in our
lives—including those that lead to suffering. This is the Divine's way of guiding
us on the road to spiritual perfection.

In practical terms, the levels of consciousness of the *sefirot* of *Hod* and *Netzach*
and the surrounding paths include prophetic visions and paranormal phenom-
ena that are symbolic forms of thought, in either pictures, words, or feelings.
This level of prophecy might also involve psychic powers such as extrasensory
perception (ESP), clairvoyance, clairaudience, precognition, and telekinesis. It is
important to note that many of us believe that when we experience these phe-
nomena, we have reached higher spiritual states of consciousness. This is not
necessarily so. We can develop incredible psychic powers and even prophecy
without integrity of the spirit or godliness. Unless we truly know ourselves and
act out of awareness, intention, truth, and an open heart, we have not reached
higher spiritual consciousness.

Kabbalists believe all prophets need to prepare themselves in order to receive
Divine prophecy. It begins with understanding our internal mechanisms and
drives. We must get to really know ourselves before we can help others, starting
by knowing our thoughts and beliefs.

Thinking: Processing Thoughts and Beliefs

The path of *lamed* is involved in reverberation and communication. To reverber-
ate is to echo words and to respond or pass on information. It involves listening,
hearing, seeing, sorting out, and transmitting knowledge. It's the area of thinking and interpretations of impressions coming through past memories or
imprints in *Yesod* as discussed in the previous chapter. If our thoughts aren't
truth, then we can't communicate clearly.

The *Zohar* explains three different ways of processing thoughts by the three primary categories of people: the wicked, the intermediaries, and the righteous ones. The wicked are those who actualize (interpret) thoughts in selfish, foolish, or evil ways. Their focus is on worldly pleasures and appeasing physical desires. Such people think and act in self-serving ways that are usually lustful, deceitful, or generally evil. These thoughts often turn into destructive actions that are considered sins in Kabbalah. Kabbalists describe these thoughts as coming from the animal soul, the thoughts of the body, the emotions or lust of the heart, or "follies of spirit," as opposed to those from the higher mind: the Divine Soul. In practical terms, they are emotionally, physically, and instinctively charged impressions based on cellular memories. These manifest in knee-jerk responses rather than through rational, intentional thought. An example might be committing to a healthy diet yet remembering how wonderful junk food tastes. Seeing a candy bar, we automatically gobble it up. Or, if we were hurt by someone, we might automatically avoid that person when we see him—now basing our behavior on the past.

As human beings, we have the ability to choose before taking action. We have the ability to transform these ruminating thoughts through the Divine Mind and the eyes of God to what kabbalists call "acquired intellect." A person who can interpret "actual" or filtered thoughts in expansive, constructive ways is known as an intermediary.

The righteous or wise ones have reached a level where they have already transformed their ways of being. They carry no old imprints other than the stamp of truth. Their thoughts and speech are pure. They see things as they are, without interpretation. They experience thoughts from the Divine Soul and act on them without instinctive physical reactions.

Kabbalah teaches that we need to know our "evil" or self-destructive thoughts—anything that blocks us from the light—in order to transform them. In practical terms this means that we need to get in touch with the self-destructive imaginative thoughts that keep us going in circles, and we need to input new ones that are expansive and keep us in union with the Divine. How can we change thoughts?

Martin Buber, a prominent twentieth-century Jewish philosopher, explains that thinking is man speaking to himself. It's what we tell ourselves internally.

In practical terms this is known as "self-talk." Our self-talk has a great impact on how we feel, the way we act, and what we attract in life. For instance, if we have an argument with a friend, and we have a stamp (*Yesod*) of not feeling okay, our self-talk will usually involve discounting ourselves or others. In this case, our self-talk might be, *She is stupid and doesn't know what she is doing.* Or *I can never get my point across. No one understands me.*

The more we repeat this type of self-talk, the more we believe it. Kabbalists teach that what we believe is significant to our psychological well-being. Beliefs form the patterns of our lives. Unless beliefs correlate with the attributes of God, however, they are invalid and limiting rather than expansive and creative. Kabbalah teaches that believing in the universal laws and living the attributes of God is the foundation of life. By following the attributes of God, which include the essence of the *sefirot*—oneness, wisdom, understanding, and knowledge, for example, rather than self-limiting thinking—we can be our divinely loving selves and evolve gracefully.

In the Eastern tradition of Jainism there's an expression: "What we believe, we conceive. What we conceive, we create." Kabbalah teaches that the body believes as true what is conceived in the mind—in images and impressions; in our imaginations and thinking. What we imagine in the form of images, feelings, thoughts, or beliefs is projected outward and therefore reflected back to us in some form. If we don't feel lovable or capable, we will often get something that we don't want and prove that we are unlovable and incompetent. Or we might interpret what comes to us in self-defeating ways to prove that we are not lovable or capable.

If we feel insecure or inept at work, for example, we might get a project to work on that is beyond our capabilities—and prove we are inept. Or else we might set it up to prove our incompetence by inefficiency, without being aware of it. This may manifest, subconsciously, in often getting to work late, having a messy desk, not paying attention to detail, or just being sloppy. We might also act in ways that provoke other people to think less of us and to berate us, such as asking questions unrelated to the topic of conversation, interrupting, acting inappropriately, or being arrogant. Then, when other people begin to degrade us, we see their discounting responses as additional proof that we are incompetent or unlovable.

Beliefs about ourselves and others are formulated on an ongoing basis, and they affect us from past lives as well as throughout our present life, even though we might not be aware of them. For instance, in a past life we may have been slaves who were constantly beaten physically, were belittled and put down, and never had a sense of who we were or felt we had the right to anything at all. We might then come into this life with impressions of being beaten (in the form of dreams or feelings) and a subconscious self-image that we don't deserve to have anything, we are not worthwhile, or we are simply evil. These beliefs form the basis of who we think we are and what we have in life.

Anytime we have something in our lives that we don't like, it's usually the result of misperceived thoughts or self-limiting beliefs—our made-up stories, our illusions. Kabbalists teach that it's important to acknowledge these interpretations of thoughts so that we can transform those that are limiting or self-defeating to new thoughts—"acquired intellect." By doing this we are choosing our will and intellect over our physical heart's desires; over our animalistic soul. In practical terms, then, it's important to know our limiting self-talk expressions. What are yours?

EXAMPLES OF LIMITING SELF-TALK

- *I am not lovable.*
- *I am incompetent.*
- *I am ruled by my past.*
- *I am not creative.*
- *I can't express myself clearly.*
- *I can't make decisions.*
- *I'm a procrastinator.*
- *I believe life is hard.*
- *I have trouble living in the present.*
- *I am lazy.*
- *I am not disciplined.*
- *Everything I do turns out wrong.*
- *I'm jack of all trades, master of none.*
- *I never get what I want.*
- *I never have time to do what I want.*

- *I can't change.*
- *I can't trust people.*
- *I am not in control of my life.*
- *I hate life.*
- *I'd be better off dead.*

Overcoming Self-Defeating Thinking

We can change self-defeating thoughts by seeing, stating, and hearing them in new ways through the creation of "affirmations." Affirmations are statements we make that we eventually come to believe. Affirmations directed to God are prayers. Ideally it helps to pray for what we want to change. Following the concept in Psalm 55:23 written by King David, "Place your burden on God, and he will carry [it for] you," the Baal Shem Tov believed that by talking to the Divine about worries, complaints, excuses, or whatever thoughts we need to change, the burdens will be relieved.

The reason for using affirmations as prayers is that to pray we first meditate, then we call on God, and then we recite the affirmation/prayer. Kabbalists teach that there is external and internal light and energy—the transcendent and immanent, the light and energy around us as well as within us. In practical terms, as we relax in meditation we open to the Divine within us. When we call on the Divine, we bring the light and energy around us, and we bond with the Divine and emanate an intense aura. When we call on God's light and love and state the affirmation/prayer, it gives an added boost to goals, visions, and intentions. We become magnetized with God's radiance and begin to attain or attract what we want without having to push or force to make it happen. Since the Absolute listens to everything we think, feel, say, and do and reflects it back to us, the more positive the self-talk and self-affirming beliefs we have, the more expansive our creativity and opportunities will be.

In practical terms, an affirmation is a positive statement that must be believable. If it isn't, then we will resist it. If we formulate an affirmation such as *I open my heart to the Divine* or *I'm living my purpose,* and we don't really believe it yet but we want to, we might change it to *I am willing to live my purpose.* If we *still* don't believe it, change it to *I am preparing to live my purpose.* This at least starts the process of change. By praying to God for the change, we have a co-partner, and it very often works. Sometimes, however, our emotional imprints are too strong for us to change a belief in this manner. This is when we have to look at the emotional piece blocking us from releasing or changing it. This is explained further when we move over into *Netzach.*

· Meditation: Changing an Old Self-Limiting Belief ·

Do a basic relaxation. Bring in the radiance of *Hod* (splendor), then picture yourself living the new affirmation in your mind. Keep concentrating on the new impression and notice how you feel, the way you look, what you're doing, and how you're relating. Then state it out loud or at least mouth it. This is setting a new "acquired" imprint into consciousness and developing a new belief at a cellular level. It leads to expansion rather than constriction.

When we develop more confidence in ourselves and begin thinking in expansive ways, we discover more of a desire to start uncovering and living our purpose.

Ox-Goad: Getting the Brain Moving

As an ox-goad, the path of *lamed* involves prodding the brain to get things going, to move toward something, to aspire, to achieve, to learn and teach.

Kabbalah tells us that humankind was put on this earth to work, to do Divine service—"to till the garden and watch over it." Work of all kinds, including manual labor, is deemed important. Many ancient kabbalists were blacksmiths, woodcutters, shoemakers, artisans, and craftsmen. They worked with their hands and lived with humility. Without work, kabbalists believe that fatigue and boredom set in. It is the Divine will for us to work, each at what is right for us.

Kabbalists believe that we also have an innate drive to find our intellectual or creative uniqueness. In contemporary life many people are "searching" for their uniqueness and purpose, but purpose is not something to be sought. It's inherent within us. It comes from what we have already experienced and know and what we have in our lives now. We need only uncover it, become more aware of it. Adlai Stevenson once said, "We can chart our future clearly and wisely when we know the path which has led to the present."

On the path of *lamed* as an ox-goad prodding us along, it's important to begin to stimulate our left-brain cognitive abilities. It begins by developing our logical, rational, mathematical talents and interests. Here we begin to ponder and pray to be shown our Divine purpose.

Along with prayers for intellectual stimulation, it helps to consider what avenue of study would challenge us. This includes the talents and skills and creative passions that we may be endowed with that need to be developed to their highest potential.

· Exercise: Questions to Ponder on Unleashing Our Left-Brain Activities and Purpose ·

The path of *lamed* reaching *hod* is involved with logic, math, and legal matters. Finding purpose begins with cleaning out the clutter in these areas and then determining what we want to pursue intellectually. It helps to first look at your office:

OFFICE

1. Are my desk drawers tidy?

2. Are my bills up to date?

3. Is my desk clear?

4. Do I have piles of "To Dos"?

5. Does my office fit the image of what I want to project professionally?

6. Is my filing up to date?

7. What legal matters do I need to handle?

8. What accounting matters need to be handled?

QUESTIONS FOR FINDING PURPOSE

1. What have I done in the past that I really enjoyed?

2. What did I win awards for?

3. What do I do now intellectually that is fulfilling?

4. What do I do that sparks my intellect?

5. What causes am I passionate about?

6. What are my hobbies?

7. What are my talents?

8. What subjects interest me?

9. What do I do that is so absorbing that I think of nothing else while I'm doing it?

10. What are the things I question in life?

11. When I read a newspaper or magazine, what sections get my attention?

12. What movies appeal to me?

13. What wildest things can I imagine myself doing that are within my capabilities?

14. If I lived to my highest intellectual or creative potential, what would be in my obituary?

15. What type of education do I want to pursue, if any?

Gematria: Path of the Heart

Lamed is the first letter of the Hebrew word *lev.* The *gematria* of the word *lev* is 32. It consists of the letters *lamed,* with a numerical value of 30, and *bet,* with a numerical value of 2. It pertains to the thirty-two paths to wisdom and connotes knowledge that comes from the heart. It involves the twenty-two paths represented by the Hebrew letters and the ten *sefirot.* Kabbalists believe that there is one letter within each of us that will show us the path to our return, our purpose. Below is the Hebrew letter chart. If any one letter stands out more than the others to you, then that might be the path on which to concentrate in remembering your purpose.

Hebrew Letters with Their Numerical Values and Signs

Letter	Symbol	Numerical Value	Sign
alef	א	1	ox
bet	ב	2	house
gimel	ג	3	camel
dalet	ד	4	door
heh	ה	5	window
vav	ו	6	peg, nail
zayin	ז	7	weapon
chet	ח	8	enclosure (fence)
tet	ט	9	serpent
yud	י	10	hand
kaf	כ	20	palm of hand
lamed	ל	30	ox-goad
mem	מ	40	water
nun	נ	50	fish
samech	ס	60	support
ayin	ע	70	eye
pei	פ	80	mouth
tzadi	צ	90	fishhook
kuf	ק	100	back of head
resh	ר	200	head
shin	ש	300	tooth
tav	ת	400	stamp

· Meditation: Hebrew Letters ·

Kabbalists often meditate on Hebrew letters to obtain the energy from the shape and sounds of the letters and thereby gain insight. Here is an exercise adapted from *The Hebrew Alphabet: A Mystical Journey* by psychologist Edward Hoffman.

Choose a letter—the first one that stands out in your mind as you look at the alphabet on the chart opposite. It is not necessary to know the meaning of the letter; just look at its shape. Write the letter down. As you write it, notice what thoughts come up for you. Contemplate the letter in detail. Observe the shape and size. Take a good look at the space around the letter and the space between its strokes. Make a mental picture of it. Close your eyes. See the letter in your mind. Meditate on it. Just be with it. Again, notice what thoughts, images, and feelings come up for you and add to your insights.

PATH BETWEEN *HOD* AND *TIFERET: SAMECH* ס

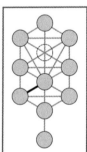

The path between *Hod* (thinking and communication) and *Tiferet* (beauty and harmony) is represented by the Hebrew letter *samech,* ס. It corresponds to the constellation of Sagittarius and the Hebrew month of *Kislev* (November–December). The Jewish holiday of Chanukah falls in *Kislev.* It commemorates the ancient miracle that occurred when one day's worth of oil burned to provide light for eight days.

The sign of the *samech* is Divine support. To begin the internal work of experiencing support and protection from the Divine and believing in miracles, meditate on the letter *samech,* ס. You can also imagine yourself surrounded and being supported by the shape of the letter while meditating.

RECEIVING AND CHANNELING DIVINE WISDOM

The shape of *samech* is round and closed like a circle. It symbolizes a wedding ring, a happy balance between independence and interdependence; support and being supported. It is a metaphor for the ability to feel supported by God, as well as supporting God.

On the path of *samech,* feeling supported by God comes with receiving and channeling God's light, wisdom, and love. Kabbalah teaches that it is God's will to impart and bestow. God created the world and humankind because of his will to receive and share.

Receiving from the Divine comes from listening within as well as experiencing and listening to what is around us or being told to us. The challenge is quieting ourselves long enough to hear what is being said or experienced. For many people, however, receiving can be threatening. Some people have trouble stopping thoughts long enough to listen within. They believe that not thinking puts them out of control.

It might be interesting to ask yourself a few questions here:

---

1. How often do I take the time to listen within?

2. For how long can I quiet my mind?

3. How close do I feel to the Divine?

4. What can I do to connect more to the Divine?

5. How do I know when I'm in touch with the Divine?

Receiving and Giving

Kabbalists teach that every personal relationship we have is a reflection of the relationship we have with the Divine. Giving to and receiving from people means showing and receiving love, affection, support, friendship, help, information, compliments, gifts, and so on.

For many people it's easier to give rather than receive. Some people experience receiving as being needy or vulnerable. Just giving and not receiving actually becomes a defense mechanism—a wall that keeps us from becoming close to others or to a connection to God. Not receiving from others can be symbolic of not allowing ourselves to receive from God. The following questions can help you determine if you are open to receiving from others:

1. How do I handle compliments?

2. How often have I received gifts or compliments by saying, "Oh, you shouldn't have," rather than merely "Thank you"?

3. How do I feel when I'm constantly giving?

4. Do I think I have to reciprocate every time I'm given a gift?

5. How well do I receive information and really listen?

6. What would it be like if God said to me, "You're great!" and I responded with, "No I'm not. What do you know?"

· Meditation: Energy Exercise on Being a Giver or Receiver ·

On an energy level, kabbalists believe that we receive with the left hand and give with the right. The left column on the Tree of Life is the female, receiving side, while the right side is the male, giving side. In practical terms, if you are sensitized to energy, there is an exercise you can do with a partner or with a group to determine whether you are a giver or receiver.

Do a basic relaxation exercise while holding hands, whether it be with one person or several. Imagine energy coming in through your left hand, going up your left arm, around your left shoulder and head over to your right shoulder, then down your right arm to the person on your right. Pay attention to the sensations in your hands and skin. Does a block of energy remain in your left hand, or does the energy flow easily? What about the energy on the right side—is it blocked in your right hand, or is it flowing out easily? When you are ready, drop your hands, open your eyes, and reflect on your experience.

Energy flow, the electromagnetic impulses within us, reflects in our personality and environment. Just as it is important for energy to flow freely between

God and us, in personal relationships it's important for energy to flow freely between two people. If it doesn't, it is experienced as a wall between the two. Furthermore, if we don't receive our partner's energy, our partner doesn't feel our love.

One of the most memorable experiences I had regarding this was twenty years ago while taking a workshop on unconditional love. There were twelve participants, and we had to choose a quality—courage, trust, love, or wisdom—on which we would meditate in groups of three. We were put in different rooms in order not to be influenced by the others. I chose love. The two other people who chose it were a man and woman from out of state. They were two of the most unappealing-looking people I had ever met.

I was repulsed by their appearance and demeanor and immediately went to the leader and told her I couldn't meditate with them. She said that since the other groups were filled I could sit it out if I wanted, but she reminded me that I was there to learn unconditional love. I acquiesced.

In the room we were told to lie on the floor with our heads together in the center like the spokes of a wheel and to meditate on love. I started to ponder love. I thought of sending love to the other two meditating with me. Then suddenly my thoughts stopped. I began to experience the essence of love that was within me as well as within the room. At that moment the man said to me, "Your energy just changed. I'm experiencing incredible love from you. It's extraordinary."

I realized then that he felt my love not when I was sending, but when I was open to receiving love—when I stopped thinking and doing, and opened to the energy in the room and the other two people. After that experience, we related on a different level, and I was more open to them and much less judgmental.

It's important to recognize that our loved ones feel our love when we remain open to their energy and "receive" their love. Also, by allowing ourselves to receive, we are constantly replenished rather than drained, and we have more to give. This is the same as our relationship to the Divine. We receive Divine energy and light when we remain open to receive, and therefore have more to give. The way of giving and sharing is through communication.

PATH BETWEEN
HOD AND *GEVURAH: PEI* פ

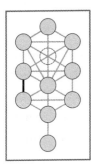

The path between *Hod* (communication, thinking) and *Gevurah* (discipline) is represented by the Hebrew letter *pei,* פ. The letter *pei* rules the planet Mercury. Thursday is its day of the week, and its direction is down. It's a double letter, and its opposite qualities are dominance and slavery—to rule or be ruled, to listen or to speak. To begin the internal work of receiving clear information, speaking from the heart, and communicating effectively, meditate on the *pei,* פ.

COMMUNICATION AND SPEECH

The symbolic meaning of *pei* is mouth: the profile of the mouth with a tooth growing from the upper gums and turning inward toward the throat. It involves communication and speech. Moving toward *Gevurah,* which signifies discipline, this path represents the disciplining of the mouth. It's knowing when to listen and when to speak—and when we do speak, it involves being in control of what we say and how we say it: directly, precisely, and assertively. It reminds us to speak from the heart.

Effective Listening

The Talmud states, "Who is wise? He who learns from every man." A wise person learns from others as well as helping them. We are each channels for one another. There is a *mishnah* (passage of Oral Law with metaphoric interpretation in the Talmud) that says you acquire wisdom when you "listen with your ears." To listen effectively is to hear, understand, and take to heart the words we hear from others. When we say the prayer *Shema*—"Hear, O Israel, the Lord our God, the Lord is One"—we are pleading to hear and be heard. We want to hear and understand others as well as be heard and understood.

To listen wholeheartedly we listen not only with our ears but also with our hearts, souls, and guts. Often we're thinking about either other things or what we'll say next while talking to someone. If when we listen to God we are at the same time busy thinking about other things or what we'll say next, what will we hear or experience? If we're busy thinking about what we're going to say before a person is finished talking, we're not totally listening. We're not "receiving" the entire message.

Communication also often manifests in competition, trying to fix things, not explaining what we mean carefully, interpreting what is being said erroneously, or just talking endlessly rather than really listening to each other. For example, a man comes home from work and as he walks in the door says, "Boy, I had a lousy day. I'm drained."

The wife, a stay-at-home mom, responds with, "*You* had a bad day! Mine was worse! The baby was sick and threw up all over the rug. Jenny needed a ride to Girl Scouts, and I couldn't find someone to take her. And I burned dinner." Mom isn't listening to Dad. She's competing with him as to who had the worse day. She's coming from her own agenda rather than really listening effectively.

Or perhaps Mom may have responded to Dad walking in and complaining about his day by offering him a drink and saying, "Just relax. You'll get over it." Trying to make things better isn't listening, either. People feel ignored.

Aside from competing, other ways of blocking communication include:

- Analyzing/diagnosing: "You are reacting irrationally."
- Withdrawing: "Let's not go there."
- Reassuring: "Don't worry. In time you'll feel better."
- Preaching: "You should always respect your elders."
- Giving orders: "Don't use that tone of voice with me."
- Criticizing: "You can't do anything right."

Giving Feedback

Real listening involves understanding and hearing what is being said and letting the other person know we truly understand. Very often someone says one thing and means another. Or we as the listener may hear something different from what is being said or meant. To make sure we're hearing correctly, it's a good practice in general to ask for clarification by saying, "What I hear you saying or wanting is _____. Is that what you mean?" This process clears up any mis-communication. It also lets the other person know we are really listening.

Communicating from the Heart: Imparting Wisdom

The path of *pei* is speaking from the heart, which means speaking from truth—the Divine heart, rather than the heart of the body that is our "longing" heart.

Imparting wisdom helps others awaken the light from within. It happens by adding value to others. This comes with listening and giving feedback that is constructive, motivating, and inspirational. When we listen to others, they feel valued. Giving constructive criticism can help others make changes and can motivate them with inspirational words. It can help guide them to be their best. This is how we channel Divine wisdom, and it's something we all need to do for each other. This means we need to think before we speak—and speak intentionally with love.

The way we speak has a significant impact on others. Language and speech are highly valued in Kabbalah. Creation took place through ten utterances. Creation manifested from language. Every time God speaks he creates something. Kabbalists believe that by saying something, it is engraved in the universe; like being carved in stone, it becomes so.

In our own speech, every word—the way it's spoken and thought, the attitude behind it, how it's pronounced, the body language, facial expressions, pitch, and tone that go along with it—gives off energy vibrations. These have an impact on our brains, our bodies, others, and the universe.

In practical terms, since the body believes that every word we think, say, and imagine is true, we need to be careful about the words we use. Talking from the "I" and speaking truth is the first step. Kabbalists believe the essential person is the soul. The soul is known in Hebrew as the *ani,* the "I." Rearranged, the letters spell *ain*—nothingness. As stated in the scriptures, wisdom comes from nothingness. When we are in touch with the nothingness, the silence within, we are in touch with our soul, our core, our own essence, which connects us to the whole—the oneness, God's presence, God's light. When we begin to define ourselves in terms of God, and channel God's wisdom and will for us, we are our own person. When we are totally honest with ourselves and others, we come from truth. When we speak from the "I" and speak truth, we come from the part of ourselves that is a part of God.

Talking from the "I" also helps us express our thoughts and feelings without imposing them on others. It helps us take responsibility for how we think and feel. This is easy to see when we examine some words and phrases we use that do *not* come from the "I," such as:

- "It" upsets me when you don't take out the garbage.
- "People think" not having children is being selfish.
- "They say" it's not appropriate to talk politics at social engagements.
- "We" do things differently.
- "Don't you" ever do that again.
- "You" make me nervous.

"You" messages, aside from using the word *you* in the second person for generalizing, can also be a way of blaming, attacking, preaching, or avoiding sharing feelings. Such messages are usually used when we don't take responsibility for our own thoughts, feelings, or actions.

- "You just don't get it."
- "You are so sloppy."
- "You always hurt me."

Look at the subject in each of the above sentences—they're not coming from the "I." Rephrasing by talking from the "I" is more direct, easier to hear, and also will make us feel more empowered as we take responsibility for our thoughts and feelings.

- "I'm upset when the garbage is not taken out."
- "I believe not having children is being selfish."
- "I don't think it's appropriate to talk politics at social engagements."
- "I do things differently."
- "I don't want you to do that again."
- "I feel unseen when you don't listen to me."
- "I get tense when you raise your voice."
- "I feel inept when I can't get my point across."

- "I hate it when I see your clothes lying around on the furniture."
- "I feel hurt by what you just did."

Although some people think talking from the "I" can be egocentric, when we express ourselves *honestly* it actually is just the opposite. It comes from the "I" of the soul. "I" messages that are truthful, self-assertive messages are noncompetitive, nonjudgmental, nonmanipulative. They are a way of sharing ourselves honestly without preconceived notions; of sharing our reactions to things rather than blaming others. They're a way of communicating from a place of neutrality so that we speak truth without control or manipulation.

Other ways we can impart wisdom to others include words of inspiration, words of motivation, words that are expansive, and words that help people feel good about themselves.

· Meditation: Offering Words of Inspiration ·

Words of inspiration come when we listen to inspiration within ourselves. That means we have an "open" ear. Begin this meditation with a basic relaxation.

Experience yourself being totally relaxed and quiet internally. Open to the light of *Hod* and imagine yourself listening within. Listen to every sound in your body: your breath, the movements of your chest, heart, and lungs. Listen to the sounds around your ears, the sounds in the room.

Now reach out for the sounds in nature, and think of hearing the sounds of the universe, then the sounds of the silent pulse of the universe—no sound. Be thankful for the silence. As you remain in silence, images, words, or feelings may come to mind. Notice any pictures that emerge. Sometimes colors may weave in or out; snapshots or movies of people, animals, entities, angels, archangels, objects, or words may come to mind. Make a mental note of them. Notice any physical sensations you may be experiencing. Identify if there is an emotional component attached to it. Make a commitment to listen to yourself; to hear, see, and feel what is going on inside your mind and body. Open your eyes and write down your insights.

· SIX ·

Netzach: Victory
Emotional Self-Mastery

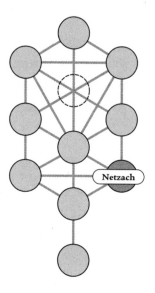

Divine Name: *YHVH Tzvaot*—Lord of Hosts

The Divine essence of *Netzach,* whose Divine name is *YHVH Tzvaot,* was described in conjunction with *Hod* in the previous chapter. On the right side of the Tree of Life, opposite *Hod, Netzach*'s overall essence is eternity or victory.

Archangel: Haniel

Haniel, also known as Uriel, is the archangel representing *Netzach.* He is the archangel of harmony and peace, the light of God. He offers us insight, artistry, and vision; assists us in determining who we really are; and shows us how to manifest our abilities and talents.

He is the archangel who helps us to be our best by filling us with confidence and self-worth. When we have self-doubt, fear, or feelings of hopelessness or indecisiveness, it helps to call on Haniel.

Patriarch: Moses

The personification of the attributes of *Netzach* is the patriarch Moses. The Bible tells us that out of the flames of the eternal burning bush God spoke to Moses, saying, "Do not come closer. Remove your shoes from your feet, for the place on which you stand is holy ground." The Kabbalah understands shoes as protection from the ground. By experiencing the earth, pebbles, and sand under his feet, Moses became more sensitive to himself, his people, and the word of God. This gave him the sensitivity to lead his people.

Moses always came to the aid of others in trouble. He saved a slave from being beaten by an Egyptian. However, his beating of the Egyptian caused him to leave Egypt. He later had to learn to control his temper. He perfected himself so he could become victorious over his instinctive reactions, loyal to his God, sensitive to his people—and therefore a great leader. Moses endured through many trials and tribulations.

Attributes: Victory, Eternity

The essence of *Netzach* is eternity and victory. It ensues when we tame our animal instincts and reach the spark within us that opens us up to intuition. In *Netzach* consciousness we achieve a level of self-mastery at which we are no longer slaves to reactive emotional charges; we overcome dysfunctional character traits and old conditioned patterns, and start living more intuitively. When we do this, we experience the eternal spark, the Divine within us. To emulate the essence of *Netzach*, ponder any of the above representations, then imagine yourself living the attributes of victory and eternity in your life. State the affirmation: *I am victorious over my instincts, impulses, repressed feelings, and actions and I am connected the eternal spark of Divine wisdom.*

NETZACH: VICTORY
(ETERNITY, INSTINCTS, AND ACTIONS,
REPEATING PATTERNS)

VICTORY: CREATING EXCELLENCE
IN OUR SEARCH FOR MEANING

Netzach, the fourth gate to enter on the Tree of Life, is the area of energy behind our instincts and actions. It's what motivates us. It is the energy of victory. Victory is winning the wars within by becoming victorious over our instincts and impulsive acting out. According to the Kabbalah, the primary motivation in the human search for meaning is to reach perfection, become one with God, and make the world a better place in which to live. We begin to create excellence in the world by focusing first on creating excellence within ourselves.

Before Abraham, Moses, and Jacob were shown their purpose, they were guided to create excellence within themselves. In all cases, they had to leave the land of their fathers and their past. They overcame adversity, tests of endurance, and suffering. They had to know their thoughts, master their impulses, develop sensitivity, humility, and kindness. They learned about themselves before they were initiated into Divine prophecy.

Often there is much adversity we need to overcome before we can uncover our purpose. We might need to learn how to control our temper, become more empathetic, be more charitable, be a better listener, what have you. This is all preparation for something much greater—our Divine mission, our destiny. Until that mission is given to us (in *Chokhmah* consciousness) or uncovered, we are in preparation. What do you still need to learn?

ETERNITY: RETURNING HOME TO OUR ETERNAL SPARK

Eternity in *Netzach* refers to reaching the energy within us that never dies, even at the end of physical life. Kabbalists often refer to this eternal spark as the backbone of existence, or the "bone of bones," called *luz*. Kabbalists believe that there is a bone in the body (around the coccyx area) that never decays and, therefore, holds the chromosomal codes of the body—which will be resurrected when the Messiah comes and all souls are united with their bodies. The *luz* carries the coding of our essence, the part that emanates from the Absolute and remains in perpetuity. The Kabbalah teaches that the soul keeps coming back life after life until it learns the lessons of Divine perfection. When we all reach this state, the souls will return to the bodies and we will all be resurrected.

In *Netzach,* after learning how to master our emotions, we begin to reach that eternal spark within us and develop the intuition that will help us unleash our soul's purpose.

PATH BETWEEN *YESOD* AND *NETZACH:* NUN נ

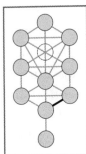

The path between *Yesod* (foundation, personal empowerment) and *Netzach* (instincts and actions, fight-or-flight response) is represented by the elemental Hebrew letter *nun,* נ. *Nun* corresponds to the constellation of Scorpio and the Hebrew month of *Cheshvan* (October–November).

The word *nun* in Aramaic means "fish." Fish represent fertility and productivity; building fertile ground in which new seeds can sprout. The numerical value is 50, which relates to the forty-nine character traits of God; the fiftieth is faith, which comes from following our intuition. The path of *nun* is a path to prophecy.

To develop faith, prophecy/intuition, and productivity, we meditate on the Hebrew letter *nun,* נ.

PREPARATION TO PROPHECY: DEVELOPING THE FORTY-NINE CHARACTER TRAITS OF GODLINESS

Nun is the first letter of the Hebrew words *nevuah* (prophecy) and *navi* (prophet). Between *Yesod* and *Netzach* is a path to prophecy. *Nun* also relates to faith. The numerical value of *nun* is 50. This correlates to the "fifty Gates of Understanding, or repentance," also known as the "fifty Gates of Return." The Kabbalah teaches that there are forty-nine gates with one above them, the gate of faith. It's the faith of understanding Divine Providence and a world beyond ourselves that is made known to us through intuition.

The forty-nine Gates of Understanding correlate to the forty-nine Hebrew letters of the names of the twelve tribes of Israel. The forty-nine gates pertain to the character traits the Israelites needed to develop during the Exodus from Egypt until they received the Ten Commandments at Mount Sinai. Observant Jews follow what's known as the "counting of the *omer*" during the seven weeks between the Jewish holidays of Passover and Shavuot. It's the time of self-evaluation as preparation for prophecy. After the seven weeks of self-evaluation, all of Israel experienced prophecy. They heard the voice of God. By developing certain character traits, we open to communion with the Divine and develop faith, the fiftieth gate.

Although we need to develop all these traits, it is believed that one of them, in particular, is for each of us the trait we need to work out in this lifetime in order to return to union with the Divine. Taken from the *Sayings of Our Fathers* 6:6, here are the character traits that are important to develop. If one stands out among all the others for you, then that just might be your particular "Gate of Return." For instance, Abraham learned how to live with kindness and to share the tradition with others as they passed by his tent. Isaac was a listener—and always listened to his father. Aaron was a great communicator and taught peace. Make a mental note of which traits you still need to work on.

FORTY-NINE GATES OF RETURN: CHARACTER TRAITS OF GODLINESS

1. Study (discussing and living the Torah by being totally aware, focused, and in the present).

2. Listening of the ear (listen attentively).

3. Ordering of the lips (proper speech).

4. Discernment of the heart (understanding from the heart of God).

5. Fear (experiencing awe).

6. Dread (mastering fear).

7. Humility (free of animal ego).

8. Cheerfulness (experiencing joy).

9. Purity (of thought—willpower).

10. Attendance on the wise (respecting and honoring scholars).

11. Cleaving to associates (honoring and debating with colleagues).

12. Discussion with disciples (learning from students).

13. Sedateness (being thoughtfully intentional or deliberate).

14. Scripture (reading and studying).

15. *Mishnah* (oral instruction on life).

16. Little business (developing business sense in moderation).

17. Little intercourse with the world (using moderation in worldly affairs).

18. Little pleasure (moderation in physical pleasure).

19. Little sleep (sleep in moderation).

20. Little conversation (learning the art of listening and speaking in moderation).

21. Little laughter (moderation in frivolty).

22. Long-suffering (conquering frustration and having patience).

23. A good heart (good-naturedness).

24. Faith in the wise (trust in advisers).

25. Acceptance of chastisements (accepting pain and suffering).

26. Being one who knows one's place (knowing when to follow or lead) and rejoices in one's portion (being content with one's lot).

27. Makes a fence for one's words (setting boundaries and guarding what is precious).

28. Claims not merit for oneself (resisting arrogance and pride or taking credit for oneself).

29. Is beloved (knowing how to be loved and experience love).

30. Loves God (opening the heart and sending love to God).

31. Loves humankind (knowing how to love others).

32. Loves justice (acts of charity and loving-kindness).

33. Loves right courses (following the inner voice).

34. Loves reproof (handling criticism and rebukes well).

35. Keeps aloof from honor (shunning honor).

36. Puffs not one's heart up with learning (not conceited).

37. Delights not in giving decisions (but in making decisions).

38. Takes up the yoke with one's associates (being sensitive to others and sharing the burdens).

39. Judges associates with leaning to merit (judging associates favorably).

40. Establishes oneself upon truth (based in reality).

41. Establishes onself upon peace (achieving inner peace).

42. Does not exalt one's heart over one's study (being composed and fascinated with learning).

43. Asks and answers (analyzing an issue with succinct questions and answers).

44. Hears and adds thereto (learning and expanding on ideas).

45. Learns with a view to teaching (learning in order to teach).

46. Learns with a view to acting (learning in order to do).

47. Makes one's teacher wise (educating the teachers).

48. Defines accurately what one hears (having an organized mind and noting precisely what is learned).

49. Repeats a thing in the name of who said it (giving credit or quoting the names of those who said what one is repeating; gratitude).

The forty-nine character traits lead to receiving the Torah (faith) and knowing it intuitively.

FISH: FERTILITY—PRODUCTIVITY

Becoming Aware and Responsible

The sign of *nun* is a fish. Fish swim in the waters of ebb and flow, and lack self-consciousness. In us the fish is symbolic of acting unconsciously, which includes involuntary responses and reacting instinctively rather than intentionally and responsibly.

The more conscious of our actions we are, and the more we cleave to the Divine character traits, the more we draw close to union with the Divine and develop a fertile ground in which to grow. On the other hand, dysfunctional character traits keep us disconnected from the Divine. We can distance ourselves from the Divine by behaving in conditioned patterns or personas rather than intentionally. Conditioned personas are formed primarily by the way we adapted in childhood in order to get attention. If we were ignored, for instance, to get attention we might now develop a persona as a trickster, and deceive people; as a comedian, and not take things seriously; or as a sad sap. These personas become habitual ways of behaving.

In more practical terms, here is a list of other conditioned patterns and personas. Do any of them sound familiar? Write down the ones that pertain to you.

- Mr. or Ms. Nice: Always obliging to others; tries to appease.
- Martyr: Gets the job done without help but usually with resentment.
- Trickster: Plays April Fool's jokes every day.
- Fool: Always makes a mess of things.
- Caretaker: Always taking care of others.
- Distracter: Changes the subject or just forgets about something.
- Shy: Doesn't speak up.
- Victim: Doesn't take responsibility; everything negative happens to him or her.
- Critic: Knows it all and criticizes others.
- Mr. or Ms. Personality: Putting on airs, always looking for attention.
- Sickly: Always has something wrong physically.
- Mr. or Ms. Accident: Accident-prone.
- Dependent/clingy: Doesn't stand on own two feet.
- Controller: Has to have his or her own way; takes control over the external world.
- Worrier: Always has problems to brood over.
- Defender: Always explaining him- or herself.
- Lazy: Lacks energy, motivation, or enthusiasm.
- Greedy: Takes whatever he or she can get—can never have enough.
- Disorganized: Hates planning and structure.
- Undisciplined: Lacks control and regimentation; jumps from one thing to the next; doesn't stay on task.
- Isolater: Stays alone—away from people.
- Procrastinator: Puts things off for another day.
- Indecisive: Can't make decisions for him- or herself.
- Supercompetent: Superman or -woman.
- False pride: Overconfident.
- Altruistic: Self-righteous.
- Space cadet: Flaky.
- Chameleon: Always changing based on location and companions.
- Performer: Always acting to impress others.

PATH BETWEEN
HOD AND *NETZACH: MEM* ☐

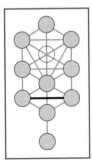

Mem is the lowest horizontal path on the Tree of Life, connecting *Hod* (thoughts) and *Netzach* (actions). It helps balance the right and left sides of the Tree of Life. The letter *mem* is the first letter of the word *mayim,* which means "water" and is associated with the womb—the life-force center. Water is also symbolic of the fluid rhythm of life and correlates with emotions and animalistic impulses. To us it can translate as the "hidden" world, corresponding to the ebb and flow of thoughts (*Hod*), feelings (the triad of *Hod, Netzach,* and *Yesod*), and actions (*Netzach*), which when made conscious and brought into balance elevate us to developing intuition and higher consciousness.

The path of *mem* is the motivating force that impels us to take action and symbolizes rebirth. The numerical value of the letter *mem* is 40, representing purification. To get in touch with our emotional acting out and our animalistic impulses, and to begin to open to Divine impulses and intuition, we meditate on the letter *mem,* ☐.

PURIFICATION: ELIMINATING CYCLICAL BEHAVIOR—FIGHT-OR-FLIGHT RESPONSE

The numerical value of *mem,* 40, represents purification; the ending of one cycle and beginning of another; or death and rebirth. Think of Noah's Ark and the rain that lasted forty days and forty nights, but culminated in new life. In another story, the Israelites wandered through the desert for forty years before reaching the Promised Land.

To eliminate cyclical behavior and conditioned patterns, becoming proactive rather than reactive to fight-or-flight impulses, we need to scrutinize our thoughts, speech, feelings, and actions.

Kabbalists teach that to know something, to make it conscious, is to experience it. In *The Path of the Just* Moshe Chaim Luzzatto states, "A person must 'feel' his actions and watch over all of his ways so as not to leave himself with a bad habit or a bad trait, let alone a sin or a crime."

In practical terms, by reviewing and reenacting our thoughts, feelings, and actions and allowing ourselves to experience them, we bring the unconscious to consciousness. Daniel Goleman, in his book of the same name, calls this "emotional intelligence." When we are conscious of our thoughts, we can change the faulty ones that create involuntary reactions or feral (untamed) impulses, opening ourselves to devout impulses. We elevate the physical to the spiritual. The first step is to notice our emotional reactions.

· Exercise: Emotional (Feeling) Reactions ·

Which emotional (impulsive) reactions do you experience most?

Anger	Hopelessness
Loneliness	Helplessness
Guilt	Jealousy
Lethargy	Embarrassment
Boredom	Anxiety
Shame	Indecision
Incompetence	Powerlessness
Unworthiness	Depression
Inadequacy	Obsessive or dependent love
Feeling overwhelmed	Other _____
Frustration	

Kabbalists teach that all the reactions listed above keep us from the light of God. Kabbalists advise that we choose any emotional quality that is difficult for us and perform a good deed with it. The concept is that as we begin to act in a positive way, we *become* it. It's similar to the idiom "Fake it till you make it." And by taking responsible action, we become more Godlike and can overcome the reactive impulses. For instance:

• Turn sadness into joy by seeing the lighter side of things and giving joy to others.

- Turn fear into faith and courage by seeing our strengths and taking action on them.
- Turn jealousy into compassion by understanding our own needs and developing our own strengths.
- Turn anger into forgiveness by facing our feelings and dealing with the issue or person with kindness and understanding.
- Turn anxiety into tranquillity by choosing peace and acting peacefully.
- Overcome guilt by making amends.

Grieving

Many times we do begin to feel more positive by doing good deeds. Other times not. We often act out of guilt or obligation. Unless we do it with a pure heart, it's not genuine. The book of Proverbs, written by King Solomon, says: "If there be anxiety in a man's heart let him quash it, and turn it into joy with a good word" (12:25). There are many different ways to release difficult reactive emotions.

Ancient mystics practiced grieving through animal sacrifice. Animals were sacrificed when people sinned—for feelings of guilt, deceit, depression, and so forth. These animal sacrifices were known as "sin offerings" or "guilt offerings." The ancient mystics would lament in front of a group of other people at the Temple by admitting their sins, sharing their vulnerabilities, and crying their hearts out while offering animal sacrifices. After the destruction of the Temple, kabbalists released their burdens and confessed their sins through prayer and meditation in the middle of the night—when they believed the transmissions were stronger and clearer.

Kabbalists teach that praying to God to alleviate the burdens of emotional reactive charges can help us overcome them. Rabbi Nachman of Breslov, the great-grandson of the Baal Shem Tov, advised meditating after midnight in an isolated place, pouring out our thoughts to the Divine. He believed that it was important to set aside an hour or more each day to talk to God. He taught that you should "make use of many prayers and thoughts, until you nullify one trait or desire. Then make use of much meditation to nullify another trait or desire. Continue in such a time and place, proceeding in this manner, until you have nullified all. If some ego remains, work to nullify that. Continue until nothing remains." The idea is to express everything within our hearts to God, whether that be regret, guilt, pride, anger, sin, shame, fear, bitterness, hatred, repentance for the past, or even thanks and blessings.

Weeping

Mem is the first letter in the word *mayim,* water. Water is soothing and purifying. Kabbalists believe tears help soothe emotions by letting them flow again. Just as the ancient mystics divulged their vulnerabilities in front of others at the Temple, it is taught that admitting our vulnerabilities to at least one other person and crying it out helps us repent for our sins. If we don't have a group to do it in, then it's advised that we talk to at least one other person about our deepest fears, doubts, sins, judgments, evil speech, thoughts, and actions. While kabbalists talk to the Divine, they often cry their hearts out in order to be heard. It is stated in the Talmud that tears open the gates to heaven. It's crying for the release of the burdens. It's getting into the bitterness, hatred, remorse, and regret so we can feel it, be with it, and experience it. We concentrate on our burdens so intently, and with such deep emotion and devotion, that we begin to weep. This releases the emotional reactive impulses and our past burdens.

In practical terms, the problem regarding feelings is that many people *think* their feelings rather than feeling them. Thoughts stay in their heads rather than being integrated into the body. Kabbalists refer to two stages of emotions: "intellectual" or thought feelings as opposed to "revealed heart" or felt feelings. Daniel Goleman in his book *Emotional Intelligence* explains it as two brains: emotional and rational. We may say we love someone, but not really feel or experience love within our heart. In the same way, we might think of God and believe in God but not really feel or know God.

Sometimes thought feelings are difficult to distinguish from felt feelings because thought feelings can be emotional. For example, we may think something is sad—the death of someone close, or a divorce—and cry deeply and often as a result of the "thought" of sadness. Yet we may still not experience the sadness within our hearts and bodies. We may not experience it on a cellular level.

As mentioned above, many kabbalists teach that in order to master the desires of the physical heart (the "body heart") or animal instincts (emotional reactive charges) within us, we must experience our thoughts, understand our feelings, know where they stem from, and express them.

These instinctive charges often stem from a childhood trauma similar to—but not necessarily the same as—what's going on now but wasn't experienced the first time. Thus we have to go back to the childhood memory and experience the feeling that we avoided then. We also probe to identify what belief we formulated about ourselves as a result of the past experience, which is most likely still being reflected now, and reframe it to something more realistic and appropriate today. It's these beliefs and instinctive charges that continue to rule us.

When we get at the core or felt feeling and understand what caused it in childhood, then determine the resultant belief and change it, we release the cellular memory as well as the emotional instinctive charges. When the emotional charges are released, we respond appropriately to the situation as it is occurring in the present moment. The right words come out at the right time.

For example, we may carry a feeling of resentment or anger toward someone who has harmed or even abused us. But underneath the resentment or anger are internal feelings as a result of being abused or betrayed—perhaps feelings of hurt or even shame for not having counteracted the incident, or for it ever happening. It's often easier to carry the anger toward others than to admit the shame within ourselves, which is what keeps us going in circles.

Instead, if we let ourselves feel the hurt or shame in the body, admit it, ask what belief we formulated that created the feeling, and change the belief, the cellular memory and emotional charges are usually released. Sometimes just feeling the feeling will release the charges.

· Meditation: (Sacrificing) Letting Go of Our Animal Instincts ·

Kabbalists use a meditation known as building, based on the work of the Maggid of Mezerich, to help overcome distracting thoughts that lead to impulsive acting out. It's based on the correspondences of the *sefirot* to the days of the creation (building) of the world, and uses the colors of the *sefirot* as described in

Chapter Two. If we're dealing with resentment (red), *Gevurah*, we bring on (green) understanding of *Binah*, the *sefirah* above *Gevurah*. We keep doing this until the thoughts and feelings subside.

The Baal Shem Tov taught that it's important to understand the basis of our behavior. The following meditation is a way to get in touch with the physical impulses and emotional correspondences in your body and to identify the core feeling in order to get to the truth.

Do a basic relaxation and center yourself. Close your eyes. When you are totally relaxed, think of something that made you sad. After a few moments, notice where tension emerges in your body. Make a mental note of the physical feeling. On a scale of 0 through 10, with 10 being the highest, how willing are you to release it? If you are willing, breathe into the tension and think of the feeling releasing. Or pray to God to release it and bring in feelings of light and love. Give yourself the time to relax again.

After a few moments of relaxation, think of something that made you angry. Notice where you feel the anger in your body. When we feel angry, it's usually the acting out of a deeper feeling. After you experience the anger in your body, ask yourself what the deeper feeling is—often deep shame or grief or powerlessness. On a scale of 0 through 10, how willing are you to release this feeling? If you are willing, breathe into it and think of releasing it, or pray to God to release it. Give yourself the time to relax again.

Think of something that scared you. Notice where the tension from fear emerges in your body. Again make a mental note of it. On a scale of 0 through 10, how willing are you to release this feeling? If you are willing, then breathe into the area of tension and mentally think of it releasing. Give yourself time to relax again.

Think of something that made you feel happy. Notice where tension emerges in your body. Make a mental note of it. On a scale of 0 through 10, how willing are you to release it? If you are willing, then breathe into the tension and mentally think of releasing it. Give yourself time to relax.

Think of something that made you feel love. Notice the changes in your body when you think of love. Make a mental note of it. On a scale of 0 through 10, how willing are you to release it? If you are willing, then breathe into the inklings and mentally think of them releasing. Give yourself time to relax again.

Think of something that made you feel joy. Notice where you feel joy in your body. Make a mental note of this feeling and make a commitment to yourself to bring it with you when you come out of meditation. Write down your insights.

Since many of us have trouble identifying core feelings, to help the process along, I've listed below a few of the symptoms that participants described after doing this exercise in groups. It's important to note that anger is an "acting out" of a repressed feeling rather than an actual core feeling. It generally manifests in the body by directing our attention away from the core feeling, which usually has to do with shame, guilt, deep sorrow, grief, or powerlessness. If we identify the anger and pay attention to it, insights will often come up that reveal the core feeling beneath it.

SYMPTOMS OF ANGER WITH UNDERLYING SHAME, GRIEF, OR POWERLESSNESS

- Tightness in the shoulders
- Tightness in the back of the neck
- Tightness in the jaw
- Clenching teeth
- Heat in the upper chest
- Weird sensations of restlessness and angst

SYMPTOMS OF FEAR

- Tightness, quivering, feeling a hole or a void around the stomach area
- Quivering in the chest
- Sweaty palms
- Blood vessels swelling in the face
- Elevated heart rate
- Nausea
- Restlessness

SYMPTOMS OF SADNESS

- Mostly constricted sensations in the heart area
- Numb sensation in the chest
- Heaviness in the chest
- Tears
- Hole in the chest
- Shallow breathing
- Sunken feeling
- Pain in the chest

SYMPTOMS OF HAPPINESS

- Excitement—almost an out-of-body sensation—"being way out there"
- An edginess similar to anger but in a positive way
- Sometimes tightness in the shoulders and neck

SYMPTOMS OF LOVE

- Heart palpitations
- Excitement in the heart area
- Sometimes tension in the heart area
- Warmth in the heart area
- Flutters in the heart area

SYMPTOMS OF JOY

- Wholeness
- Centeredness
- Whole-body peacefulness
- Satisfaction
- Balance
- Elation

Core feelings might include: sadness, fear, shame, guilt, loneliness, ineptitude, insecurity, helplessness, hopelessness, powerlessness, love, happiness, and joy. After we identify the core feeling, we can ask ourselves what belief created this feeling. When we become aware of the belief, which is usually false—against the attributes or character traits of the Divine—we can then change it as we did in Chapter Five, *Hod*.

· Meditation: Elevating Feelings to the Divine ·

Do a basic relaxation exercise to center yourself and release tension. Now think about something that is bothering you. Tune in to your body. Is there any area in which you're experiencing pain or tension? Focus in on it. Focus all your attention on that area. Breathe into the tension. What is the tension telling you? See if any images, imprints, or insights come up around the pain or tension. Ask for the emotional feeling beneath the physical impulse. Identify the core feeling. Keep focusing on the visceral feeling in your body. Ask what this feeling reminds you of from sometime earlier in life—even back to childhood. Often imprints will emerge from the past, such as times when you were left alone and felt betrayed or abandoned by the people in your life. Betrayed and abandoned (feelings generally ending in -ed) are not core feelings. They are how you feel as a result of what other people did to you.

Dig for the deeper core feeling. Ask yourself what you are experiencing as a result of being betrayed or abandoned. Perhaps you feel loneliness, shame, fear, helplessness, hopelessness, sadness. Just be with these deeper feelings and breathe into them. Ask what these feelings remind you of from your childhood. If any insights or images come up, probe to understand what happened, then ask what beliefs you formulated about yourself as a result of these experiences. Ask yourself if these beliefs are expansive or constrictive. If they are constrictive and self-limiting, then change them to something more expansive and believable.

When you've explored a feeling to its core, gotten to the original belief, and changed it, the feeling often subsides on its own. If not, ask God to take away the feelings. Surrender and "sacrifice" these feelings to God. Plead to be released from these feelings. Tell God, "I give this up to you." "I let go and let God." "I choose peace." After letting go of these "feral" or emotional impulses we open to the devout impulses. The devout impulses are often experienced as feelings of warm tingles (soft pins and needles), lightness, peacefulness, expansiveness, openness, confidence, strength. Embrace these new sensations. Remember these devout feelings. Bring them with you as you begin to come out of meditation. When you are ready, open your eyes while you continue to pay attention to the "devout impulses" with your eyes open. Write about your experience.

Working with a client on this, I had her relax and do a body scan. She noticed tension in her shoulders and neck. I had her pay attention to that area and ask what was causing it. "I'm angry," she said. "I do all the work in the house. No one ever helps me." I told her to stay with the anger and see what was beneath it. "I really feel overwhelmed by all the work." I asked her to dig deeper into what she felt as a result of being overwhelmed. She said, "I'm tired. I'm not feeling well. I've been having chest pains." I asked her to dig deeper still, to a core feeling. She told me, "I've been avoiding going to a doctor because I'm afraid he'll find something seriously wrong with me. I guess the feeling is really *fear*. That's it, it's *fear* I'm experiencing. It's holding me back from going to the doctor."

To get to her belief, I had her tune in to the fear and ask what this feeling reminded her of from her past, when she may have felt it before. She remembered her mom being sick and always being afraid of doctors. And because Mom was sick, she always wanted family members to do all the work. That was one of the ways Mom got attention. With this insight, the client was able to release the fear. After identifying the fear and releasing it, she was capable of dealing with the issue rationally. She made an appointment to see a doctor. Furthermore, she acknowledged that she really wasn't doing any more work than she had previously, when she was happier. She really didn't want her family to help. She was feeling overburdened with fear because of her health and wasn't doing anything about having it checked out. The doctor eventually diagnosed indigestion.

The more we practice identifying physical charges and core feelings, identifying where they stem from in childhood, and releasing them and changing the beliefs in meditation, the quicker we will take charge of ourselves. Furthermore, the more we practice identifying these physical impulses and emotional feelings in meditation, the more easily we will be able to identify them spontaneously in the moment while dealing with people. We will therefore avoid relating emotionally and begin to communicate in new ways, opening ourselves to new experiences.

PATH BETWEEN *NETZACH* AND *TIFERET: YUD* ׳

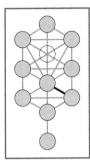

The path between *Netzach* (instincts and actions) and *Tiferet* (beauty) is represented by the Hebrew letter *yud*. The Hebrew root of *yud* is *yad*, signifying both "hand" and "power." On the path between *Netzach* and *Tiferet*, it is the compelling force that catapults us forward.

Yud correlates to the constellation of Virgo and the Hebrew month of *Elul* (August–September).The numerical value of *yud* is 10, representing the ten *sefirot*. Standing for *yechidah,* the highest level of soul, *yud* symbolizes its connection to Divine unity and oneness. As the first letter of the Tetragrammaton, this also indicates its union with the Divine.

Yud is the path that bridges the gap between heaven and earth. Reaching up to *Tiferet,* it begins the path to wholeness and beauty. To ignite the spark that initiates change, liberating your talents and innate abilities, meditate on the letter *yud,* ׳.

GOD TAKES US OUT OF SLAVERY WHEN WE BRING OURSELVES OUT OF SLAVERY

The sign of the *yud* is a hand, representing the hand of God reaching to bring us out of slavery. The *yud* is considered "king over action," as stated in the *Sefer Yetzirah.* On the path of *yud,* between *Netzach* (unconscious actions) and *Tiferet* (beauty, self), we begin to come out of slavery when we take charge of our actions. In practical terms, this happens by the way we speak.

Kabbalists believe speech is the seat of emotions. Whether speech is internal in the form of self-talk or external as what we say to others, it creates our feelings, which affect the way we behave. To behave spontaneously in loving ways, we want to come from a place of truth without emotional charges. We therefore need to master our emotions while speaking to others. This involves releasing physical and emotional impulses spontaneously. If we acknowledge the physical charges and emotional feelings when they arise to either ourselves or others, we remain open to the Divine. Many people think they're expressing feelings when, in fact, they are expressing thoughts. For instance, people often believe that just by saying *I feel,* they're expressing a feeling. They may say, "I feel *as though* you want to get back at me." "I feel *as if* you're trying to put me down." "I feel *that* your behavior is irrational." "I feel *you* always take me for granted." "I feel *like* I'm the one doing all the work." What are the feelings in these statements? Stating a feeling with terms like *as though, as if, that, you,* and *like* is expressing thoughts or thought feelings, not felt feelings. By not acknowledging the actual felt feeling, there is no release within ourselves, and therefore we often act emotionally and irrationally. This automatically catapults us into making excuses, blaming, or attacking.

To truly express feelings, it helps to identify our physical reaction and the emotional counterpart to what is being said, and to express it as such: "I feel anxious. My heart is pounding," Then dig for the emotional counterpart: "I feel so sad," or "I feel hurt by what's happening." In this way we acknowledge and release the physical charges and emotional reactions spontaneously, automatically opening ourselves to the higher energies. If we cleave to light and love, the right words come out at the right time. We explain why we feel the way we do or ask for what we really want from the other person without making excuses or attacking. Releasing the physical impulses spontaneously and expressing the emotional counterpart (again, even if it's just to ourselves) put us in touch with the silent pulse, the Divine, and what comes out is intuitive and right for all.

A client reported feeling very empowered when she started using these techniques. Miraculous things started happening, sometimes on a small scale and other times on a large one. While redecorating the house, for instance, she wanted paint matched to a color on her wallpaper. When she walked into the paint store, she asked if she could have it matched by the next day. The man, whom she knew, said in his usual rough voice, "Can't you see the sign, PAINT MIXED TO MATCH IN 48 HOURS? I'm too busy. I can't do it."

She was crushed and would have normally stormed out, saying she would not shop there anymore. Instead, this time she tuned in to her body. She realized she had a charge up her spine and was very disappointed and sad. She said, "I'm so disappointed and sad," then explained where she was coming from. "It's my parents' fortieth anniversary and I'm having a party this weekend and really wanted the project finished. I'm painting the walls myself and won't have enough time to finish if I don't get the paint by tomorrow." He kept reiterating that he couldn't do it. She maintained her calm and said, "I really understand that you're busy and I'd appreciate anything you can do for me." By the time she got home she had a message on her voice mail. "Your paint is ready. You can pick it up whenever you want." Many other incidents similar to this happened as well. My client told me she realized she was in charge, not by controlling but by letting go of the "charges" and simply stating the truth without an attitude.

When we practice the power of accurate expression of feelings, we begin to elevate ourselves to the Divine. We are "king over action." We begin to come out of the slavery of the past, leaving our animal soul behind. We're on our way to becoming *tzadikim*—righteous, responsible people.

LIBERATING OUR CREATIVITY AND TALENTS: DEVELOPING PERSONAL PURPOSE

The Hebrew letter *yud* shares the same root as *yad,* power. *Yud* is the single point of primal force and energy. It's symbolic of the point that exploded outward in the Big Bang. It's the thrust of creation. It's the energy that can help liberate our creativity and talents. *Yud* is the first letter of the Tetragrammaton, symbolic of connection with the Divine. It comes with choice and intention. It comes with choosing how we want to live. We can live our highest potential every moment by choosing the highest and best way to respond to people in each moment. And we can choose to live our Divine purpose. The choice catapults us into receiving ideas and opportunities.

In furthering our desire to uncover our purpose, along with defining our intellectual studies, talents, and skills, the Kabbalah teaches that our purpose often emerges from our greatest challenges. In each lifetime our goal is to work on a different trait or attribute of God. We keep coming back until we've learned all the lessons. Our goal in each lifetime is to manifest the learning of that trait in some way. This usually shows up in the challenges we have in life.

Rabbi Nachman of Breslov said, "In seeking to sanctify God's Name, each person has something in his life that is more of a barrier for him than anything else. This is precisely the barrier he has to break in order to serve God."

An example might be Christopher Reeve and his challenging triumph over trauma. After a horseback riding accident and severe spinal cord injury, he was paralyzed from the neck down. He then turned his attention to working, along with his wife, Dana, to raise money for research and helping people suffering with similar injuries. He became an inspiring role model for moving on despite tremendous suffering.

People are generally shown their purpose in the situations that arise in their lives. Some may not be as traumatic as paralysis, but nevertheless offer hints as to what we might want to work on and pursue as a career. I had a client who noticed her role was as a caretaker to her mother and father. Her mother was depressed for many years and stayed in bed more than going out. Her father became ill later in life, and she had to care for him as well. She was now dealing with a husband who was suffering from terminal cancer. While caring for her mother and father, she thought she'd played the role of caretaker well. She later realized, however, that she hadn't done it with compassion. She was given a situation in her adult family that repeated her childhood pattern. With her husband, however, she learned how to caretake with compassion—which she realized was her true calling. She started volunteering at a hospice and plans to write a book on it.

· Exercise: Questions to Ponder on Discovering Our Personal Purpose ·

1. If I died tomorrow, what regrets would I have?

2. What challenges have I had in life that helped me gain wisdom?

3. What challenges have I had to overcome?

4. What hardships have I endured?

5. What do I still resist?

6. What have I learned from my experiences?

7. What experiences have I had that few others have had?

8. What unfinished business do I still need to work on?

9. What type of vacations do I like to take?

10. What books do I take with me on vacation?

11. What are my creative talents?

12. What do I love to do creatively that's totally absorbing?

Taking the First Step at Living Our Dream

Living our personal purpose means taking small steps first—both personally and professionally—and then letting things evolve. If we have an inkling of what we want to do but are not sure, we can put ourselves into the environment in which we think we would like to work. Many of us don't really know what we want until we start doing it. Then, if our heart goes into the doing, we know it's right. Sometimes finding our purpose comes via the process of elimination. We need to take action first.

- If you think you would like to teach but aren't sure, volunteer as a teacher's aide.
- If you like to paint, then buy paints, set up a section of your house as a studio, and start painting.
- If you like acting, take a drama course.
- If you need more education to pursue a particular area of expertise, look into schools that fit your schedule and budget.
- If you have an expertise in some particular area, start offering workshops yourself.

The minute you take the first step, you are beginning to live your dream.

PATH BETWEEN
NETZACH AND *CHESED: KAF* כ

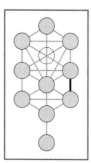

The vertical path between *Netzach* and *Chesed* is represented by the Hebrew letter *kaf,* כ. As a double letter, it has two opposing qualities: life and death. The letter *kaf* corresponds to the planet Venus and the day of the week Wednesday. Its direction is up.

The sign for the letter *kaf,* כ, is the palm of the hand. It is symbolic of the creation of something special—of potential and actualization. *Kaf* is the first letter of the Hebrew word *kavanah,* intention. Kabbalists teach that many obstacles come our way to keep us from reaching our goals. We need *kavanah,* along with deep devotion, to overcome them. To do the internal work of sticking to goals by improving willpower, focus, and direction, meditate on the letter *kaf,* כ.

MAINTAINING FOCUS AND ENDURANCE

Kaf is the first letter of *kavanah,* intention; it comes from the root word *kivein,* which means "to aim." In order to achieve what we want, we need to stay directed and maintain focus. We need determination, perseverance, and endurance.

In practical terms, endurance as a primary attribute of *kaf* is the fortitude, staying power, and patience to stay focused on something until we understand it or complete it. Rabbi Yitzchak Ginsburgh in *Alef-Beit* describes the tip of the *kaf,* כ, as the crown; it represents "crowning achievement."

As mentioned previously, we are constantly being tested as to whether we're following animal impulses or devout impulses. It's the choice between following what we want as opposed to what's right for us. For example, we may set the intention of painting a few hours each day. When the phone rings and a friend asks us to go shopping, however, we are caught off guard and forget our intention. The following day at breakfast we start reading the newspaper and then turn on the TV news. A friend calls and we talk for a while and decide to meet for lunch. Before we know it, the four hours we intended to paint are gone. Again, we forgot our intention.

· Visualization: Maintain Focus ·

A way to maintain intention and focus is to start the day by opening to the Divine. Do a basic relaxation. Close your eyes. Call on Divine light. Then imagine yourself accomplishing what you want to do for the day. See, think, and hear yourself accomplishing each step in detail in a relaxed manner. Notice what it feels like as you accomplish it. When you are ready, open your eyes. After meditation and throughout the day it helps to keep Divine light and love in mind, radiating an image of accomplishing each thing step by step.

· SEVEN ·

Tiferet: Beauty

Self/Soul, Harmony, and Higher Consciousness

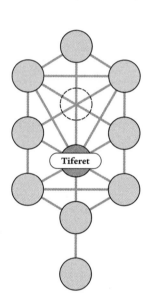

Divine Name: YHVH—Eternal God of Creation

The Divine name for *Tiferet* is YHVH (pronounced *Adonai*). As the central point on the Tree of Life, it is the pillar of balance between both the upper and lower worlds, and the right and left columns representing severity and mercy. The letters *YHVH* bring everything together.

Archangel: Michael

The archangel representing *Tiferet* is Michael, who is known to be "like unto God." Michael is the chief of hosts. Michael is also known as the guardian of Israel. He is the custodian of the keys to the Kingdom of Heaven—to God's Divine Chariot. The *Zohar* states that Michael brings the souls of the righteous before God. He brings courage for experiencing the spiritual life and following our own path.

Patriarch: Jacob

Jacob deceived his blind father, Isaac, into thinking he was his twin brother, Esau, in order to receive Esau's birthright. When Esau subsequently threatened to kill him, Jacob was urged by his mother, Rebecca, to flee his homeland and go to her brother Laban in Haran to find a wife. By nightfall, traveling north alone, Jacob lay down using a stone as a pillow and fell asleep. He dreamed of seeing angels ascending and descending a ladder. He described it as coming to "none other than the house of God, and this is the gate of heaven" (Genesis 28:17).

After this dream Jacob traveled approximately four hundred miles to his uncle Laban's home in Haran. There he met Laban's daughter, Rachel, and fell in love. He worked for Laban for seven years in order to marry Rachel. As the bride walked down the aisle veiled, Jacob did not know that it was actually Leah, Rachel's sister. Laban told him afterward, "It is not so done in our country, to give the younger before the firstborn." Jacob worked for another seven years to get Rachel as his second wife. Jacob eventually produced twelve children who later symbolized the twelve tribes of Israel. (The personalities of these sons correspond to the essence of the constellations.)

Years later, when Jacob wanted to return to his homeland, he feared Esau and his four hundred waiting men. During the night, Genesis tells us, "a man wrestled with him until the breaking of the day." Jacob is thus known as the patriarch who wrestled with God. The lessons here are of wrestling with and subduing our internal instincts and drives, not being deceitful, meeting obligations, and having faith in the Divine.

Attribute: Beauty

In *Tiferet* consciousness we are in touch with our self, our hearts are open, and we come from truth. We begin to open to higher consciousness and feel the connection to all that is, to the Absolute, and to the beauty in life. To emulate the essence of *Tiferet,* use these concepts or else imagine living with Divine presence and seeing the beauty in life. At the end of the meditation, state the affirmation: *I am in touch with my soul, which connects me to the Divine, and I see the beauty in life.* Give thanks for the ability to communicate.

TIFERET: BEAUTY
(SOUL, WATCHER OVER THE EGO)

Tiferet on the overall Tree of Life is third from the bottom in the middle column. The essence of *Tiferet* is beauty or harmony. It is the beauty of Divine presence. It is the union of the *Shekhinah,* the bride, the exiled feminine part of God, with the bridegroom, the male side, essence and being. It is the middle *sefirah* between heaven and earth, between body and mind. *Tiferet* is the point that many paths flow to and from. And because of its ability to communicate with the higher worlds as well as the lower, it is known as the Seat of Solomon. Hindus compare this level of consciousness to God's presence in man: the Atman. Christian kabbalists see it as the Christ center, or incarnated God. It is individualized man known as the place of adornment.

BEAUTY

In *Tiferet* consciousness we are balanced. Life has meaning. Harmonious relationships give us added pleasure. Our feelings well up at the sight of a beautiful painting or while hearing a wonderful opera. Our hearts open and we experience the Divine within. When we come from *Tiferet* consciousness, we come from an open heart. We are compassionate. The right words emerge at the appropriate times.

In opening the heart we also open to higher realms of existence—the spiritual realm. The Divine name for *Tiferet* is YHVH. As the central point on the Tree of Life it is the pillar of balance between the upper and lower worlds, integrating the physical and the spiritual realms. It also is the central point of balance for the right and left columns on the Tree of Life, representing severity and mercy. The Divine name YHVH brings everything together in balance.

To maintain this openness and remain centered and balanced, kabbalists use several meditations on the Divine name YHVH. Here is one of them.

· Meditation: The Divine Name YHVH ·

The four-lettered Divine name for *Tiferet,* YHVH (read in Hebrew from right to left, ‎י ה ו ה‎), often depicted as the Tetragrammaton (the Hebrew letters written vertically)—is the root of all of the other Divine names in the Torah and symbolic of the entire Tree of Life. The *yud* pertains to *Chokhmah,* wisdom; the first *heh* pertains to *Binah,* understanding; the *vav* incorporates the six *sefirot* of *Chesed* (loving-kindness or mercy), *Gevurah* (judgment or justice), *Tiferet* (beauty), *Hod* (victory), *Netzach* (splendor), and *Yesod* (foundation). The second *heh* represents *Malkhut,* action.

When we meditate on the Divine name, kabbalists warn that it should be done silently to ourselves—not out loud. Meditating on the Divine name can bring on very strong energies, sometimes making us dizzy or even nauseated. If this happens, then stop the meditation.

To begin, Aryeh Kaplan in *Meditation and Kabbalah* recommends exhaling completely before meditating on the *yud,* then inhaling before the *heh,* exhaling before the *vav,* and inhaling before the final *heh.* Do this silently and very slowly, repeating the name as a mantra several times. Notice what happens in your body.

RUACH: HIGHER SELF—HUMAN SPIRIT

As we move up the ladder into *Tiferet* and the surrounding areas, we begin to awaken to our higher self, the level of the soul known as *ruach*—human spirit. This is the level of objective watcher over the ego; the observer. It's like watching ourselves from above ourselves. We begin to see ourselves objectively and can change what is not divinely driven.

Sometimes this self or *ruach* level of soul is likened to Sleeping Beauty. It is the part of ourselves that is often asleep, awakening only when we break through the old patterns of the animalistic ego. And when we do awaken to this level of the soul, kabbalists say that we begin to approach the Gates of Paradise. We open to spirit guides and other celestial beings. We open to the beauty and essence of the Divine.

Kabbalists believe that there are several ways this level of soul can awaken. It can happen spontaneously through trauma or else through conscious study, meditation, and practice. It is the level where we might have a glimpse of some extraordinary events such as seeing angels, having near-death or out-of-body experiences, or feeling the oneness of everything. We may also hear voices. At this level such peak experiences often come and go and we're left with the essence of the experience, which is sometimes negated or forgotten altogether. For example, a client of mine said that when he was severely hurt in a car accident he saw himself hovering over his body, watching the paramedics take care of him. Then he experienced himself going through a dark tunnel. At the end of the tunnel he found himself engulfed in an incredibly brilliant light. He described it as an experience of peaceful serenity. An angel met him and told him he was with God. He had never experienced such awe. The angel told him that he would have to go back and heal. He then felt himself being pulled back into his body. He said he'd never spoken about his near-death experience before, thinking it was a hallucination. Not believing in angels, he forgot about the incident until taking his first workshop five years later. During one of the meditations he saw the same angel.

Our goal is to be more aware of these Divine episodes and understand what they are telling us.

PATH BETWEEN
YESOD AND *TIFERET: RESH* ﬧ

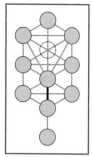

The path between *Yesod* (foundation) and *Tiferet* (beauty), the moon and sun, or the ego and the self, is represented by the Hebrew letter *resh*, ﬧ. The path of the *resh* corresponds to the planet Saturn. The opposite qualities are peace and war. *Resh* is the first letter of the Hebrew word *rosh,* which means "head" or "beginning." It's also the first letter of the Jewish New Year, Rosh Hashanah. This day is for Jewish kabbalists related to doing *teshuvah,* or repentance. It is also the first letter of the Hebrew words *Ruach Hakadosh,* Holy Spirit. It signifies gaining knowledge through intuition. This comes with shedding even more of our past. *Resh* also opens the words *refuah,* healing, and *rofeh,* healer. To work on healing the past and getting into deeper levels of consciousness, we meditate on the Hebrew letter *resh,* ﬧ.

LETTING GO OF THE PAST: VALUES, MORALS, AND ETHICS

The Hebrew root of *resh* means "poverty." Its connotation is being impoverished morally and ethically and having values that lead to wrongdoing, as in the word *rasha*, wicked person or evildoer. In practical terms, on the path of *resh* as we continue to let go of the past, we deal with morals, ethics, and values. Aside from breaking old patterns (which we covered in *Hod* and *Netzach*) and learning to forgive (we will get into this in *Chesed*), it's learning to actualize Divine values and standards as opposed to following our parents' values, conditioning, or our own destructive values.

The *Zohar* mentions values, morals, and ethics sporadically. Subjects include humility, trust, repentance (replacing evil with good), hospitality, pride, arrogance, anger, evil speech, miserliness, drunkenness, wisdom and folly, and delivering a rebuke.

- Humility is one of the primary goals in Kabbalah. It's humbling ourselves to the greatness and power of the Divine and using that energy to transform evil into good. Humbling ourselves, in practical terms, means letting go of our ego, our animalistic tendencies, and our emotional charges in order to open to the higher soul.

- Trust is having faith in the sustenance of nature and God and our own ability to remain open to these energies by not harboring or manifesting alien or evil thoughts, speech, or deeds.

- Repentance comes with replacing anything we've done that's considered evil with good. It's promoting love among people, as opposed to hate.

- Hospitality is a commandment expressed in Genesis and demonstrated by Abraham and Sarah, who invited everyone into their tent. It's being open and generous to others.

- Pride is considered a sin in Kabbalah. It's associated with boasting or holding a charge of superiority. But instead if we have "a broken spirit" (sacrifice our emotional charges and open ourselves to God), it is taught that we are honored.

- Arrogance of rulers is related to rulers sinning. When a person reaches a leadership role and sins, it's indicative of a "haughty" heart. The "haughty" heart manifests when someone seeks recognition or worships the self rather than God. We strive for humility.

- Anger is part of the evil inclination and therefore considered a sin. In practical terms, shame is often the underlying core feeling of anger. If we admit the shame or grief, we open to truth. We strive for understanding and acceptance.

- Evil speech is one of the greatest sins in Kabbalah. The Torah says, "Keep your tongue from evil." It is taught that an evil tongue, including gossip, brings on evil spirits. We strive to inspire and motivate.

- Miserliness—collecting or hoarding money for the self for personal use—is considered another sin in Kabbalah.

- Drunkenness is also a sin. It keeps us from awareness. Kabbalists believe that it inflames pride and an overbearing spirit. It is a sin to pray when drunk. We strive for clarity and awareness.

- Wisdom over folly is important—yet we still need folly to know wisdom. Folly in the form of playfulness or relaxation is necessary to give us a break from forcing rather than being in the flow. Too much folly or playfulness, or sinful folly, however, is destructive. It is important to understand both sides.

- Delivering a rebuke can teach others how to be in the light of the Absolute rather than continue evil thoughts, speech, or deeds. As suggested in the *Zohar*, however, it needs to be done with love, and at first in secret. If not accepted, then it should be done among friends; if it's still not accepted, then it can be done openly.

· Exercise: Values, Morals, and Ethics ·

In practical terms, to continue to separate from our past it's important to distinguish our own morals, values, and ethics from those of our parents. Here it helps to look at our parents' values and what we've picked up from childhood to see if we want to follow these today. Keeping in mind the values, morals, and ethics mentioned above that are divinely guided, write out what you saw or heard your parents say or model for you regarding the following areas and what you either took on for yourself or rebelled from:

1. Work ethic:

2. Money:

3. Religion:

4. Culture:

5. Recreation:

6. Eating:

7. Parenting:

8. Relationships:

9. Sex:

10. Socializing:

11. Career/achievement:

Next to your answer write down what decisions you've made about how you would behave now in each of the above areas.

1. Were you the type who did whatever your parents said? How does this affect you today?

2. Were you the rebellious type? If so, how are you still rebelling today?

3. Do you still believe these childhood decisions to be true for you as an adult?

4. How have you adapted in general to the role modeling and decisions you've made?

5. What do you really value today in each of the above areas?

6. Do your values coincide with the attributes of God?

Redo the exercise with your current self in mind. Notice where you might be either rebelling or adapting to your parents' or other values rather than living divinely.

If there are any other areas in your life that need reevaluating, then by all means do it.

OPENING INTO HIGHER STATES OF CONSCIOUSNESS: DEVELOPING INTUITION AND PROPHECY

On the path of *resh*, in the middle column passing through the triad of *Hod*, *Netzach*, and *Tiferet*, we begin to open to the higher realms of existence. We begin to awaken. By paying close attention to our thoughts, constantly releasing feelings, and being repentant, we are more in touch with the internal messages or mental images that come to mind. Often these images and messages seem to come from nowhere, and can therefore be understood as coming from beyond ourselves or a higher state of consciousness. We may begin experiencing ESP and mental telepathy, and often connect with a spirit guide. Dreams become more symbolic as well.

· Meditation: Developing Higher Consciousness ·

Resh is the first letter of the Hebrew word *ruach*, which means "wind" or "breath." Maimonides taught that combining breathwork with mental, physical, and emotional healing, we reach higher states of consciousness. Hindu and Buddhist philosophies teach concentration on breathwork as well.

To get into higher states of consciousness, Abraham Abulafia used a three-stage breath meditation including inhalation, retention of breath, and exhaling twice as long as inhaling while expressing one of five vowel sounds at a time: *holam* (o), *qamatz* (a), *hiriq* (i), *tseireh* (e), and *qubutz* (oo). Each sound influences a different sphere of the body and acts as an internal message that produces better blood circulation. As reported by Marc-Alain Quaknin in *Mysteries of the Kabbalah:*

- **O** (*holam*) acts upon the center of the thorax and the diaphragm, and tones the heart.

- **A** (*qamatz*) acts upon the esophagus, the upper three ribs, and the upper pulmonary lobes.

- **E** (*tseireh*) acts upon the throat, the vocal cords, the larynx, and the thyroid.

- **I** (*hiriq*) vibrates upward, toward the larynx, the nose, and the head, and dispels migraines.

- **Oo** (*qubutz*) acts upon all the abdominal viscera, including the stomach, the liver, the intestines, and the gonads.

· Meditation: Finding Our Inner Guide or *Maggid* ·

When we are totally balanced and in tune with mental imagery, we begin to awaken to higher consciousness and a sense of being guided. Some say they actually hear an internal guide talking to them. Kabbalists call this inner guide a *maggid*. They believe we each have our own *maggid*—our internal guide whom we can contact and use as support. Angels, guardian spirits, animals, plants, and trees are all forms of spirit guides.

Do any basic relaxation—or you may just want to meditate on the Hebrew letter *mem* (מ), the first letter of the Hebrew word "maggid," and wait for insights. If nothing comes, then imagine yourself walking through a beautiful meadow. The air is clear, the sun shining, and you feel very light and free. There's an aroma of mixed flowers as you pass a garden of wildflowers. You breathe in the aroma. Then you look out at the other end of the meadow. There is a cluster of entities. Some are in human form, others are angels and archangels, and still others may be animals. One of these entities stands out among all the rest. This entity is smiling at you. Smile back.

This entity slowly starts crossing the meadow to greet you. Ask the name. Listen closely to the first thing that comes to mind. Move closer to this image. Ask if he or she has a message for you. Listen for it. It may come instantly, or it may come later on. Notice what images, thoughts, and feelings are going on inside your body and how it feels to be in the presence of your *maggid,* your guide. Embrace the presence and now give thanks for showing up. Make a commitment to stay connected. Slowly begin walking back. When you are ready, open your eyes. Write about your experience.

When we begin opening to higher consciousness, we need to be careful because sometimes we begin feeling very powerful, develop a sense of false pride, act superior, and may even tend to control or judge others.

PATH BETWEEN
TIFERET AND *GEVURAH: TZADI* צ

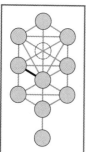

The diagonal path between *Tiferet* and *Gevurah* is represented by the Hebrew letter *tzadi,* צ. *Tzadi* correlates to the constellation of Aquarius and the Hebrew month of *Shvat* (January–February). In Hebrew the word for "Aquarius" is *dli,* literally "pitcher" or "bucket." The sign of Aquarius looks much like a water carrier.

Because of the angles and bent shape of the letter, *tzadi* is likened to a fishhook, which represents bending to our higher self. *Tzadi* is the first letter of the Hebrew word *tzimtzum,* Isaac Luria's process of creation. It involves contraction and expansion and is symbolic of either taking or letting go of control. *Tzadi* is also the first letter in *tzadik,* the righteous one. To do the internal work to develop righteousness, know when to take control or let go of control, and bow to your higher self, meditate on the Hebrew letter *tzadi,* צ.

TZADIK: RIGHTEOUS PERSON

Tzadi opens the Hebrew word *tzadik*—a righteous or wise person. A *tzadik* is nonjudgmental, noncritical, nonoffensive. A *tzadik* has no expectations of others. A *tzadik* lives with honesty and integrity; with high morals and ethics. A *tzadik* knows the right way to respond using the right words at the right time in every situation. A *tzadik* lives in a state of equanimity and creates goodness in the world. A primary goal of Kabbalah is for us all to become *tzadikim* (plural)—wise and righteous.

Becoming Nonjudgmental, Noncritical, and Free of Attitudes

To become a *tzadik,* a wise one, one of the first things we need to do is to overcome being judgmental. Kabbalists consider being judgmental toward others evil. There is a Talmudic saying: "Whoever is greater than his fellow, his inclination (for evil) is also greater." We've all heard "Love thy neighbor as thyself."

The Baal Shem Tov taught that when we do judge or criticize another, it's usually an indication that we are finding some fault within ourselves. For instance, a person might always be late for appointments. We might criticize him for always being late. Yet we are obsessively early because we may have had a problem with tardiness in the past. Or else we might see someone who is the life of a party and judge her for being too outgoing, loud, self-absorbed. Yet inwardly, we would like to be like her—outgoing, the center of attention. We may judge a critical parent, a lazy spouse, an unruly child, a strict boss, manipulative friends . . . yet they are only reflections of ourselves.

Kabbalists believe that whenever we think poorly of others, through judgment or criticism without mercy, we commit sins. These are major transgressions that lead to evil inclinations, often manifesting in having emotional reactive charges or attitudes toward people, rather than coming from equanimity. Attitudes manifest when there are expectations. Therefore it's important to let go of expectations.

Many years ago I taught classes on parent effectiveness. Although most of the parents said they were using the right communication techniques, only about half said they had success. Upon further exploration I found that those who weren't successful had hidden agendas and expectations while using the right communication techniques. They wanted things to turn out their way. I realized then that it wasn't just about having the right communication techniques; the right attitude was needed as well. Kabbalists believe fixed expectations of outcomes come from selfishness or ego. If we have hidden agendas or expectations when we communicate, the transaction comes across as convoluted, confusing, and often manipulative and charged. We have an attitude. For example, if you're having a disagreement with a spouse and fully expect to get your way, you will probably fight till the end. There's no room for hearing the other side or listening to options to reach an amenable solution.

· Exercise: Judgments and Expectations ·

Judgments and expectations in relationships are usually based on decisions we made very early in life about how people should be, or the way we would like them to be. Below is an exercise to see what expectations or judgments you might have of the people in your life. Write out the ending of each sentence.

Column A	Column B	Column C
A mother should be . . .	My mother is . . .	As a mother, I am . . .
A father should be . . .	My father is . . .	As a father, I am . . .
A wife should be . . .	My wife is . . .	As a wife, I am . . .
A husband should be . . .	My husband is . . .	As a husband, I am . . .
A daughter should be . . .	My daughter is . . .	As a daughter, I am . . .
A son should be . . .	My son is . . .	As a son, I am . . .
A brother should be . . .	My brother is . . .	As a brother, I am . . .
A sister should be . . .	My sister is . . .	As a sister, I am . . .
A granddaughter should be . . .	My granddaughter is . . .	As a granddaughter, I am . . .
A grandson should be . . .	My grandson is . . .	As a grandson, I am . . .
Friends should be . . .	My friends are . . .	As a friend, I am . . .
A boss should be . . .	My boss is . . .	As a boss, I am . . .
A co-worker should be . . .	My co-workers are . . .	As a co-worker, I am . . .

Compare how you think the people in your life should be in Column A, and how you actually experience the people in your life in Column B, and then how you see yourself in Column C. Then ask yourself the following questions:

1. Are the people in my life the way I want them to be?

2. What expectations do I have of each one?

3. Why can't I accept them for who they are?

4. Who can I not accept?

5. Who am I still trying to change?

6. What am I judging in this person?

7. Have I at one time done the same thing, for which I feel embarrassment or guilt that I haven't resolved?

8. Do I have a silent wish to be like this person?

9. Have I gone overboard in doing just the opposite?

10. Do I want what the other person has?

11. In what ways am I still judging myself?

12. How are these judgments and expectations serving me in my life?

13. What are these judgments and expectations stopping me from doing for myself?

14. Am I the way I would like others to be?

15. What expectations do I have of myself that are unmet?

· Meditation: Overcoming Expectations ·

Do a basic relaxation. Set an intention to overcome whatever expectations you struggle with. Think about the person you are judging. Notice what you are feeling. Reach for the core feeling. What is it about yourself that makes you feel this way? What self-talk or beliefs are going on about yourself? Determine what in the other person is you—or what lesson you are learning from this other person. See yourself as the other person, as if you are one, soul to soul. Now think about your feelings toward the person. Usually a genuine attitude of gratitude emerges for having been shown our inequities so we can now make changes that lead to spiritual perfection. Give thanks to the person for showing you the way. When you come back, write down what you are grateful about.

Another good meditation to practice being nonjudgmental is to learn to be with everything and anyone you come in contact with, without reacting—responding, yes, but not reacting.

· Meditation: Mindfulness ·

Do a basic relaxation, then just sit and be mindful of whatever is happening. Notice what is going on without reacting; just be with it. Try this for twenty minutes at a time. Eventually your body will begin to follow this practice during daily activities.

Preventing Criticism and Judgments by Communicating from a State of Harmony, Truth, and Oneness

To overcome judgmental attitudes and behavior, seek to connect with your heart and say what you feel rather than blaming others. Talking about your feelings and needs instead of accusing someone else makes a big difference in how what you say is received by the listener. Talking from the "I" expresses yourself without an attitude of blame. Saying, "You're so cold and closed off," sends an entirely different message from, "I feel lonely and alone and I need to understand what's going on." The first is an attack. The second explains—without blame or criticism—how you feel, where you're coming from, and what you need. When there's no intention to blame or criticize, but only a true desire to communicate to the point of understanding, the right words often come automatically.

To speak from the heart, communicate from a place of authenticity, and give effective feedback, you must be totally honest with yourself and others.

HONESTY

A *tzadik* lives with honesty and integrity. The path of *tzadi* is part of the triad of *Tiferet, Gevurah,* and *Chesed.* This is the area of essential speech: speech that comes naturally from the heart. Kabbalists believe when we come from the heart, the right words come out at the appropriate times, even without our knowing the right communication skills. Alternatively, though, using the right communication skills can keep us connected to this level of openness. It comes with listening from our hearts and giving feedback that is truthful, loving, and helpful—giving value to others.

THE WORD

As I've mentioned several times previously, words, the way we say them, and what we mean when we say them are of the utmost importance in Kabbalah. The *Sefer Yetzirah* translated by Aryeh Kaplan explains that words are studied in three ways: *sefer* (text), *sefar* (numerical value), and *sippur* (meaning). These three terms also describe the way the *sefirot* are defined.

- *Sefer* is the physical form or text of a word. In the *sefirot* it defines universal space and stands for the recording of information.

- *Sefar* stands for the numerical value of the letter. When it comes to the *sefirot,* this is where all events and actions are measured and weighed.

- *Sippur* is the telling or means of communication. It's the way God communicates with humans and humans communicate with God.

Just as God created life through the sounds of the Hebrew letters, we create our lives through words. Everything we say, how we say it, and what we mean by it—whether it is in English or any other language—has an impact on others as well as on the Divine realms. It creates an impulse, a vibration.

Looking at the Tree of Life, we can see that thoughts, feelings, and intuitions all come from different levels of consciousness and, therefore, come with different vibrations. In practical terms, our speech gives off sounds, vibrations, and meanings. If the word doesn't correspond to the meaning, there is a mixed vibration, a mixed message, a mixed "recording." For instance, if we say "I feel" and instead express a thought, there is a mixed vibration. In turn, if we say "I am tired" rather than "I feel tired," it's another mixed vibration. If we say "I am" anything other than the attributes of the Divine, there is a mixed vibration.

When expressing ourselves it is thus important to distinguish among observations (what we see as real), thoughts (interpretations of information, including beliefs, perceptions, assumptions, expectations), feelings (physical sensations and their emotional components), intuition/ESP (hunches, dreams), actions (our attitude, speech, and behavior), and being (who we are). Very often we express opinions—rather than observations, thoughts, or intuition—as feelings; feelings as thoughts; or observations as perceptions. In class one night, for example, I did an exercise where a woman stood in the middle of a group of seated participants who did not know her. I asked them to describe what they saw. A person sitting in front of her said, "I see an attractive woman who has a soft heart and is very loving."

I asked the person sitting in back of her what he observed. He said, "I see a woman probably in her fifties, who knows her stuff, and thinks a lot about what she does."

I asked someone to the left of her, who said, "I see a huge aura that shows she's very creative and spiritual."

I asked the person sitting to the right what he saw. He said, "I see a woman in a black suit with a white blouse. She has long black curly hair, brown eyes, and is wearing glasses." He was the only person who was accurate.

The Talmud says: "We see things not as they are but as we are." It's the same as seeing things through the proverbial rose-colored glasses. The three former participants all offered interpretations, including assumptions or perceptions, based on where *they* were coming from, without really knowing the woman in the middle.

Knowing the differences among observations, thoughts, perceptions, assumptions, feelings, and intuition helps us keep our discussions accurate. Here are some of these distinctions:

- Thoughts: These are generally interpretations drawn from what we have heard, read, and observed. They may incorporate value judgments in which we decide that something is good or bad, right or wrong. Or they may include beliefs, perceptions, projections, assumptions, opinions, and theories—all varieties of interpretations or conclusions based on thought.

- Perceptions: These are interpretations of what we see, and may not be factual. For example, we may see a plant with brown leaves and think it's dying when actually it's shedding its fall leaves.

- Projections: What we think of someone can be based on our own experience, not the person. As in the previous exercise, another participant describing the woman in the middle said she was attractive and nice. The woman didn't know her. How could she say she was nice? That's a projection, possibly because the woman reminded her of someone else she knew.

- Assumptions: There is a saying that when we "ass-u-me" something, we make an ass out of you and me. Assumptions are misperceived expectations of something about to happen. They are conjectures, not necessarily what is. Assumptions are not truths. Therefore, we can never "assume" anything. We want to know the facts, what *is*.

- Beliefs: Beliefs are what we formulate as a result of observing repeated outcomes to repeated experiences. They are also viewpoints about what we think is true but may not be.

- Observations: What we see as real. The facts.

- Feelings: When it comes to the expression of feelings, it's important to distinguish between thought and felt feelings, as discussed under *Netzach*. Core feelings are expressions of what our body is experiencing and the emotional counterpart. The importance of identifying and expressing the core feeling is that it releases emotional charges and allows us to respond honestly from our true feelings, rather than in transference from an emotional reaction.

- Intuition: When we have an intuitive sense about something, we express it as a hunch. A hunch is an inkling, sensation, or image of something for which we have no proof.

BEING: "I AM THAT I AM"

When we say "I am," we need to think about what we are experiencing at the moment. If it is anything other than the attributes of God, then it is not what we are, but rather how we think, how we feel, or what we are sensing.

Saying "I am" and adding anything other than the qualities of the Divine is totally disempowering. When God described himself to Moses, he said, "I AM THAT I AM." If we are in God's image, and say we are anything other than the qualities of God, then we're going against the source of who we are—ourselves and God. Remember that our perceptions of ourselves and what others think of us are not the same as who we are. This is an important distinction.

When someone asks "How are you?" the usual answer might be "fine"—or "miserable," or "sick." Kabbalists may take the opposite stance and explain by deduction. It might be compared to being told, "Don't picture a pink elephant." What do you see in your mind's eye? The pink elephant. The universe only receives the mind's impressions. Below are some examples:

- Instead of saying "I am miserable," say "I am not great."
- Instead of saying "I am unhappy," say "I am not happy."
- Instead of saying "I am sick," say "I am not well."
- Instead of saying "I am tired," say, "I am not energetic."
- Instead of saying "I am ignorant in these matters," say, "I am not smart in these matters."

By putting things this way, the words *great, happy,* and so on become the goals, rather than words such as *sick, tired,* or *unhappy.* It sets up a different impression in the mind.

On this path of honesty, aside from talking from the "I" and distinguishing among thoughts, feelings, and intuition, we must be in sync within ourselves. That means thoughts, feelings, and intuition all have to portray the same message. Very often we say one thing and do another, or think one thing and say another. If we are not honest within ourselves, the message is not clear to others. We give double messages, not truth.

Kabbalists teach that thought is the root of speech. If the speech does not coincide with the thought, then what is said does not get its life force from pure thought, but instead from animalistic ego thinking, the shadow side of ourselves. If the words are false, the interpretation and message are corrupted.

In practical terms, if we say "I love you" to someone, yet are unaffectionate and never there for the person, we're not in sync. If someone asks us to do something very inconvenient, and we say we'd be happy to do it yet do it with resentment, we're not in sync. The messages need to be whole and honest. When we speak from the "I" and say "I think" or "I feel," we must truly know and understand what we think or feel, and not just talk from the "top of our heads."

INTEGRITY

Along with honesty, a *tzadik* has integrity. Having integrity means living up to our own words, doing what we say we will do, and meeting our obligations. It's "walking our talk." How much integrity do you have?

---

1. How often have I promised to invite someone over for an evening without ever actually extending an invitation?

2. How often am I late for agreed-upon times for appointments, dinner engagements, parties, and so forth?

3. How do I respond when someone asks my opinion on a new outfit—and I really don't like it?

4. When have I lied about something to save my own skin?

5. When and to whom have I told white lies?

6. How honest am I with myself?

7. How honest am I with others?

8. When have I reneged on obligations?

9. When have I not fulfilled my promises to myself?

10. When have I not fulfilled my promises to others?

11. What percentage of the time do I "walk my talk"?

Remember, whenever we do not follow our own words or live up to our obligations, we go against ourselves. Our souls go back to sleep. We are our own worst enemies.

REFLECTION ON COMMUNICATION

The path of *tzadi* moves us closer to the *sefirah* of *Gevurah*, which deals with discipline. It means disciplining ourselves to speak honestly, kindly, and compassionately. To refrain from judgments and criticisms and express ourselves without attacking, we speak from the "I." When we use "I" messages and our thoughts, feelings, and intuition are in sync, we come from truth, and a clear message is received. We come from the "I" of the soul, not the ego.

Setting our minds to talking from the "I" and expressing thoughts, feelings, intuitions, and requests accurately is like learning a new language—and it can change our attitude and our world. It will keep us in a state of harmony and equanimity and therefore keep us in the flow. When observations, thoughts, feelings, and actions are all in harmony, then we are "at-one-ment." When we are in our "oneness," we are in sync with the life force that generates our energy. We are in touch with the greater truth. When we are honest with ourselves, we experience inner peace. When we are honest with others, we experience living our truth and channeling Divine wisdom. We are on our way to becoming *tzadikim*.

Acceptance: Knowing When to Let Go and When to Take Charge, When to Be Quiet and When to Speak

Tzadi is the first letter of the Hebrew word *tzimtzum*, the process of contraction and expansion. A *tzadik* accepts what comes and knows when to let go and when to take charge.

Since everything that we experience comes to us from Divine will, then we must accept what comes and do the best we can with it. For many people, accepting what comes often means having to let go of control and having to have things our way. If we're busy controlling things, we stop Divine Providence from showing us what we need to learn.

We often try controlling things in our personal lives or with other people. In our personal lives, for instance, if obstacles come along to stop us from reaching a goal, we may keep pursuing it and pushing ourselves to make it happen. The universe, on the other hand, may be telling us we belong somewhere else.

Kabbalists believe it's important to set goals but at the same time remain nonattached to the outcome. Letting go of the outcome of a goal makes way for mystical or magical events to play their part. The purpose of letting go of outcomes is that although we have a goal, we may also be led onto a new path. Sometimes we're guided by choice. Other times we have no control over it. For example, a couple in a business partnership may have an overall goal of expanding their business. After a number of years, however, one person might want to end the partnership and buy out the other, or to dissolve the business altogether. Here the other party has no choice. She or he has to let go of the business. Illness is another obstacle that might prevent us from reaching a goal. Such obstacles show us that we need to either learn something before we achieve the goal, or else be on a different path altogether. Sometimes we're tested to see just how much we need to either learn or persevere in order to reach our goal. We can generally keep pursuing our goal as long as we have the power to do something about it. Whenever we no longer have control, we need to let go and remain open to other opportunities.

When we do get what we want, kabbalists often use the expression, "It's *bashert.*" Daniel Schwartz in *Finding Joy* defines *bashert* as a "predestined path that is shaped by a combination of God's will and our own receptiveness to opportunity. Over the course of a life it will take us in directions not initially seen or anticipated."

We have to let go of controlling other people or other people's lives as well. This allows others to experience what they need to learn. For instance, when children make mistakes, a parent often steps in to protect them, rather than letting the children learn the consequences of their actions (within reason, of course).

Many people are troubled by letting go, thinking they're playing a passive role and could be doing more. By taking a step back, however, we can look at when it's appropriate to take charge or to let go. It's the difference between making things happen or letting them happen.

· Exercise: Knowing When to Let Go and When to Take Charge ·

Here's a way to decipher when to take charge and make things happen, and when to let go and let them happen: Make a list of every ruminating thought that plagues you. It might be concern about a job; worry about a sick friend or a daughter who wants a divorce; or things you tell yourself you "should" be doing. Then take another piece of paper and draw a line down the middle to create two columns. On the top of one column write: THINGS I CAN DO SOMETHING ABOUT. Over the second column write: THINGS I HAVE NO CONTROL OVER. Look at your first list to determine what you have control over. If your job problems are caused by a change in tasks and you are not up to it, you may have no control. Still, you do have control over what you want to do about it. If it's affected by your attitude toward your boss, and there's something you can do about this, put it in the column THINGS I CAN DO SOMETHING ABOUT. A daughter getting a divorce is your daughter's problem, and there's nothing you can do about it. Put it under the column THINGS I HAVE NO CONTROL OVER. Wanting to change your attitude about a friend is something you have control over. You can change if you want to. Put that in the column of things you do have control over. To help determine whether you have control over something or not, it helps to ask the question *Whose problem is it?* If it's not your problem, you have no control over it, and therefore can't do anything about it.

For the things we have no control over, we can pray to God for the highest and best good or blessings for the people or things we are worried about. We can also work on ourselves to overcome wanting things to be our way when they can't and learning to let go of control. We can pray to God to let go of control as well. This can begin with saying prayers such as:

- *I let go and let God.*
- *This is out of my hands and in God's hands.*
- *Divine Providence is manifesting what is right for the good of all now.*

When it comes to the THINGS I CAN DO SOMETHING ABOUT, start taking charge. But do it one step at a time.

PATH BETWEEN
TIFERET AND *CHESED: CHET* ח

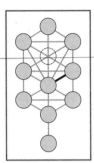

The path between *Tiferet* and *Chesed* is represented by the Hebrew letter *chet,* ח. The path of *chet* corresponds to the constellation of Cancer
and the Hebrew month *Tammuz* (June–July). *Chet* carries the numerical value of 8. Turned sideways it is the symbol for infinity; beyond
space and time; stepping into the unknown. It is also the foundation
of sight. *Chet* is the first letter of the Hebrew word *chai,* which means
"life" and has the same numerical value as *oheiv*—he loves. It is symbolic of having love and harmony in life, which is what allows for
good health. For love, vitality, good health, and harmony, meditate on the letter
chet, ח.

SIGHT: BEAUTY IS SEEN IN THE DETAILS

Chet equates to the foundation of sight. This path helps us see the intrinsic beauty
in life, in others, and in creation. When we see the beauty in others and life, there is
love. With love, there's vitality and healing.

At this level we are able to see the essence of things, their core beauty. In order
to perceive the essential nature or beauty in things, according to the *Sefer
Yetzirah,* it is essential to "make each thing stand on its essence." It is said in the
Sefer Yetzirah that "when a person perceives the true spiritual nature of a thing,
he also elevates that thing spiritually."

In practical terms, beauty, essence, and meaning come with being detail-
oriented. When we delve into what we see in detail, we can experience the core or
essence beyond the appearance. This is beauty.

Ways of practicing this include listening carefully or seeing something in such
detail that we reach its core. When you look at a painting, look at it with the eyes
of an artist. See the negative and positive shapes, the shapes around each object
in the picture, as well as the picture as a whole. Notice the colors, shadings, textures, views. Notice the background. Notice how you feel looking at the entire
picture. What's going on in your body? What are you experiencing?

Listen to the sounds of an orchestra. Learn to distinguish the sounds of the different instruments.

When we look at something in close detail, we see not only the whole picture but also its minute parts. When we pay attention to our experience of it, that's when we see beyond what is actually there. We have deeper "inner sight." That's when we connect with the beauty of what is—the essence.

Opening to the Beauty of the Divine: Open to the Beauty in Our Own Lives

Chet is the first letter of the Hebrew words *chazak* (being strong) and *chutzpah* (having guts). Although sometimes *chutzpah* is used as a pejorative, indicating that someone has a lot of nerve, in this case it refers to having the guts to open to the unknown, the abyss, the void of the infinite. In opening to the infinite, we see the beauty in the Divine. To open to the beauty of the Divine, we need to open to the beauty in our own lives. Take the time to see beauty in everything you have and do. See everything from new perspectives.

- If you don't have anything to love, start loving what you have. Look at yourself in the mirror. Take a good look at your eyes. The eyes are the windows of the soul. See the beauty inside.
- Appreciate yourself: your breath, movement, sense of smell, taste, touch, sight, hearing.
- Look at your surroundings in detail. Surround yourself with beauty. In your house, have beautiful scents around—perhaps fresh flowers. Play soothing music.
- When walking along a garden path, take in all the aromas of the flowers, the grass, the air. Appreciate the ability to distinguish similarities and differences, the ability to breathe, the ability to think, to speak, to walk, to talk. Bless your abilities.
- See the beauty in everything you do even if it doesn't appear to be beautiful: Comfort a sick child; visit people in hospitals; see the wisdom of your years. If you see a person handicapped with Parkinson's disease struggling to balance soup on a spoon and dripping some while putting it into his

or her mouth, think of the courage and fortitude it takes to eat soup at all. See the beauty of it. Bless it. Bless everyone with whom you come in contact. Blessings in Kabbalah generally mean asking the Divine to help people see and be in the light.

CREATING HARMONY

On the path of *chet* we communicate in ways that create more harmony. To do this we need to learn to speak in details rather than generalizations—to speak in ways that are unarguable. That means there is no generalizing or labeling. For instance, we might say someone is lazy, ungrateful, or even wonderful. These labels can be argued. We might tell a child his painting is great, but he might not believe it. But instead if we say, "I like the painting because of the colors you used and where you placed every object," that cannot be argued. It works the same way when criticizing or giving directions. If we ask a child to clean her room and she makes the bed but leaves the rest a mess, we might be upset. Yet a child may think a clean room means making the bed. Had we instead explained that to us, "clean the room" means putting shoes in the closet and picking up the toys from the floor, the child might have understood our instructions better. Speaking in detail also gives more meaning to what we are talking about. We don't talk in code that way. Practice seeing and thinking in details. It creates more harmony and beauty in our lives.

As we begin to see the beauty in our lives, we begin to experience beauty in ourselves and come from our own love—the love that comes from within, our own natural state.

ENTERING THE ARCHWAY:
REMEMBERING WHO WE ARE

Career Values

With a numerical value of 8, *chet* signifies beginnings. The eighth day after the seven of the previous week is a new week. *Chet* is also represented by the symbol of an archway or gateway: the beginning of a new life, a path of transformation.

As we move closer to *Chesed,* when we free ourselves from the past, we become our own person, come from our own truth, and awaken our higher self, the human spirit, *ruach.* It's remembering who we are. As Zusya, an ancient rabbi, said before he died, "In the world to come they will not ask me, 'Why were you not Moses?' They will ask me, 'Why were you not Zusya?'"

On the path of *chet* we return to a previous state of existence. Ascending the Tree of Life, we've been practicing our hobbies, using and refining our skills and talents, increasing our education, and defining our role toward uncovering our Divine purpose. Now determining our career values helps expand our visions toward unleashing our purpose. What values are important to you regarding your career? Write them down.

Creativity	Team participation
Flexibility	Winning
Adventure	Teaching
Learning	Leadership
Security	Spirituality
Love	Pleasure
Independence	Relationships
Sincerity	Cleanliness
Autonomy	Beauty
Freedom	Children

Look back at the career lists you made in *Hod* and *Netzach.* Review what you highlighted and notice where you can combine your skills, interests, greatest challenges, and career values. Now choose five areas that have the most value for you and prioritize them. Notice which ones you most excel in. Think about what area you might want to concentrate on and expand in order to become an expert. This type of practice and questioning helps us unleash and define our Divine purpose and live life anew.

Gevurah: Strength, Justice
Self-Discipline and Boundaries

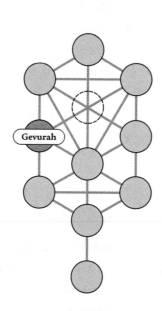

Divine Name: *Elohim*

The Divine Hebrew name for *Gevurah* is *Elohim,* God the Just. In the spiritual world this is the name that serves Divine justice and Divine punishment. It is the Heavenly Court that determines judgment: feast or famine, life or death. Each one of us is created through judgment, based on righteousness (responsibility) or wickedness (foolishness), and judgment determines our body size, shape, structure, and nature; number of days we will live; and the type of sustenance we will have in life. As we stand before this court we are told what size, nature, and status we will have. With the knowledge of what will happen to us, we are in compliance.

The body and environment we come in with are a result of Divine Providence, but what we do with them is up to our free will. The way we act creates what we merit in each lifetime—the amount of awareness, consciousness, or energy and light we come in with. Favors are bestowed on the righteous.

Archangel: Samael

Samael represents *Gevurah* on the left side of the Tree of Life. It is the evil inclination, *yetzer hara*. Samael—often represented as Satan in more contemporary times, or the devil, Lucifer, in ancient scripture—was not the evil angel that he has become known as. He plays the role of adversary under God's control. As the evil inclination, Samael shows himself as the tempter in whatever form need be, such as the serpent tempting Eve in the Garden of Eden. He can come in the form of a person, animal, or entity and constantly tempts our own integrity and righteousness, showing us our imperfections and what we need to work on.

Patriarch: Isaac

Isaac is the patriarch representing *Gevurah*. Fearing his own death while Abraham tied him down on the altar to be sacrificed to God, Isaac represents the fear of God. Isaac preached the accountability of actions. He told people that they were being judged by God and that there are consequences for actions.

Attributes: Justice, Strength, Discipline

The attributes of *Gevurah* are justice, strength, discipline. We are nonjudgmental, have courage and strength, and are disciplined in living our lives and following our career paths. We have faith, are in awe of Divine Providence, and are humble before the power and awesomeness of the Absolute. To experience the essence of *Gevurah* we can bring on any of the above representations or we can imagine experiencing justice, strength, and discipline with the awe of God. At the end of the meditation, state the affirmation: *I am disciplined and stand for due justice and mercy. I am in awe of God and thankful for Divine presence.*

GEVURAH: JUSTICE/JUDGMENT— FEAR OF GOD, AWE OF GOD

Gevurah is the next gate to enter on the Tree of Life. Diagonally above and across from *Tiferet* on the left side, *Gevurah* represents the fear and awe of the Absolute. *Chesed* is horizontally across from *Gevurah* on the right side and represents love of God and loving-kindness and mercy toward others. Kabbalists consider fear and love to be the two core emotions of the intellect. At this level of consciousness we have the ability to use our intellect and choose to develop positive attributes of righteousness, charity, loving-kindness, and strength while avoiding the mundane, materialistic desires that lead to devastation, rebelliousness, cruelty, and death.

When we choose the former, we begin to experience the awe of God. In experiencing the awe of God we begin to experience the greatest good—the love that comes from closeness to God; the love of God, which is represented in Ch*esed*. If we experience too much love, however, we may go overboard and become self-sacrificing, overly giving, self-indulgent, self-confident, self-righteous. Being overly loving and giving can burn us out (by the fire). We're thrown off balance. Imbalance separates us from the Divine. The fear of separating from the Divine keeps us on our best behavior and respectful of the power and awesomeness of Divine Providence. The fear, or really awe, of Divine Providence is what keeps us humble. It reminds us of the source of strength and power.

Gevurah represents judgment, justice, strength, or discipline. In *Gevurah* we have the skills to be nonjudgmental; we know when to take control or let go of control. We know how to set boundaries, defend ourselves, and confront without attacking. We are courageous and have the determination and will to use our power wisely. When we do this, we have the faith and courage to follow what's right for ourselves and others.

JUDGMENT: BEING TESTED

In *Gevurah* we are constantly being tested to see if we are worthy of entering the "orchard," the Garden of Eden. But who is the judge? Kabbalists believe that in the spiritual world, judgment comes from the Divine Court—the governing power of several houses of the "flames of fire." Every creature is afraid of it and in awe of it. It is a fire that devours, consumes, and can annihilate everything. It is also a fire that can heal and sustain life.

In practical terms, since the soul is in the image of God and derived from God, it is God who judges himself. According to Isaiah Tishby in *Wisdom of the Zohar,* "Moses de Leon sees the punishment of the soul as a kind of self-inflicted punishment on the part of God, since the soul is God's 'own essential being.'" In the physical world, if we're a reflection of the Divine, and the Divine knows right from wrong, then we have an innate sense of right and wrong, and therefore punish ourselves for wrongdoing. We are our own judge here on earth. Since people are fearful of being consumed by the fire, they fear God's wrath and punishment. In the physical world, however, it isn't God who punishes us. We punish ourselves. We are accountable mostly to ourselves, and we reap the consequences of our own actions in the form of what happens to us in life. We get back what we put out.

A client told a story of immediate cause and effect. While driving to work, someone tapped her car in the rear. There were no dents in the car, and no one was hurt. Yet she still was angry and cursed the other driver. While driving home that night she accidentally rear-ended someone else's car. Again, fortunately, no one was hurt, and there was no damage. Upon realizing the synchronicity, my client chuckled at the dues she paid as a result of her cursing.

When we act in ways that are destructive, we experience separation, disconnectedness, and fear. When we act responsibly and for the good, we experience the awe of God's power, might, and strength. We experience more light, love, and joy.

The work here is to overcome our evil urges, the *yetzer hara,* open to the awesomeness of the Divine, and remain humble. R. Bachya ben Joseph ibn Paquda, in *Duties of the Heart,* says, "Desires for worldly pleasures are unable to dwell in the heart together with a love of God."

EVIL SPIRITS: *YETZER HARA*

There are differing points of view regarding the origination of evil. Some kabbalists explain it as the residue coming from the destroyed worlds prior to this one. Some describe it as a world that existed before this one that was the proto-type of the *sefirot*. These *sefirot* did not interact with one another, however, instead creating what kabbalists call a universe of chaos (*tohu*). The *sefirot* as vessels would receive Divine light but not be able to give as God gives, and therefore are shattered. Isaac Luria called this the "Breaking of Vessels." The shards fell into a lower spiritual dimension, which is considered the source of all evil. The other opinion is that evil comes from *Gevurah,* the world of judgment and justice, and originated with Adam and Eve eating from the Tree of Knowledge and thereafter knowing good or evil. In any case, kabbalists believe that there is a realm of darkness on this earth, and that demons (evil spirits) are constantly leading us there.

Lilith, the wife of Samael, is considered the ruler of the evil forces. In mythical literature Lilith was actually Adam's first wife, before Eve. She was made from dust and equal to Adam. She refused to lie down under him in a missionary position in intercourse, however, and this enraged Adam. She left the Garden of Eden and when she wouldn't return, a curse was put on her—one hundred of her sons would die every day. She believed her purpose was to put a curse on every unborn child.

Many demons are considered to be spirits of people who died suddenly and violently and haven't yet acclimated to death. These spirits often hover over cemeteries or fly around the earth haunting people and houses.

It is also believed that demons can enter the body of a sick person. This is known as a *dybbuk*—a clinging soul; in more modern terminology it might be known as a "walk-in." Such a soul can actually enter and control a person's body. It is considered demonic possession. King Saul flying into a wild rage without reason is one example of such possession.

To avoid demons, Hasidic mystics use a variety of methods, including tying a red twine with seven knots around the left wrist, and wearing amulets. Most Jews affix *mezuzot* on doorposts. Western kabbalists often wear amulets with mystical writings and magical symbols either affixed on them or inserted within. Magical incantations, specific meditations, and prayers are said to vanquish the demonic evil. One often used to ward off evil or cure illness is *abracadabra*. This is recited as an incantation.

ABRACADABRA
ABRACADABR
ABRACADAB
ABRACADA
ABRACAD
ABRACA
ABRAC
ABRA
ABR
AB
A

Kabbalists believe a way to ward off the Angel of Death is the giving of *tzedakah*, charity. There is a story of Rabbi Akiva of the second century being told by a stargazer that his daughter would die on her wedding day. As the bride was getting dressed, a poisonous snake crawled up her dress. While putting on her bonnet, however, she stuck one pin in and pierced one eye of the snake. The second pin pierced its other eye. When she walked out to greet her father, he saw the dead snake dangling from her neck. "What did you do that succeeded in saving yourself from death?" he asked.

She remembered that earlier in the day the bell had rung, and since everyone else was busy she'd answered the door. It was a beggar asking for money. She gave him a few coins. Rabbi Akiva responded, "*Tzedakah* saves a person from death."

Another kabbalistic practice to ward off the evil spirit if someone is near death is having that person change his or her name. And if someone is ill in your family, you may want to make a donation to charity.

· Meditation: Archangels' Cube of Protection ·

To remain protected, kabbalists often picture themselves surrounded by the archangels. This is particularly done at night before going to sleep as protection from evil spirits while the soul leaves the body.

This meditation can be done at any time. As you meditate on each archangel, allow yourself to experience the quality and essence it represents. At the end, just be with the energy of all the archangels surrounding you in the total protection and awesomeness of the Divine. Give thanks for their presence.

Do a basic relaxation. Close your eyes. Picture yourself surrounded by archangels on all sides, as well as from above. On the right is Michael, who is a messenger of God and represents the love of God. Take your time and call on Michael. Let yourself experience the essence and the images. Gabriel is on the left, representing the fear and awe of God. Again, take your time and call on Gabriel. Let yourself experience the essence and the images. Continue to do the same with all the other archangels. Uriel is in front, representing the belief in and light of God. Behind is Raphael, who guards us from negative or misinterpreted foreign thoughts and represents the healing power of God. The *Shekhinah* is above the head and represents the feminine presence of God as well as God's existence and providence.

Kabbalists teach that the best protection to ward off the evil eye is to live responsibly and not give in to evil inclinations. We need to subdue our own evil inclinations. We must also make amends for the past.

PATH BETWEEN
GEVURAH AND BINAH: GIMEL ג

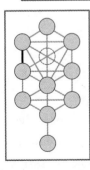

The path between *Gevurah* (discipline, strength) and *Binah* (understanding) is represented by the Hebrew letter *gimel,* ג. The vertical path of *gimel* corresponds to the planet Mars; Monday is its day of the week, and north is its direction.

The double meanings of *gimel* are "wealth" and "poverty." The word *gimel* is a derivative of the Hebrew *gimul,* often interpreted as the giving of either reward or punishment. Reward comes when we choose good over evil. That's when there's wealth.

The sign of *gimel* is a camel. It's symbolic of wandering through the desert until we are nourished within sufficiently to sustain ourselves and also help others. To become totally independent and overcome evil and do good, we meditate on the letter *gimel,* ג.

OVERCOMING EVIL INCLINATIONS: *YETZER HARA*

The path of *gimel*, in practical terms, is the area of consciousness that tests our ethical and moral characteristics, our inclinations toward greed, lust, excessiveness, instant gratification, arrogance, lying, stealing, cheating, and harboring anger. Aside from these obvious crimes, scoffing, slander, gossip, idle chatter, and holding back when we see an injustice instead of righting a wrong are all considered evil.

Lashon Hara: Evil Speech

The Talmud states, "An unrefined word should never pass a man's lips, for the Torah goes out of its way and uses eight extra letters to avoid an unpleasant word."

Evil speech is considered a major transgression in Kabbalah. Part of evil speech is gossiping. Miriam was punished with leprosy when she spoke to Aaron about Moses being so involved with Divine communication that it separated him from intimacy with the Cushite woman he had married.

Kabbalists believe gossip can be very harmful to others even if it isn't meant that way. Gossiping to kabbalists includes: talking about someone who is not in our presence even if what is being said is true; listening to what others say about another person; and talking about a person even while leaving the name out. Talking about another can influence the person we are talking to and therefore create more animosity.

Slandering, bad-mouthing, blaming, and attacking others are equally demeaning. According to kabbalists, the only time derogatory words are acceptable is if they act as a warning involving doing business or marrying a person who is involved in wrongdoing. Aside from this, we need to discipline ourselves not to engage in slander or gossip.

Another transgression is not speaking up when we witness injustice. Kabbalists believe we are just as much at fault as the one committing the crime if we don't speak up to right the wrong. Still, kabbalists teach that it's important to serve justice with mercy—to discern what is right and wrong, and to give punishment in a way that is fair without personal vindictiveness or revenge. That means leaving judgment up to a jury or court. For example, if a child is intentionally hurt, it's not up to us to get a gun and hurt the accused. It's up to a jury to decide the punishment. In the higher realms, celestial justice means affirming the rightness of things for the good of all.

Kabbalists teach that in order to overcome evil speech, we need to repent, confess our wrongdoing, and avoid believing everything that is said or heard.

Coming Out of Exile: Repenting by Overcoming All Evil Inclincations

The path of *gimel,* represented by the sign of the camel, is symbolic of moving through the desert, pursuing, and enduring. It involves developing understanding and using wise judgment, which increases our wealth. Poor judgment leads to poverty. The lesson is to become assertive through strength and awe of God as opposed to judgment, criticism, destruction, and the fear of God.

Following the path of *gimel* to release ourselves from exile in the mundane, materialistic world, we must overcome *all* evil inclinations. If we have incurred any injustice for anyone, consciously or unconsciously, or if we are carrying around any anger, resentment, guilt, fear, or need for revenge, we keep ourselves separate from God. We must resolve it. We begin repentance by spiritual stock taking.

· Meditation: Heavenly Tribunal and Spiritual Accounting ·

Kabbalists teach that the Heavenly Tribunal is a court we sit before at the time of death in order to hear judgment. As mentioned in *Yesod,* during this time there is a life review when we are judged on merits and demerits, then sentenced. Here in life, the best judge is ourselves. Let's take a look at what we have.

Do a basic relaxation. Visualize yourself going on a long trip. Eventually you come to a tunnel. Go through it very slowly. This tunnel takes you into the heavenly realms of existence. At the end of the tunnel you come upon a resting place, where you sit down. There is radiance around you, and you are engulfed in quiet serenity. Before you is a presence; three others are behind. It's the *Shekhinah* with three ministering angels. One angel has recorded your deeds, the other sets the reckonings, and one has been with you since you left the womb.

They ask you to come with them as they take you to the Heavenly Tribunal. Sitting before this tribunal you are given a life review in detail, and judgment is made. Here you have a glimpse of your own life reeled out in reverse. You are told that the best judge of your life is you. Think of the people in your life, the things you've done, the times you were angry, you gossiped, and you didn't speak up to right a wrong. Think about who you may have harmed in your life by evil thoughts, speech, or actions and the impact of your behavior on them. Think of who might have harmed you and what feelings you might be harboring—anger, resentment, wanting revenge, hopelessness, despair, doubts, fears. Think about the choices you made and why you made them. Think about your childhood with your parents, what they did, how they treated you, the way you responded, the beliefs you formulated, and the decisions you made about how to live life because of them. Make a commitment to forgive them all. Open your eyes. Write down your experiences, feelings, and insights.

Spiritual Accounting: Becoming Accountable for Our Actions

In practical terms, to overcome evil and to make amends we reflect on and work to understand the motives for our past misdeeds or inappropriate behavior, admit our mistakes, pray never to repeat them, and do good deeds. Some kabbalists actually request the same or a similar situation to manifest to assure that we have learned our lesson.

Below is a detailed list of people with whom injustices may exist, followed by a list of questions. Write the names of those with whom you may have some emotional charges or unfinished business. Prioritize the ones you want to work on. Continue thinking about it.

1. Spouse or significant other:

2. Members of my family:

3. Friends:

4. Neighbors:

5. Employer(s):

6. Employees:

7. Clergy:

8. Doctor:

9. Dentist:

10. Haircutter:

11. Waiters, waitresses:

12. Salespeople:

13. Cashiers:

14. Myself:

15. Anyone else:

1. Who in my life has hurt me?

2. Whom have I criticized, or whom do I still criticize in my life?

3. Whom am I intimidated by?

4. Whom have I gossiped about?

5. To whom have I been dishonest?

6. Whom do I still judge?

7. How do I judge or criticize myself?

8. Toward whom do I still harbor resentment?

9. In whom have I instilled guilt?

10. Who instills guilt in me?

11. With whom do I always have to have my own way?

12. With whom do I lose my temper?

13. With whom am I possessive?

14. Whom am I jealous of?

15. Whom do I not listen to?

16. Who do I believe has slighted me?

17. Whom do I need to forgive?

18. By whom would I like to be forgiven?

19. What mistakes do I still feel guilty about?

20. What painful memories have I not resolved?

21. What issues have I denied or avoided?

22. Whom do I keep judging and criticizing?

Kabbalists believe pleading with all our hearts to erase the transgressions leads to mercy. It makes us humble, and crushes the spirit of evil husks and the *sitra achra*—the other side or evil spirit. We will work more on forgiveness when we move into *Chesed*.

OPENING TO DIVINE INSPIRATION

On the path of *gimel,* the sign of the camel is also symbolic of the Angel of Death. According to Rabbi Yitzchak Ginsburgh in his book *The Hebrew Letters: Channels of Creative Consciousness,* it's "the process of weaning so a person learns to be independent," and it is "the obligation to emulate God by giving to others."

A camel moves through the desert very slowly, in extremely hot, dry climates, yet endures and perseveres. Camels have the resources to survive. This is symbolic of our own inner strength and endurance.

Coming out of exile involves developing the resources needed to survive through the desert. We no longer need to follow the emotional charges, childhood decisions, or old patterns and conditioning that have plagued us from the past. We are now guided by our own connection to our internal source of wisdom and truth, the Divine. With this connection come inspirational impulses, creativity, and acts of loving-kindness. On the path of *gimel,* moving closer to *Binah,* we come from a strong sense of vitality and inner strength as opposed to needing adrenaline to motivate us.

Coming from vitality as opposed to adrenaline is the difference between force and flow, fear and faith. Many people use fear as a motivator. They think if they fear not getting the next customer or client, it will motivate them to market more. Or if they fear getting hurt, it will keep them safe. People unconsciously wait until the last minute to do things, so fear crops up and motivates them. Fear gets the adrenaline flowing. We may get energized, but right after we accomplish what we want we often go into a downslide. We are energized by personal pressure rather than Divine inspiration or passion—the action that comes from inner strength and faith. But if we instead come from love and faith, not fear, we will accomplish things more easily and effortlessly. The goal is to keep God always in our mind and before our eyes: "I place God in front of me always" (Psalms 16:8). This is the internal resource that helps motivate us and protect us as long as we work to defend ourselves.

· Meditation: Divine Guidance ·

Kabbalists believe that we carry the wisdom of our forebears within us dating back to Adam and Eve. When we get into the vibration of these energies, we can derive more wisdom.

Do a basic relaxation. Imagine yourself on a mountain. It's so high, you're above the tree line. You can see all around you. As you look around, a circle forms around you with all your immediate family, children, mates, brothers, and sisters. Another circle forms around them with their relatives. And a larger circle forms around them with all your ancestors dating back to Adam and Eve. Within each of them is a part of you. And you are some part of them. Throughout the ages, the wisdom that you each have to share is glowing in every heart.

As you listen quietly, each one is giving you a message—together it comes out as a song, a melody. It's your own personal melody from God. Listen to it, remember it, hum it, dance to it. This is your own song of truth, of purpose. Keep it with you to guide you. Take it back with you. This is a song you can keep with you to remind you of your ancestral and Divine guidance. Give thanks for it. Write about your experiences.

PATH BETWEEN
GEVURAH AND *CHOKHMAH: ZAYIN* ז

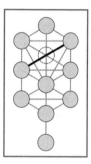

The path between *Gevurah* (strength) and *Chokhmah* (wisdom) is represented by the Hebrew letter *zayin,* ז. An elemental letter, *zayin* corresponds to the constellation Gemini and the Hebrew month of *Sivan* (May-June). It also correlates to the foundation of motion and the left foot. The sign of the *zayin* is a sword and stands for self-discipline and defending our boundaries. To do the internal work on this, meditate on the Hebrew letter *zayin,* ז.

SELF-DISCIPLINE: LIVING OUR PRINCIPLES

The letter *zayin,* shaped like a sword, acts as a weapon to defend ourselves from transgressions and evil. It's defending life rather than causing more death. It's defending beauty instead of destruction. It's defending our creativity. It's defending our boundaries. It's defending our peace. This could pertain to nations, personal relationships, or our own sense of self.

In practical terms, just as the universe follows cosmic laws and boundaries in a systematic plan, the path of *zayin* involves law and order. It includes rules, boundaries, and discipline. When we go against universal laws, the consequences are usually harsh. When justice is followed, there is strength.

On the path of *zayin,* coming from *Gevurah* to *Chokhmah,* self-discipline is extremely important. Self-discipline involves staying on path by setting boundaries for both ourselves and others.

Disciplined Daily Plan

Kabbalists believe we need an ordered daily plan. It is taught that discipline brings us closer to God. Being aware of every moment is a key component of living kabbalistically. This means understanding every experience or lesson by keeping our minds alert, constantly striving to reach our highest potential.

Kabbalah teaches that time wasted is a transgression. Time is to be used for learning and teaching, family life, parenting, livelihood, and celebration. Free time is used primarily for self-purification, spiritual study, and living the attributes that make us more loving and joyful. Watching TV or just letting our minds wander is okay if it's for the purpose of clearing the mind, but not if it's prolonged. Sleeping too much can also sap our energy and is considered a waste of time. It is part of our task to develop alertness and self-awareness.

In spending time valuably, it helps to know why we are doing what we are doing and what we're getting out of it. To see how you are spending your time, keep a detailed hourly calendar for a week. Notice where you may be wasting time on prolonged phone conversations, watching too much TV, just zoning out, or sleeping too much. See if you can create more balance and order in your life.

To consider what might not be important, look at each segment on the calendar and ask yourself:

1. What am I getting out of spending time this way?

2. What am I learning from spending time this way?

3. What am I teaching by spending time this way?

4. How is spending time this way serving me?

5. Do I really need to spend time this way?

If the answer to the last question is no, then you might be able to find a way of deleting the activity from your life.

· Exercise: Setting Boundaries in Relationships ·

Following the path of *zayin*, we need discipline. Part of a disciplined daily plan is to set boundaries with others. Very often we let people take advantage of us and our time. Being disciplined in setting boundaries sets up the guidelines for other people to help safeguard our time, our emotional energy, our physical stamina, and our space. It is letting them know how we want to be treated regarding time, speech, and actions. We want time spent with people to be valuable and the transactions to be nourishing, not draining.

---

1. Make a list of the boundaries that are unacceptable to you regarding relationships—people making demands, taking advantage of you, having demeaning behaviors, wasting your time, and so on.

2. Make a list of people in your life who overstep these boundaries.

3. Make a list of how to communicate these boundaries to others.

When you need to communicate boundaries, remember the discussion in previous chapters about talking from the "I" and explaining yourself. Doing this, you don't blame or attack—just express how you feel, why, and what you want because of it. It's important to maintain such composure. This takes a lot of discipline.

· Exercise: Discipline in Careers ·

Self-discipline in careers means continuing to develop our skills and talents in the areas in which we are interested. Kabbalists believe that we need to constantly practice and refine our craft by improving our skills, techniques, and talents, educating ourselves further, and doing new things in our field.

1. What have I done recently to refine my craft or vocation?

2. What new skills have I learned?

3. What courses have I taken to improve my skills?

4. What new techniques have I implemented?

5. What else can I do to expand and refine my craft?

NINE

Chesed: Loving-kindness, Mercy

Forgiveness and Unconditional Love

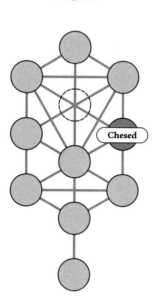

Divine Name: *El*—Almighty God

The Divine Hebrew name for this *sefirah* is *El,* Almighty God. The English translation is "mercy," "compassion," or "grace." It's the center of repentance and gratitude. This is where harsh judgment is passed by the Heavenly Court. It is taught, however, that one righteous man who reveals himself can help overcome the power of this judgment. With repentance and mercy there is grace.

Archangel: Zadkiel

The archangel representing *Chesed* is Zadkiel—sometimes spelled Tzadkiel, as in *tzadik,* the charitable one, the righteousness of God. Zadkiel is best known for preventing Abraham from sacrificing Isaac on the altar after God had asked Abraham to do so. Because of this Zadkiel is known for stopping us from acting on our untamed animal instincts. He is the archangel of cosmic laws and works toward fulfillment and abundance. This includes prosperity, expansion, generosity, mercy, clarity, and good memory.

Patriarch: Abraham

The patriarch representing *Chesed* is Abraham. Abraham is known as the father of all religions and a mystic with incredible talents for prophecy, leadership, and faith. Some kabbalists believe that the metaphysical information in the *Sefer Yetzirah* came from Abraham. It is speculated that he not only passed the information down to Isaac but also sent the teachings he received from God to Ishmael, his son by the concubine Hagar, who eventually settled in what is now called India.

Abraham's qualities of compassion, humility, righteousness, and hospitality were unsurpassed. Abraham and his wife, Sarah, always acted out of compassion for humankind. They invited family, friends, and even strangers into their tents and offered all of them food and rest. Abraham and Sarah had a wish to perpetuate love to future generations.

Personal Attributes: Loving-kindness, Mercy

The attributes of *Chesed* are loving-kindness and mercy. It's the world of forgiving, pouring out our love to others, and being creatively productive. To meditate on the essence, we imagine ourselves living the attributes of *Chesed:* loving-kindness and mercy. At the end state the affirmation: *I am merciful, pardoning, creative, kind, loving, compassionate.*

CHESED: LOVING-KINDNESS, MERCY

The Divine name *El*, Almighty God, resonates with the qualities of the infinite power of God's love, which include infinite unconditional love, unrestrained giving, generosity, and greatness. It is the level of consciousness that involves serving humanity through loving-kindness, creative freedom, blessings, and grace.

Opposite *Gevurah*, *Chesed* is the area of *yetzer hatov*, good or godly inclinations. It means loving and caring for one another and the world, as well as continuing to develop our creative potential. Sometimes, however, good inclinations can be taken to extremes. Love or creativity can go overboard, as when we love obsessively and even smotheringly, or work obsessively hard on a project. *Chesed* therefore needs the discipline of *Gevurah* to balance it. When balanced, *Chesed* is the level of consciousness of experiencing grace.

EXPERIENCING GRACE

What is grace? It's that feeling that emerges when we experience a sense of the miraculous. It's the openness to the love of God that fills us with the feeling of being divinely guided and blessed. It's experiencing Divine presence within us and around us. This can manifest in many different ways.

While writing this chapter I was struggling to define grace in a few short paragraphs. That evening my husband and I went to Barnes & Noble for coffee. Every table was taken. There was, however, one man sitting alone reading the newspaper, and my husband asked if we could join him. He nodded and continued reading. Then suddenly the man picked up his head, looked at me, and asked, "What is grace?" I was stunned. My husband looked at me in amazement because I'd been trying to verbalize grace to him in the car driving over. He asked the man why he'd asked that—was it something he was reading in the newspaper? "No," he said, and explained that he had met with a minister that afternoon and they'd pondered the concept but he still wasn't sure he understood what it really meant. It was something he had questioned for a long time.

I began a long explanation about feeling good about ourselves, being loving, and ended by saying, "It's a connection to something greater than ourselves. It's that feeling that emerges when we experience a sense of the miraculous." I kept groping for words. "It's the openness to the love of God that fills us with the feeling of being divinely guided and blessed. It's experiencing Divine presence within us and around us." The man nodded in agreement and asked, "But what does that have to do with daily living? How do you experience it?"

"It's something we receive," I said and explained that grace can manifest in many different ways. For example, in the delivery room when a baby is born there is usually a sensation of the miraculous, of awe. Celebrating a holiday with all your family around, children and grandchildren all playing together cohesively, you may look around and say, "This is as good as it gets." Working on a difficult project, you might suddenly break through to a new level of understanding and creativity. You might hug someone and immediately feel a soul-to-soul connection. Or in desperation one day you may break down crying hysterically and suddenly see an angel bringing a message of inspiration and hope. In each case you feel you've been blessed or touched by the hand of God. These blessings are all signs of experiencing grace. Grace is a feeling that awakens from within when there is unconditional love, service, and gratitude.

The man nodded and said, "This I can understand." He smiled, thanked me, and left the table. He didn't know that his question forced me to come up with a more specific answer. He was my angel. And another experience of receiving grace.

INFINITE, UNCONDITIONAL LOVE

Kabbalists distinguish two types of love. The first is love that is revealed from God—the love that comes to us and through us. It is infinite and unconditional Divine love. The second is the love that originates from the animal soul—physical or interpersonal love. In order to explain infinite, unconditional love, it's important to understand how it differs from personal love.

Interpersonal love is the love we experience when we are involved in a relationship with another person. It can be a romantic relationship between two adults, or a nurturing relationship between parents and children, among friends, or among siblings. Most of these are based on conditions. They are generally contingent on getting personal needs met. In a romantic relationship, for example, we are often attracted to people who are our opposites. If we're creative we might seek out someone more intellectual and logical. If we're passive we might be attracted to someone more aggressive. This person fills the gap in order to make us feel more complete. And if the person doesn't do that, we try to change him or her. On the other hand, if we choose someone similar to us and that person reflects what we don't like within ourselves, we also try to change the other person.

Kabbalists believe infinite or unconditional love has no preconceived notions, expectations, or conditions attached to it. It is not contingent on how we feel about other people or how they feel about us. Instead, it's the love that emanates from the Divine through us. When we resonate from this part of ourselves, we come *from* love—with no conditions. It's what we bring to the relationship, not what we can get from it, that makes a difference.

Unconditional love manifests when we are centered and balanced. It's when we are clear channels for the Divine and open to giving and receiving from the Divine. A way to maintain balance is through breath.

THE PATH BETWEEN
GEVURAH AND *CHESED*: ALEF א

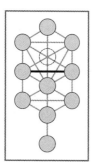

The path between *Gevurah* and *Chesed* is represented by the Hebrew letter *alef,* א. As the first letter of the words *Ein Sof,* it stands for the infinite. The sign of *alef* is that of an ox, strong and stubborn. *Alef* is often depicted in the form of a person with outstretched arms in motion, signifying action, renewed energy for creating a new project or a new way of being. To experience a state of oneness as well as renewed energy for creativity and living our Divine purpose, meditate on the letter *alef,* א.

ALEF AS BREATH

The shape of *alef,* א, is two *yuds,* like apostrophes with one upside down, and a diagonal *vav,* ו, separating the two *yuds,* י. It's similar to the Chinese image of yin-yang representing opposites, ☯. The top *yud* represents the water above and the joy of being close to God. The bottom *yud* represents the lower waters and the bitterness and sorrow of feeling separated or far away from God.

As one of the mother letters, *alef* corresponds to the element of air. Crossing the chest on the human body, *alef* relates to breathing.

Alef is the first letter of the Hebrew alphabet and has no sound. It's the emanation from nothingness, the breath before creation, the breath of God. Its numerical value is 1. It begins the Hebrew word *echad,* which means "one" and represents the Divine unity we experience when we enter the still silence—the nothingness. In nothingness there is everything. We are in touch with the infinite, which gives us the energy we need to create.

The *alef* as the horizontal path in the middle between *Gevurah* (strength) and *Chesed* (mercy) is also the median between *shin*—the horizontal path between *Binah* (understanding) and *Chokhmah* (wisdom)—and *mem,* which is the horizontal path between *Hod* (splendor, reverberation, thinking) and *Netzach* (victory, instincts, action). In the psychological world *shin* represents fire and can be an overabundance of shame. *Mem,* on the other hand, represents water, which to humankind represents a lack of sensation, or depression. *Alef,* representing air, is the temperate zone between fire and water and represents *revayah,* temperance or abundance. It is taught that certain ways of breathing can help balance the energies and therefore help us overcome cravings, bad habits, or inertia, opening us up to nothingness, which in turn opens us to oneness, love, and creativity.

Deep-breathing exercises are extremely important in Kabbalah. Breathing with the sound of *alef, ahhhhh,* can help overcome cravings and extremes. It helps balance the energy between the world above and the world below as well as loving-kindness (*Chesed*) and restraint (*Gevurah*).

· Meditation: Balancing the Energies Between *Gevurah* and *Chesed* and the Upper and Lower Worlds ·

To help balance energies, concentrate first on exhaling and let out a sigh with an *ahhhh,* the breath of *alef.* Make sure your throat is relaxed and your mouth is open wide. As you breathe out with the *ahhhh,* notice what happens in your throat, mouth, body, and mind, and in particular around your chest. Then breathe into your diaphragm with your stomach extending on the inhale—as if you're blowing into the farthest part of a balloon first and watching it bulge out—and continue the inhale, filling your lungs. Continue to move up to your shoulders, even rounding your shoulders somewhat to fill your lungs totally. Hold for a few seconds before exhaling. Then begin to exhale slowly, releasing the air from the top down, and again let out the sound *ahhhh.* Repeat this several times. Since this exercise is so energizing, if you get dizzy or light-headed, stop.

As we balance the energies between *Gevurah* and *Chesed,* we are more open to Divine energies and living in a state of oneness and grace. To accomplish this during the day, we must remember to stop from time to time and breathe deeply through the diaphragm.

THREE MOTHERS

In the Soul, male and female,
are the head, belly, and chest.
The head is created from fire,
the belly is created from water,
and the chest, from breath,
decides between them.

—*Sefer Yetzirah* 3:6

OPEN TO THE ONENESS THROUGH LOVE

Alef is the first letter of the word *ahavah,* love. It pertains to the love of God and, out of that love, the passion to live and work with loving-kindness. To love totally is to love the sustenance of all life—the Absolute—the Divine. When we open our heart to the Divine, there's room to be filled with Divine love.

· Exercise: The *Gematria* of Love ·

Ahavah has a numerical value of 13: *alef* = 1, *heh* = 5, *bet* = 2, and *heh* = 5, for a total of 13. The Hebrew word for "one" is *echad,* which also adds up to 13: *alef* = 1, *chet* = 8, and *dalet* = 4, totaling 13. Adding both together, we get 26, which is the numerical equivalent of the Tetragrammaton, YHVH: Y = 10, H = 5, V = 6, and H = 5. Kabbalists consider that God is love and God is one. Comparing this to YHVH, love and oneness equal the unity of the four worlds and the name of God. Furthermore, if we simply add up the digits of 13 which are 1 + 3 = 4, we find that each word is a numerical value equivalent to the four worlds and the name of God, symbolizing unity. Love here is God's love, which is unconditional. To experience God's love, we can meditate on the Hebrew word *ahavah;* while doing that, we think about the greatness of God, the awe-inspiring oneness and unity. When we open our hearts to this energy we experience pure love.

PATH BETWEEN
CHESED AND *BINAH: KUF* ק

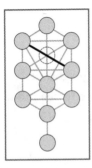

The path between *Chesed* (loving-kindness) and *Binah* (understanding) is represented by the Hebrew letter *kuf,* ק. It corresponds to the constellation Pisces and the Hebrew month of *Adar* (February–March). The organ is the spleen. The sign of *kuf* is the back of the head, or hindbrain. It's the primitive part of the brain that reacts instinctively in expressing mercy and loving-kindness. The numerical value of *kuf* is 100, which is considered a number that completes a cycle. To draw us closer to God, bring on holiness, mercy, loving-kindness, and love of God, we can meditate on the Hebrew letter *kuf,* ק.

MERCY/FORGIVENESS

As we move from *Chesed* to *Binah* on the path of *kuf,* we begin to let go in forgiveness. *Kuf* is the first letter of the Hebrew word *korban,* sacrifice. The sacrifice is letting go of the temptation toward negativity or meanness—which means sacrificing or giving up the old charges of resentments, anger, and remorse. It happens by forgiving.

The Talmud tells the story of a non-Jew who came to the ancient Rabbi Hillel and said, "I wish to convert to Judaism, but only if you teach me the entire Torah while I stand on one foot."

Hillel said, "What is hateful to you, do not do to your fellow man. . . . The rest is mere commentary."

As explained in the *Zohar,* the letter *kuf* represents imitation. The spiritual aspects of this path pertain to imitating the ways of God as opposed to imitating the ways of man and giving in to evil inclinations. If we've done something that is hateful to someone or someone has done something that is hateful to us, we must imitate God in mercy and compassion. We must learn to forgive.

Moses Cordovero of the thirteenth century identified thirteen attributes of mercy. He saw these attributes as a reflection of *Keter.* Here are Cordovero's attributes of mercy. While reading them, think about how many you follow:

CORDOVERO'S THIRTEEN ATTRIBUTES OF MERCY

1. Patiently bear insult and be good to those who insult you.

2. Patiently endure evils performed by your neighbor.

3. Pardon sin and wash its stain away.

4. Regard yourself and your neighbor as one. Always wish your neighbors well. Never say anything negative about them and never desire to see them suffer or be disgraced. Rejoice in your neighbors' good fortune and be grieved at their misfortunes as if they were your own.

5. Do not stay angry with others, even when they persist in sinning. "It is a religious duty," says Cordovero, "to encourage your neighbor lovingly, and perhaps this way of dealing with him will succeed."

6. Show mercy to those who offend or provoke you by recalling their good qualities.

7. Do not harbor resentment against anyone who offends you. If your neighbors repent of a misdeed, show them "a greater degree of kindness and love than formerly."

8. Always remember the good your neighbors have done and forget the evil they have done.

9. Do not hate or judge those who suffer. Welcome those who suffer and are punished, and save them from their enemies. Do not say of those who are suffering, "Their sufferings are the result of their sins," but have compassion upon them.

10. Be truthful and upright.

11. Go beyond the letter of the law when dealing with the good and saintly. We should choose as our friends those who are good, and we should be extremely compassionate and patient with them.

12. Do not behave cruelly toward the wicked or insult them, but have mercy upon them and try to help them improve.

13. Recall the good deeds others have done from the day of their birth. When others are unworthy, remember that there was a time—even if it was in infancy—when they did not sin.

If we get into the habit of thinking like this, Cordervero said, everyone will be found worthy of our prayers and mercy.

The path of *kuf,* mercy, connotes having compassion for others even though they may have hurt us or sinned. It is also important to have mercy for ourselves for our misdeeds. Kabbalists believe that when we've been harmed by others or ourselves, it's really as a way to show us what we need to learn for our souls to evolve; therefore it's actually a blessing. Dr. John Dimartini, a worldwide lecturer, author, and workshop leader on consciousness evolution, describes forgiving as for-giving thanks for showing us the lesson we need to learn. It's having gratitude toward the people in our lives and the way they treat us—the evil and the good.

We must remember that kabbalists believe that everything we have and everyone in our lives are a reflection of ourselves telling us something about ourselves. We come into life situations as a result of the lessons we need to learn to perfect our souls. This means everyone in our lives is a channel, showing us who we are and what we need to change about ourselves. If we are still carrying around anger, resentment, or remorse, these are things we have to resolve.

In practical terms, forgiving or having mercy on others is really for ourselves, for-giving up or letting go of the emotional charges that we might still be holding on to that block us from the Divine. Nevertheless, the process of forgiving actually brings on a release and a deeper connection to the good.

Many people think forgiving is giving in to or surrendering to the other person, as if acknowledging that the person is right. This is not so. Kabbalists believe that forgiving either another or ourselves is actually freeing ourselves of burdens. Rabbi Zalman Schachter-Shalomi, the contemporary kabbalistic leader of Jewish Renewal, often uses the metaphor that if we keep holding on to feelings of anger, resentment, or wanting revenge, we are actually punishing ourselves. By holding on to these feelings, it's as if we are keeping the other person in prison. However, in order for that person to stay in prison, he or she needs a warden. And who might that warden be? Us, of course, which means we are in prison along with the prisoner. To free ourselves, we need to let go in forgiveness and compassion. Almost all other spiritual practices teach forgiveness as well.

Kabbalists teach that we erase the past through forgiveness by opening our hearts to make room for the radiant light to enter and then doing *teshuvah*, repentance through actions. When we ask for mercy for or from others and ourselves, we open to the grace of God and allow the light to transcend between us.

· Meditation: Forgiving Others ·

Go back to the list of people you would like to forgive or whose forgiveness you seek for past misdeeds (see page 165). Choose one.

Do a basic relaxation. Imagine the other person through thought, images, feelings, or essence. Notice what you're experiencing in your body. Take the time to tell the other person the feelings you have been harboring over the years and why. Notice any insights or new feelings that may crop up. Just pay attention to the person, probing for more and more insights, and continue to verbalize your insights to the other person in your mind.

When you feel you've explored all areas sufficiently, take a step into the other person's shoes. Become the other person, who is now talking to you. As the other person, explain why you did what you did and where you were coming from. Explain the things in your life that provoked this behavior. Take all the time you need. As you explore this, you begin to understand more from the other person's perspective and frame of reference.

Now step back into your own shoes. On a scale of 1 through 10, with 10 being the highest, how ready are you to let go of these feelings and either forgive or ask to be forgiven for them? If your answer is 9 or higher, then tell the person you're ready to release the harbored feelings, and either forgive the person or ask for forgiveness. If you're at less than 9 in readiness, then tell the person you're willing or preparing to let go. Redo the exercise in a few days to see actually how ready you are to let go. Write about your experience.

In order to feel a total release, after forgiving the other person we also need to forgive ourselves for holding on to these feelings for so long. Here is a self-forgiveness exercise.

· Meditation: Forgiving Ourselves ·

Very often we may not even feel as angry at people who've hurt us as we are at ourselves for having allowed it to happen, for going against our intuition or our own words, for our own response, or for holding on to the anger or resentment that has kept us from experiencing the light or essence of Divine presence. We need to release these feelings. We follow the same process of asking for forgiveness described above, but now we are asking forgiveness of ourselves.

Do a basic relaxation. Now picture yourself in your mind through thought, images, feelings, or essence. Notice what feelings you have been harboring over the years and why you have been harboring them. Think back to all the times these feelings emerged. Point out specific events. Notice the feelings emerging inside you now. Be with them, experience them. Notice any new insights or new feelings that may crop up. Just pay attention to them as you keep probing for more and more insights.

Now step into your own shoes and behaviors of the past and tell yourself why you acted as you did. Notice the circumstances and where you were coming from. Notice how you feel. When you feel you've explored all areas sufficiently, step back into your own shoes as you are now. On a scale of 1 through 10, with 10 being the highest, how ready are you to let go of these feelings? If your answer is 9 or higher, then take a look at yourself and forgive yourself. Open your heart to yourself. Notice the changes in your body. Write about your experiences.

Making Amends with Others

Continuing on the path of *kuf*, to truly repent, kabbalists believe we need to go beyond just internalizing the forgiveness or even actually verbalizing it to another by saying, "I forgive you." We need to take action by expressing our mistakes and then doing deeds of kindness.

In practical terms, in making amends with others, practicing good communication skills helps. As discussed earlier, remember to talk from the "I," express feelings, and explain the reasons for your feelings and responses. Then ask to be forgiven or forgive, whichever the case may be: remember—no "you" messages or blame.

Then we can show our penance by opening our hearts in many ways. Offer to be with the other person, or to help out. If he or she is ill, we can make a visit to the hospital. Or we can simply help out in general—painting the house, adding a deck, watching the animals, babysitting the children: being there, having a relationship.

If we are angry at ourselves, we can by start by being good to ourselves. Buy something special—get a massage, do something healthy. Such acts of loving-kindness release us from the past and keep us open to the light.

LIVING WITH LOVING-KINDNESS AND COMPASSION

The path of *kuf* between *Chesed,* loving-kindness, and *Binah,* understanding, leads to serving God in the best way we know how. The best way to serve God and others is to be kind. Mother Teresa said, "Be the living expression of God's loving-kindness—kindness in your face, kindness in your eyes, kindness in your smile, kindness in your warm greeting."

To kabbalists being kind means kindling the light within ourselves and helping others kindle their lights. This is what is meaningful to people. This is what adds value to people. This is the meaning of being "of service" to others and God.

Kindness is doing something when we don't have to, out of the goodness of our hearts. This might mean giving to a beggar, listening to a friend, or playing with a child. Listening to people is extremely important. This is when people feel valued.

Holiness: Simple Ways of Serving Others and Showing Loving-kindness

Kuf is the first letter of the Hebrew words *kadosh,* holy, and *kavanah,* intention. On the path of *kuf,* set an intention to live with mercy and kindness, to live with holiness. Through mental focus and determination, we can aim our thoughts and actions to imitate God and create a life of godliness. Here are simple ways of showing loving-kindness:

- Look at people with soft eyes.
- Smile warmly.
- Make eye contact.

- Listen with your heart, gut, and soul.
- Be affectionate. Hug.
- Tell people that you care about them.
- Be supportive of people in what they are doing.
- Let other people be themselves.
- Send birthday cards.
- Stroke people by telling them what they mean to you and cheering their success.
- Give without any attachments: no expectations or preconceived notions.
- Extend goodness in the world.

· Exercise: Manifesting Our Creativity in the World ·

The path of *kuf* involves manifesting our creativity in the world. To do the work of *Chesed* and continue to unleash our purpose, we can ask ourselves the following questions:

1. What contribution can I make today?

2. What do I do personally that I value in life?

3. What strengths do I have that I can draw upon?

4. What do I like about myself?

5. What have I done successfully? What am I a success at, in any area of my life? Make a list.

6. When we give to others, we give to the world. How can I let my energy flow out to others and the world?

   a. Love: g. Friendship:
   b. Time: h. Touching:
   c. Money: i. Special talents and abilities:
   d. Volunteering: j. Companionship:
   e. Affection: k. Physical energy:
   f. Appreciation:

Keep praying to know your Divine purpose. Begin to trust what you are attracted to. If you are drawn to certain types of people or situations and find them nurturing, trust this inspiration. Go back to your list of interests and talents and see what you are drawn to now.

PATH BETWEEN
CHESED AND *CHOKHMAH:* BET ב

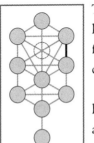

The path between *Chesed* and *Chokhmah* is represented by the Hebrew letter *bet,* ב. As a double letter, its opposite qualities are wisdom and folly. *Bet* corresponds to the moon, which is cold and damp. The direction of the *bet* is south. The day of week is Sunday.

The sign of the letter *bet* is a house, which signifies the universal home of the *Ein Sof.* The letter *bet* represents the potential for growth and creativity.

Bet is the first letter in the Hebrew word *beracha,* blessing. It's remaining open to receive Divine light and blessings as well as offering blessings. To be at home in the world, psychologist Edward Hoffman, author of *The Kabbalah Deck of Cards,* suggests counting our blessings and meditating on the Hebrew letter *bet,* ב.

HOSPITALITY

The shape of the letter *bet,* ב, with the door open to the left, symbolizes our openness to welcoming visitors into our homes. Abraham and Sarah were open to receiving anyone who passed by their tent. A home is very important to kabbalists. It is the place where we want the *Shekhinah* to reside. We need to bring light, love, and people into the home. It's important to think about how hospitable you are. Is your home a sanctuary for other people and for God?

· Meditation: House of Love ·

Do a basic relaxation. Picture yourself back in ancient times, living in the desert in a tent. Your tent houses the *Shekhinah,* the female side of God. The light and love inside the tent radiate not only throughout the tent but also outside it, and to all those who pass by. You want people to experience this light and love, and therefore you invite them into your tent. In the tent you offer them food, drink, and song. Their hearts open in your abode, and light and love abound. Notice how you feel in the sharing of God's love. Write about your experiences.

BLESSINGS

Making Peace with Suffering

Hasidic Jews teach that following the Torah means embracing the lessons, even if it's difficult. God offered the Torah to everyone. Only the Jews agreed to adhere to the lessons in the Torah, which include happiness and prosperity in the world to come, the spiritual world. They further believe that in suffering, there are lessons to learn; therefore suffering isn't always bad. The suffering is in learning the lessons of godliness and accepting the challenges that come to us. These may involve losing a job, the death of a loved one, or marital stress. This may involve learning to face these painful experiences in merciful, couragous, and loving ways. What is important is learning how to deal with suffering.

The path of *bet* represents blessings. Kabbalists believe that everything we encounter and have is a blessing, a lesson to learn. There is a story about Rabbi Akiva, who always saw the good in things. One day he was walking through a village asking for a place to stay. None was offered. Rabbi Akiva kept reiterating, "All that God does is for good." He left the town and on the outskirts found a field where he could lie down. He had with him a rooster, a donkey, and a lamp. Overnight the lamp was blown out by a wind, a weasel ate the rooster, and a lion killed the donkey. He said, "All that God does is for good." It later turned out that after he left the village, it was taken over by an army and all the people in the village were killed. Had the rooster not been eaten and the donkey killed, Rabbi Akiva would have arisen early to ride back into the town. He, too, would have been killed. Instead he escaped unnoticed and unharmed. Upon hearing this news, the rabbi said, "Didn't I tell you that all the Holy One, Blessed be He, does is for good?"

WHEN SUFFERING, ASK: "WHAT IS THE QUESTION FOR WHICH THIS IS THE ANSWER?"

As previously observed, suffering can manifest in many ways—the loss of a job, the death of a loved one, marital stress, or illness. These are certainly painful experiences, but the way we respond to them can indicate changes in our attitude about them and how we move on in spite of them. Kabbalists believe that our reality is the answer to questions we ask internally. When we have something in our lives that we don't like, and don't know why we have it, kabbalists probe and ask, *What is the question for which this situation, dilemma, feeling, or reality is the answer?* By questioning in this way we can often come up with a deep insight as to how we got to where we are. We can then determine where we want to go.

For example, a client, Fran, went back to school at age thirty. After receiving her bachelor's and master's degrees in marketing, she worked for a public relations agency. Fran was very creative and networked a lot. She enjoyed what she was doing. Working with the man who hired her was a blessing. When he left, however, a new director was brought in. She wasn't accustomed to working with someone who was so rigid and inflexible. Extremely unhappy, Fran was forced to look at what was going on. She knew that whatever she was finding fault with in another human being was usually a projection of herself or at least something she needed to look into and discover about herself. Fran finally asked herself, *What is the question for which this situation is the answer?* A few days later she had an insight.

She had been subconsciously asking herself, *Am I doing what's right for me? Am I living my purpose? Why don't I feel fulfilled?* Her original reason for going back to school had been to gain the knowledge and credentials to open her own public relations firm. She is basically a very independent, creative person who needs autonomy. This situation was showing her that she wasn't following her own intention or truth. She had already gained the experience she needed. With this realization, she made sure she first had enough reserves, both financially and emotionally, to get along on her own. Then she quit her job and gave herself three years to make a go of it. Today she has a thriving public relations firm. In thinking back to when she started, she realized that the turmoil she experienced at the agency was truly a gift, a blessing helping her see what she needed to do. It catapulted her into making a change.

If there is something in your life that is causing you to suffer, ask yourself: *What is the question for which this is the answer?* The answer will be a question.

Often when something has happened that has made us suffer, and we do some deep soul searching in retrospect, a feeling of gratitude emerges from deep within us for how we've grown or what we've learned. When we are grateful for the lesson, we experience the grace of God. With this grace comes a feeling of wanting to serve, to return such incredible love. Being of unconditional service to others means living with loving-kindness and compassion. Being of service to God means pursuing our creative endeavors and sharing with others.

Blessings—Gratitude

The path of *bet* is the path of blessings. God's blessings come whenever God reveals his essence in anything. When we bless God or, as stated by Aryeh Kaplan in the *Sefer Yetzirah*, "When we say that God is 'blessed' (as in 'blessed be He'), this means that His essence is brought down so as to interact with his creation and 'bless' it." When we bless God, we are acknowledging him and asking him to come down here to earth. When we send blessings to others, we are bringing God down to them. Saying a blessing merely states that *I am aware of you* or *of my connection to you.* Blessings can also be given for the simplest things, like the food on the table, going to a movie, watching something inspirational on TV, or helping a friend. Abraham Abulafia taught that we must say one hundred blessings a day—no more, no less. Just the act of blessing gives us joy.

It's easy to notice how blessed we are with joyful elements in our lives. It's more challenging to bless sorrow, lack, or what we may deem as curses. Notice how you feel when you walk past a handicapped person and instead of feeling pity, you offer blessings. The same applies if we feel depressed, anxious, or ill. Feeling sorry for ourselves or others gives off negative energy. We're putting out feelings of lack to the universe. Blessing others is helping others be in the light. Blessing each element in our lives—whether happy or sad, joyful or sorrowful—returns it and us to oneness. Start now by recognizing and blessing what you have in life.

· Exercise: One Hundred Blessings a Day ·

Practice saying a hundred blessings a day. Give blessings for everything in life, the joys and the sorrows, for all are communications from the Divine. Bless:

Our children	Entertainment	Joy
Relationships	Helping a friend	Sorrow
The food we eat	Study groups	Illness
Our health	Intellectual pursuits	Anger
Waking up	Forgiving	Depression
Going to sleep	The clothes we wear	Rejection
Friends	Tasks accomplished	Doubts
Family	Our misery	Fears
Jobs	Bad fortune	Household
Careers	Good fortune	Home
Interests	Sadness	Everything we have
Hobbies	Happiness	God

· TEN ·

Daat: Knowledge
Inner Knowing and Spiritual Union

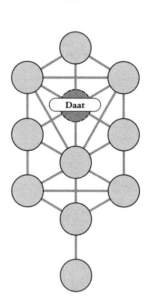

Daat—The Non-*Sefirah* of Inner Knowledge

"With wisdom [*Chokhmah*], God established the earth, and with understanding [*Binah*], He established the heavens, and with His knowledge [*Daat*], the depths were broken up" (Proverbs 24:3–4).

Daat is known as a quasi- or non-*sefirah*. Some Kabbalah schools believe *Daat* should be included in the *sefirot* instead of *Keter* since *Keter*—as the infinite *Ein Sof*—actually came before creation. They explain *Chokhmah* as the first *sefirah* of creation. Other schools use *Keter* instead of *Daat*. Some schools use *Daat* moving up the Tree of Life and *Keter* coming down. Some kabbalists describe *Daat* as a third brain, the connection between *Chokhmah* and *Binah*.

Keter, the unknowing and hidden, is considered the internal aspect of the Divine, while *Daat* is the external manifestation of *Keter*—the expression of God. It's the way we communicate knowledge to the world. As a quasi-*sefirah, Daat* is the abyss separating the three supernal intellectual *sefirot* from the seven lower emotive *sefirot.* It is the interval between the transcendent and immanent. It is the empty space where creation begins, often seen as darkness, or the abyss of ignorance. It is separation from God. *Daat* is also the coming together of *Chokhmah* (wisdom or Divine inspiration) and *Binah* (understanding and Divine thought). It represents the union of cosmic opposites, or the sexual union of man and woman.

Attribute: Inner Knowing

The attribute of *Daat* is knowledge. To us, it's inner knowing. Inner knowing comes from experiencing our thoughts and feelings—and therefore Divine knowing. To experience inner knowing, meditate on *Daat* and state the affirmation: *I know my own thoughts and follow Divine intuition.*

DAAT (KNOWLEDGE)

Daat consciousness is the inner knowing as well as the external manifestation of the Divine.

The central column on the Tree of Life is known as the Tree of Knowledge or pillar of consciousness. It represents the knowledge of evil and good, which converges in *Daat*. Kabbalists believe that when we know evil and good and unite the opposites on the Tree of Life, we live in a state of equilibrium, harmony, balance, and love. Seeing the dualities in everything, we release the one-sided perceptions that cause tensions and anxiety (our animalistic egos) and open to the oneness of Divine knowledge. Kabbalists refer to this state as equanimity. When we are in equanimity, we become channels for Divine will.

INTELLECTUAL LEVEL OF SOUL: *NESHAMAH*

As we move into the overall large triad of *Tiferet* (beauty), *Binah* (understanding), and *Chokhmah* (wisdom), with *Daat* (knowledge) in the middle, we open into the soul level of intellect and higher consciousness known as the *neshamah*. This is cosmic consciousness, the transpersonal world known as Divine spirit and often referred to as messianic consciousness. Christian kabbalists believe the Messiah has already come. They describe *Daat* as the Holy Spirit or Holy Ghost. Jewish kabbalists believe the Messiah will be here when we all reach this level of consciousness. Franz Kafka said that the Messiah will come the day after he is no longer needed. According to Maimonides, Messiah consciousness is knowing God; therefore, "In those times, there will be no hunger or war, no jealousy or rivalry. For the good will be plentiful, and all delicacies available as dust."

In practical terms, messianic consciousness is a level at which we become channels for Divine inspiration. This is the world of mystical union with the Divine known as *Ruach Hakodesh* (Holy Spirit).

· Meditation: *Neshamah* ·

We can connect to the *neshamah* by meditating on the name and the essence. Do a basic relaxation. First concentrate on the lower level of the soul, *nefesh.* Think about the body and the soul within the body. Meditate on the word *nefesh.* Sit with the name for as long as you need and let yourself experience the essence. Notice what happens in your body and if any insights come up.

Concentrate on the *ruach,* the emotional level of the soul. Sit with the name for as long as you need and let yourself feel the essence. Notice what happens in your body and if any insights come up. Then concentrate on *neshamah.* Sit with the name for as long as you need and let yourself experience the essence. Notice what happens in your body and if any insights come up. Write about your experiences.

PATH BETWEEN *TIFERET* AND *KETER* PASSING THROUGH *DAAT: DALET* ד

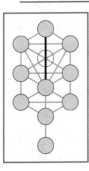

The path of *dalet* connects *Tiferet* and *Keter* while passing through the quasi-*sefirah* of *Daat. Dalet*'s day of the week is Tuesday, and it correlates to the sun.

Dalet is the first letter of the Hebrew word *deveikut*—devotion or cleaving to God. It means having faith in the Divine. It represents our humility and ability to ask for and be open to God's presence and gifts. When we are humble and open to the gifts of the universe, we know intuitively what we are here to do.

Dalet is the door that opens to the senses, knowledge of our bodies, knowledge of others, and knowledge of God's plan for us. It is the door to the radiant light of the *Ein Sof Or.* The numerical value of *dalet* is 434 (*dalet* = 4, *lamed* = 30, *tav* = 400), the same as *likdosh,* to sanctify (*lamed* = 30, *kuf* = 100, *dalet* = 4, *shin* = 300). To cleave to the Divine in humility and open to the senses and the spark that motivates us into action, meditate on the letter *dalet,* ד.

TAKING A LEAP OF FAITH: SURRENDERING AND CLEAVING TO THE DIVINE

Dalet opens the word *deveikut,* which means cleaving to the Divine—bonding with God and having faith. What does it really mean to have faith? And what is it that we are to have faith in?

Kabbalists say God is unknowable, indescribable, and hidden. If that is so, then what is God? Daniel C. Matt in *The Essential Zohar* writes: "God is a process of becoming. God is godding." God is known as the "I am that I am," or "I am that I am becoming." God is also the source of all that is. If we are in the image of God, then we are the source of all that is in our own lives, and what we have faith in is what we are becoming. And since there is also a greater source of all that is, the source that created all of existence, we also have faith that there will be a continuation of God's energy and light and the sustenance of all creation. Henceforth, having faith is having faith in ourselves and in our ability to connect with the source of all being, remaining open to Divine radiance.

Cleaving to God means surrendering ourselves and attaching to the source of all energy and light, the source of all being. This involves taking a "leap of faith" to trust in God, rather than just believing in God. When I teach Kabbalah workshops, I usually ask how many people believe in God. Approximately 95 percent will raise their hands. When I ask how many have surrendered and cleave to God, about 3 percent raise their hands.

This is an important distinction to work through. Do we just believe in God? Or do we live our lives by surrendering and cleaving to the Divine? And what is it that we are surrendering and cleaving to anyway?

Some people think surrendering and cleaving to the Divine is letting go of everything and aimlessly meandering through life waiting for God to make things happen. That is not the kabbalistic way. Surrendering ourselves means letting go of our animalistic tendencies—misinterpreting thoughts, emotionally reactive impulses, and conditioned patterns—by elevating the shadow side of our egos to goodness. Cleaving to the Divine is attaching to the essence of the Divine energies: the Divine attributes. We can therefore bond with the source of being by attaching or cleaving to the attributes of God, which include the attributes we've been working on while ascending the Tree of Life: oneness/will (*Keter*), wisdom (*Chokhmah*), understanding (*Binah*), loving-kindness/compassion (*Chesed*), justice (*Gevurah*), beauty (*Tiferet*), victory (*Netzach*), splendor (*Hod*), stability/foundation (*Yesod*), and kingship (*Malkhut*). To cleave or attach to the Divine, we need to live in a willful state of animalistic ego surrender and focus on the Divine. Kabbalists refer to this state as equanimity.

Equanimity

Equanimity is being in a state of total objectivity as opposed to reactivity of the animalistic ego. We are neutral in all our responses, and we act accordingly. The *Zohar* states, "Who attains the mystery of cleaving to God will attain the mystery of equanimity, and if one attains the mystery of equanimity, one will attain the mystery of aloneness. Having attained the mystery of aloneness, this person will attain the Holy Spirit. And from there, prophecy, and he will prophesy the future." To foresee the future means having a vision and following it.

When we are in a state of equanimity and cleave to the Divine, we are open to Divine inspiration. We are in the "flow" of life. To reach this state means going beyond ego control, attachments, and having to have our own way, and instead being able to accept what comes. In Kabbalah the concept of equanimity is similar to the Eastern concept of nonattachment. When faced with any obstacles or adversity, we maintain self-control and remain poised, calm, and objective without getting attached to a particular outcome. We're flexible and resilient, like a tree that moves with the wind. If this tree were rigid, it would snap, but because it's resilient and soft it bends and remains strong. Accepting what is and doing the best we can keeps us in the flow.

In Kabbalah it is taught that equanimity is one of the highest levels we can reach. It is beyond emotional reactions. There is an ancient account of a sage who came to one of the meditators and asked to be accepted into the society of meditators. The meditator replied, "My son, blessed are you to God. Your intentions are good. But tell me, have you attained equanimity or not?"

The sage said, "Master, explain your words."

The meditator said, "If one man is praising you and another is insulting you, are the two equal in your eyes or not?"

He replied, "No, my master. I have pleasure from those who praise me, and pain from those who degrade me. But I do not take revenge or bear a grudge."

The other said, "Go in peace, my son. You have not attained equanimity. You have not reached a level where your soul does not feel the praise of one who honors you, nor the degradation of one who insults you. You are not prepared for your thoughts to bound on high that you should come and meditate. Go and increase the humbleness of your heart, and learn to treat everything equally until you have attained equanimity."

Many people think of equanimity as a passive state because of its neutrality and objectivity. Actually, however, it is a very active state. By cleaving to the Divine and remaining neutral and objective, we resonate and harmonize with the pulse of the universe and become clear channels for the Divine. Devout impulses give us the knowledge, passion, and motivation to take action and do our Divine work. When we respond from the higher energies of the universe, extraordinary things take place: healing, prophecy, creativity, purpose, and ecstasy. This is equanimity in action.

HOW DO WE KNOW WE ARE NOT IN EQUANIMITY?

When we are not in equanimity, the universe provides opportunities for us to come back into balance. For instance, we might be elated at work about a huge sale and an opportunity to earn a lot more money. We are excited about our accomplishment and rather "full of ourselves." We come home from work and the kids are screaming and everything is chaotic at home. Our spouse immediately scolds us for something we forgot to pick up on the way home. If we are down and feeling depressed, on the other hand, we might read something that motivates us, or someone might call to lift our spirits. Following the laws of expansion, contraction, and equilibrium on the Tree of Life, when there is too much elation or deflation and we don't cleave to the Divine in either gratitude or faith, something occurs externally to balance it and show us we're not in harmony. If we maintain balance and constantly cleave to the source of energy of the Divine, however, we won't have the extreme highs or lows of the ego state and become a victim of circumstances, but instead will maintain a state of truth, love, and joy and be co-partners in creating our lives.

The traits of equanimity include composure, calmness, levelheadedness, self-control, poise, and passion. There are specific signals to let us know we are not in equanimity.

FEELING DISCOMFORT IN OUR BODIES

- Stomach discomfort
- Heart pounding
- Anxiety
- Losing temper

FEELING EITHER SUPERIOR OR INFERIOR TO OTHERS

- Judging
- Criticizing
- Holding grudges
- Wanting revenge
- Blaming others
- Building cases against people
- Feeling insecure
- Withdrawing from confrontations

MAKING DEMANDS OF OTHERS

- Telling people what to do
- Getting the last word in

BEING UNFORGIVING

- Holding on to anger
- Resentment
- Animosity

BEING UNPRODUCTIVE OR UNCREATIVE

- Feeling lethargic
- Having no direction
- Finding no meaning in life
- Feeling depressed

BEING TOO HIGH

- Feeling manic
- Feeling overly excited
- Blood vessels seemingly ready to burst

MAINTAINING EQUANIMITY: REFLECTION THROUGHOUT THE DAY

A way to maintain equanimity is through constant reflection. Kabbalists believe reflection, meditation, and prayer throughout the day keep us in constant touch with Divine presence. They allow us to see ourselves and make the changes we'd like instantaneously; and therefore remain in a state of active equanimity.

Starting now, we can practice this by reviewing ourselves in segments of time. Kabbalists suggest meditating and praying upon awakening, between breakfast and lunch, between lunch and dinner, and before bed. During these times we can observe ourselves to see what might be stopping us from feeling creative, connected, loving, and divinely inspired at all times. Then we can pray to release the obstacles.

The benefit of meditating in segments throughout the day is that we can stop and look at where we may be thinking irrationally, repressing a feeling, or harboring resentment or anger; we can see where we are not in a state of peace or equanimity. When we stop, reflect, and tune in to ourselves, an insight may come up to solve the problem, and we might state a spontaneous prayer for whatever we might need: healing, eradicating emotional charges, understanding inappropriate behavior, or performing a deed. This sets the seed for deescalating the impulsive emotional charges and responding more appropriately next time. It also prepares us for future behavior by giving us new images and resources (acquired intellect) on which to depend. For example, your boss denies your request for a day off because he or she has a deadline on an important project and needs your help. Although you had no real plans for that day, you get very angry, feel helpless and taken advantage of, and want to scream. You go into your office completely discouraged and angry. You can't work. You have no desire to complete the project and maybe even think of quitting.

If you meditate and go into the feelings, you can "let go and let God." Scream internally to God to help you let go of the anger and resentment and to under-stand the implications. While doing this, you may experience an insight on how to handle the situation, or simply a feeling of letting go and knowing that for whatever reason, this is where you need to be. Then picture yourself relating to your boss objectively.

If we do this throughout the day, it keeps us in a state of equanimity. If we cannot do it throughout the day, then it's a good practice to do it nightly. That way we resolve the issues and sleep more soundly.

Devotion to God: Living in the Present— Experiencing the Oneness

Continuing on the path of *dalet,* passing through *Daat,* to maintain our devotion to the Divine and remain in equanimity, we need to live in the present. When we are in the present, we are here now. We are balanced. We are aware. We are alive and enlivened. We experience what is happening to the fullest extent, giving meaning and value to what we do.

Words and Phrases That Keep Us Out of the Present Moment

In practical terms, the way we think and speak actually indicates whether we are in the present. Here are some words or phrases that indicate we're not in the present moment:

- *If only . . .*
- *What if . . .*
- *Yes but . . .*
- *I should . . .*
- *I would . . .*
- *I could . . .*
- *I ought . . .*
- *I'm trying . . .*
- *I hope . . .*
- *I must* or *I have to . . .*
- *I have so many problems . . .*
- *I can't . . .*

When we say *If only,* we take ourselves out of the present and tend to regress into past regrets and thinking about something we have no control over now. "If only I hadn't said that, maybe she wouldn't have left."

Saying *What if* takes us out of the present and puts us into the future of worrying about something we have no control over now. "What if I don't go out with him tonight—maybe he'll never call again."

Saying *Yes but* gives us excuses why we can't do something. "I would like to walk on the beach every morning but I don't have time because I have too many other things to do." The *too many other things* take precedence over the desire. If we change the *but* to *and,* however, it can open our minds to options for achieving what we want. It puts the dilemma on the same level as the desire. "I would like to walk on the beach every morning and I don't have the time. Gee, maybe I can make the time by getting up earlier."

If we say *I should, I would, I could, I ought,* we're creating mental clutter. These phrases are wishy-washy messages, not real intentions. They often come from our conditioned past—the things we were told to do by our parents or the decisions we made as children but really don't want to do now.

Saying *I can't* blocks us from creating anything. We can do most things within our physical and mental capabilities as long we put our minds to it.

I'm trying and *I hope* are ambivalent messages. *Trying* or *hoping* to pick a pen up leads to rolling the pen on the table; *I am picking up the pen* leads to picking it up. Change *I'm trying* or *I'm hoping* to *I'm doing.*

Saying *I must* or *I have to* creates force rather than flow. If you close your eyes and say to yourself, *I must buy a new car today,* and pay attention to your body, how do you feel? Now say to yourself, *I am buying a new car today,* and think about how your body feels. There's generally more pressure or tension when we say *I must* or *I have to.*

When we begin to speak in the present, we begin to live more in the present moment. And when we live in the present, we are freed from worry, regret, tension, and anxiety and therefore have more access to Divine light and love in everyday living. Feeling connected to the Divine, we feel empowered with goodness and knowingness. We know who we are. And when we really know ourselves, we also understand others at a much deeper level.

KNOWING OTHERS AS OURSELVES

If I can accept the negative part of me

I can accept the negative part of you

Never to judge or cut down

Because we are all one.

—Penny Cohen

The path of *dalet* is also the path that opens us to the knowledge of others. Our love for God must manifest in our love of others. Kabbalistically this means knowing others as intimately as ourselves and treating them as we would like to be treated: "Love thy neighbor as thyself."

To kabbalists, God is the beloved. Rabbi Akiva stated, "The 'Song of Songs' not only depicts the love between a shepherd and his beloved, but is also a song of love between us and God."

In practical terms, relationships are the metaphoric manifestations of our closeness to the Divine and knowing God in the real world. In romantic relationships we experience being "in love" or "in union with" when we experience each other's energy; that overall soul surrounds us. We are on the same frequency. When we are that open to another, we often experience extrasensory perception and mental telepathy, even when we are not together. Many times couples have this at the beginning of a relationship; then the ESP dwindles, either because we were hurt by the other person or because we become judgmental, critical, and disrespectful. We close off from light, love, and our mate.

In *Netzach* we worked on identifying and knowing our own feelings and how to master them. Now we deal with knowing others and dealing with others as ourselves.

Genesis 4:1 says, "Adam knew Eve." Knowing others as ourselves means knowing them deeply and intimately. It's more than just physical knowing, but mental and spiritual knowing as well. It involves listening to and being with someone with our entire being—heart, soul, and gut—and hearing and *feeling* at a deep level what is being said or felt. It's feeling the other person's feelings and understanding where he or she is coming from, without taking them on as our own.

If we cleave to the Divine—protect ourselves in light and love by drawing God around us and within us—we come from unconditional love. When we allow ourselves to feel the other person's feelings—as we did our own in *Netzach*—and reflect them back, we will not personalize them and take them on as our own, become protective or defensive, or go on the attack. We will feel them but not absorb them. And furthermore, if we should absorb them, we can still release them.

For instance, I was coaching a woman who was feeling great at having secured a new client at work. That evening her husband came home from work very down. He told her a close friend at work was getting a divorce. This news hit my client's husband hard. She tried soothing him, commenting on how common divorce was and how lucky they were to have a solid marriage. But that evening she had trouble sleeping and felt anxious although she didn't know why. Suddenly it dawned on her: she had internalized the deep sadness her husband was feeling. Her own parents were divorced, so she knew this sadness, but she'd avoided feeling it when her husband was down. She hadn't helped him identify the feeling or allowed him to be sad. He felt unheard, and she absorbed the sadness into her own body.

The following morning she worked on releasing her feelings of sadness, as we did in *Netzach*. Ironically, about half an hour later she received a call from her husband saying he was feeling a lot better despite everything that was going on. He'd experienced the release himself.

Kabbalistic healers are known to intentionally take on other people's feelings or even illnesses and release them through their own bodies. If we experience and feel what the other person is feeling, being with it and reflecting the feelings back, we remain in equanimity. We won't take the feelings on as our own, and the other person will really feel heard and understood. If we feel the feeling with the other person, we are in sync, and there is an experience of oneness between us. This is what allows for real emotional intimacy and communion. This is true knowing. When we unite with people like this, we bring more light into the world. We actually unite with God.

In *Daat* we begin to be powered by Divine spirit as opposed to our animalistic ego. We constantly keep our hearts open to God and the world around us and experience what is going on. This relates not only to other people, but to our communities, other nations, and the world as well. We can feel the distress in our communities, other nations, the world, and elevate it to Divine light and love through the power of prayer. The more people we have doing this, the quicker we will have peace in the world.

· Meditation: The *Shema* ·

Everything is one. When we see ourselves as one with everything else, we experience the oneness of God. It's for this reason that Orthodox Jews say a prayer known as the *Shema* three times a day. *"Shema Yisrael, Adonai Eloheinu, Adonai Echad."* "Hear, O Israel, the Lord our God, the Lord is One."

KNOWING GOD'S PLAN FOR US: FINDING OUR UNIQUENESS

On the path of *dalet,* when we cleave to the Divine there is a natural tendency to crave God's plan for us; we are motivated into service. It's in this state that we begin to experience *Ruach Hakodesh* (Holy Spirit)—Divine inspiration. Along with praying to be shown our Divine purpose, seeking to know God's plan for us is helped in practical terms when we can identify our uniqueness.

Kabbalists believe that we must do and be our best in all our actions. This is how we begin to live our potential. When we practice our trade, skill, or vocation for a very long time, and reflect on what we are doing and how the rules apply, we are aware of the intricacies of the craft or role we play. When we know it so well, we can expound upon it and do something new with it or around it so that it makes an impact on others or the world. This is expressing our uniqueness. It's the potential for doing something special. This is when we become masters rather than just professionals. This is when we become leaders.

For instance, a client who is a psychotherapist had for many years been successfully helping parents become more effective, as well as helping families develop more fulfilling relationships. At that point, she was still just a professional. After reflecting back on what made her so successful, however, she realized that she had a keen grasp of metaphor; she could take any scenario and make up a story that people could relate to that would help them break through their obstacles. Each story addressed a particular issue.

After writing down some scenarios, she realized there was a pattern to how she put the symbols together. She did not learn this from someone else. It evolved while she worked with clients. What she did was unique. When other psychotherapists started asking how she did it, she decided to write a book on it. Once she made the decision, ideas for other books came to her easily and effortlessly. She felt she was truly being guided. She became a master in her field rather than just another professional.

Kabbalists believe that once we make a decision, the Divine goes to work for us.

· Exercise: Questions to Ponder on Developing Our Uniqueness ·

Hopefully we've taken steps to live our personal purpose. To determine what is unique about what we do, and how we are doing it, ask the following questions:

1. What do I know about my work that no one else knows?

2. What do I know about my work that no one else has experienced?

3. How is my work different from that of others in the same field?

4. What makes me successful at this?

5. What am I doing right?

6. What patterns have I followed that make my work unique?

7. What systems do I use that are unique?

8. What message is coming from my heart about my work?

9. What am I really good at in the work I'm doing?

10. How do I actually perform in comparison to others that makes my work unique?

11. In what areas have I integrated my own thinking or techniques?

12. What is unique about what I do?

An awareness of this individuality and the conscious decision to continue developing it are what set the master apart from the professional. That's living our uniqueness.

· ELEVEN ·

Binah: Understanding
Discernment, Vision, and Repentance

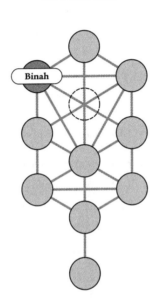

Divine Name: YHVH—God the Creator

Binah, the *sefirah* above *Gevurah,* heads up the left column of severity. The Divine name is YHVH, vocalized as *Elohim. Binah,* understanding, is where God created all things in the form of holy angels called *Elohim.* These angels are the foundation of differentiating between heaven and earth, and distinguishing one thing from another. *Binah* is also responsible for directing the flow of energy from the two upper *sefirot* passing through *Daat* to the six lower extremities. As the third *sefirah* from the top and the seventh *sefirah* from the bottom, it ties together all the *sefirot,* the upper and lower worlds.

Coming down the Tree of Life, while *Chokhmah* is everything and the source of giving, *Binah* distinguishes one thing from another and is therefore the source of restriction,

207

restraining the flow of spiritual energy into thought and then down to the lower *sefirot*. It's considered the *Shekhinah* of the upper world—the heart of the upper, spiritual world that gave birth to the lower world.

Archangel: Zaphkiel

The archangel representing *Binah* is Zaphkiel, also spelled Zafkiel or Tzaphkiel. Signifying God's knowledge, he is the eye of God that watches and sees all. He is a symbol of understanding the mystery of the unity of all things. Zaphkiel governs the art of meditation. He is also called the Beholder of God, and as such he helps us understand the patterns of our life and the part we played in each incident as well as the overall scheme.

Matriarch: Eve

The matriarch representing *Binah* is the great mother figure Eve. Eve represents the first separation (from Adam) as a result of eating from the fruit of the Tree of Knowledge. After she convinced Adam to eat from the tree, the two became aware of being naked before God and separated from pure spirit. For the first time humankind knew the difference between good deeds and evil ones. Exiled from the Garden of Eden, they were clothed in animal skins and had to work for their survival. To return to the Garden, they needed to work on developing higher consciousness. Eve is the mother of all creation and understanding.

Personal Attributes:
Rational Intellect, Understanding Patterns

In *Binah* we are the creator of our own life, and see things rationally and logically through the eyes of God. We understand the dynamics of our relationships as well as our own relationship to God. We become the master of what we do, develop our own uniqueness, and determine how we can benefit others. We live in a constant state of equanimity and productivity. To experience these attributes internally, meditate on *Binah* or any of the above representations. Or else meditate on the essence and at the end of your meditation state this affirmation: *I am living my uniqueness and sharing with others in God's Divine plan.*

BINAH: UNDERSTANDING

Binah consciousness is understanding from God's perspective. At this level of holiness, *Binah* consciousness involves perceiving the "principle of principles and the foundation of foundations," as stated in *Sha'are Orah* (Gates of Light) by Joseph Gikatilla.

It is understanding at its ultimate. It's understanding creation. It's understanding the structure, patterns, and overall dynamics of the workings of the universe. It's understanding the origin of the Ten Commandments and the laws that rule the universe, governments, nations, businesses, people. It's understanding the energies in the cosmos and how they affect our lives. It's understanding our relationship to these energies and to that of the Absolute. It's understanding the underlying dynamics of relationships. It's understanding and living the fifty Gates of Understanding, as well as understanding the thirty-two paths to wisdom. It's the understanding of the mystics who discovered the mysteries of the Kabbalah. It's understanding from God's perspective.

Binah is also future-oriented. It is often called the world to come. It is here that we are welcomed out of the darkness and into the light. It is here that the upper *Shekhinah* resides. This is the area of true freedom and joy. As stated in *Sha'are Orah,* "For anyone who merits cleaving to her [upper *Shekhinah*] will never know worry and will never be found wanting, because it is she who cleaves to the higher Spheres in the innermost houses." This is the highest level of *teshuvah,* return or repentance.

Kabbalists consider *Binah* consciousness to be the ultimate redemptive state. It is the state in which we are totally devoted to God, living in the present, working toward channeling God's work. We are in a constant state of preventing evil by doing good. We are giving back the gifts we received.

Binah consciousness involves the left-brain, or logical, intellect. It is rational thinking and a sense of understanding at a very deep level. With a singular focus, we weed out one thing from another.

PATH BETWEEN
TIFERET AND *BINAH: AYIN* ע

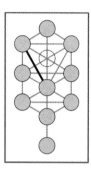

The path between *Tiferet* and *Binah* is represented by the Hebrew letter *ayin,* ע. *Ayin* corresponds to the constellation of Capricorn and the Hebrew month of *Tevet* (December–January). *Ayin* is king over anger. Kabbalists believe anger is a sin or evil inclination that must be tempered through discernment. *Ayin*'s sign is an eye, symbolic of seeing things from all sides.

The numerical value of *ayin* is 70. This is an important number in Kabbalah: seventy languages, seventy nations, seventy names of God. The path of *ayin* is the path of discernment and vision. To develop these qualities, meditate on the letter *ayin,* ע.

ANGER

The *Sefer Yetzirah* states that *ayin* is king over anger. One of the goals on the path of *ayin* is to obliterate anger. Kabbalists teach that anger is a despicable trait. The *Zohar* compares it to worshiping idols. Moses was told he could not enter the Promised Land because he struck a rock in anger when there was no water. He lost faith. When angered, we are considered to have lost faith, to have lost our connection to God.

Kabbalists believe that if we can maintain a state of humility when being insulted, we elevate our anger to higher consciousness. When we feel angry, it's important to pray to God to release the anger. Here it helps to acknowledge the embarrassment or shame underlying the anger. This process was covered in *Netzach* and dealing with feelings.

In *Binah* consciousness a primary source of anger is toward ourselves and the spiritual shame of not living our truth, not following our purpose, not living up to our potential, not following God's will for us. We need to start serving God and humankind. It helps to develop a vision.

Having a Vision

The sign of *ayin* is an eye. *Ayin* is the first letter of the Hebrew word *einayim*, eyes. *Ayin* involves seeing things and understanding them in depth, which comes with being perceptive, insightful, having foresight and a vision of the future. Vision is extremely important in Kabbalah. In Proverbs 29:18 it is said, "Where there is no vision, the people perish."

Having a vision gives us direction and focus. Prophets throughout time have always had visions. They had a sense of purpose within themselves and in the larger perspective of Divine order while dealing with the mundane. Some people are born with a sense of purpose. They seem to know at an early age what they came to earth for. Others have to work at unleashing it. And some of us wait to receive our calling. It is stated in *Sha'are Orah,* "Except for Moses all prophets needed to prepare themselves and to direct their attentions toward prophecy before prophecy will descend upon them."

Kabbalists believe that we are all sought out to receive Divine revelation or prophecy, but it's only the select few who earn it, be they common people or royalty. Those who are chosen to lead understand the rules and laws, make a deep commitment to following them, and achieve mastery. A person who performs at this level can do miraculous things that lead to what is called *tikkun olam,* world repair.

Divine prophecy often doesn't materialize until something happens—the right situation or a new idea. This is where *Chokhmah* consciousness emerges. We can prepare for it by sowing the seeds, and then waiting for the "aha." Sometimes the "aha" is like the Big Bang. Other times it's subtle and evolves gradually.

Part of our preparation for Divine revelation is choosing the path and waiting for the opportunity. There is a Talmudic expression that God leads a person along a path he or she has chosen. Kabbalists believe when we choose our path, the Divine works with us. Choosing our path through vision offers direction and focus. If we have nothing to look forward to, there is nothing to get up for or work toward. We begin to stagnate, get bored, and lose interest in what we are doing.

Drawing closer to *Binah* on the path of *ayin* represents the future. The future is known by understanding cause and effect, which means knowing the past. It's similar to the way a doctor might see the pattern of a particular bacterium caus-ing a particular illness repeated over and over again, and thus comes to diagnose and cure it. By seeing what the patterns and themes in our lives have been show-ing us, we can understand the path we have been on, determine the messages we have been given, and ascertain what we believe is needed in this world that we can offer. We can develop a vision.

In practical terms, a vision is our image of what is possible—how we can make a difference in others' lives, our field of work, community, nation, the world. It comes with reflecting on our experiences, knowing our skills, values, needs, and passions, and refining what we do to the point of uniqueness, which we have been working on while ascending the Tree of Life. Now we can create a vision for the future.

For example, I have a client who is a teacher. She always wanted to be a teacher and couldn't see herself doing anything else. After teaching for five years, how-ever, she described herself at work as feeling "flat." She wondered if this was all she had to look forward to. She needed something beyond her comfortable daily routine to focus on. She needed a vision for the future.

She began integrating her passions with her experiences. As explored earlier, some ways to determine our passions are to notice what we do on vacation as well as what books we take with us. In this client's case, most of her vacations were sports-oriented or nature-related, or involved visiting Third World coun-tries. The books she brought along to read were on personal and spiritual growth. She also enjoyed working with at-risk youth.

Thinking about combining her teaching with outdoor activities gave her a sense of excitement and focus. Wanting to work with at-risk youth gave her a sense of pur-pose. The more she focused, the more ideas and opportunities started to flow. She had noticed that many urban, underprivileged children rarely got out of the city. Many had little opportunity for lessons in personal growth. She developed a vision of taking these children out of their environments and offering personal growth workshops in the mountains. Her vision helped prioritize her goals. She saw chil-dren going to schools in geographic areas where they could be in touch with nature and challenged physically, academically, and personally.

Her short-term goal was to start networking and looking for programs that would offer outdoor events and physical challenges for youth, similar to Outward Bound programs. She also wanted to offer workshops on personal development. A week after determining her new vision, she actually received a call from her brother's friend offering her a summer position with an Outward Bound–type program. This was the beginning of living her vision and eventually starting a school of her own.

To help determine a vision, we look at what we believe people, our communities, our nation, and the world need, as well as future trends in our field of endeavor where we can make a difference. Here are some questions to ponder:

1. What are the future trends in my field where I can make an impact?

2. What do I think people need in general that I can offer?

3. What are people in our society yearning for that I can help with?

4. What is needed in my community?

5. What does our nation need that I can help with?

6. What is missing in the world that I can contribute?

· Meditation: Developing a Vision ·

Do a basic relaxation. Imagine yourself hiking up a high mountain. Walk slowly up step by step, overcoming many obstacles—waterfalls, streams, mud, and slippery trails. Negotiate each obstacle slowly and patiently. As you glance out, you see the heavens opening up to you. You are embraced by peace and harmony. As you continue toward the top, begin to shed your old clothes. See yourself in new attire. Notice what you look like as you reach the top.

At the top you feel like you are beginning a new adventure. You look over the vastness of the land. You're in awe of the peace and serenity. Then, looking out into the universe, you see an archangel coming toward you. He comes down to greet you. He wants to take you on a trip. You hold his hand. By his side you fly over the earth. You breathe in evenly and deeply, taking in the Divine air.

You think about what is burning within you that you can share with the world and make a difference. Looking down at the earth, see what's going on and what it is that people need that you can offer. Develop a vision for the future. Make a commitment to live out this vision and be the best you can be. A feeling of warmth fills your body. You are inspired to start living your dream. You are eager to come back down to earth and get to work. The archangel sets you back down on the mountaintop.

You thank the archangel. Then you start descending the mountain. Your clothes change again into the new apparel that fits your new image and the new work that you will be doing.

You are deeply focused on the hike down, paying attention to every step. An excitement builds in your body. As you reach firm ground, you are motivated and directed toward living your vision. Write about your experiences.

Every artist has a message. Every business has a message. Every person has a message. What is yours? If you had one thing that you would want to share with people, what would that be?

- A mother said, "I want people to learn how to enjoy life by living in the present, just as children do."
- A doctor said, "I can help motivate people to take better care of themselves and their health."
- A director of human relations in a major corporation said, "I have a vision of corporations integrating more skills for human potential in their training programs."

What is your vision? What can you offer to benefit humankind?

PATH BETWEEN
BINAH AND *CHOKHMAH: SHIN* 𝖜

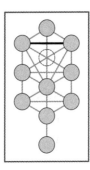

The horizontal path connecting *Binah* (understanding) and *Chokhmah* (wisdom) is represented by the Hebrew letter *shin,* 𝖜. As a mother letter, it correlates to the element of fire. *Shin* is the first letter of the Hebrew words *shalom,* peace, and *Shabbat,* Sabbath, which pertain to harmony. It's being connected to the Absolute where there is satisfaction, peace, and harmony rather than grasping or desiring, and where our focus is singular. To accomplish this, we meditate on the Hebrew letter *shin,* 𝖜.

FOCUSING ON GOD AND PURPOSE

The letter *shin* represents fire. The three-pronged shape of the *shin,* 𝖜, looks like flames and makes a hissing sound, just like the sound of the letter *shin.* A fire can work like a laser light and can focus on one particular place or object at a time. A fire also rises upward.

Fire can burn away negativity. To burn out negativity, we need to overcome dualities in our thinking and be totally focused on the good. When we direct all the energies of breath, speech, heart, and soul toward one given task, it's like a laser burning in our hearts that lights the way to creation.

What we focus on, we attract. It can be ideas, people, or opportunities that come to us. By setting an intention (*kavanah*) with deep concentration (*deveikut*), sincerity, purity of thought, and focus, we have directed thought. Directed thought makes things happen. Without intention and directed thought, we are in touch with everything; too much comes in too fast, and we can't decipher the one from the many. In *Binah* consciousness we sort out the one from the many. We have understanding.

Gematria and Meditation on *Shin* to Bring on the Spirit of God

The numerical equivalent of the letter *shin* is 300. The Hebrew state of *ruach Elohim* involves the spirit of God. If we add up the numerical value of the letters of *ruach Elohim,* it equals 300 (*resh* = 200, *vav* = 6, *chet* = 8, *alef* = 1, *lamed* = 30, *heh* = 5, *yud* = 10, and *mem* = 40). If we meditate on the Hebrew letter *shin,* we can bring on the spirit of God, YHVH (pronounced *Elohim*), which involves peace and harmony.

· Meditation: Gazing ·

A Kabbalah meditation exercise called gazing involves maintaining such a directed focus while gazing at an object that we obtain the essence of what we are focusing on. To understand the workings of the universe and the significance of astrological signs, kabbalists gaze and contemplate the patterns of the stars that form the constellations. By contemplating each pattern, we see pictures of the signs emerge. In his book *The Heavenly Ladder,* psychologist Edward Hoffman suggests looking even beyond to decipher Hebrew letters in the sky. If one stands out more than the others, then keep meditating on it. Watching the sky often gives us a connection to God. Relish this connection. Write down your insights.

JOY

The Hebrew letter *shin* is the first letter of the Hebrew word *simchah,* joy. Kabbalists believe joy is the end result and essence of living spiritually. Rabbi Nachman of Breslov said of joy, "Try to be as happy as you possibly can. Search for your good points in order to make yourself happy. The main source of strength within is joy."

In *The Pathways to the Way of God,* Moshe Chaim Luzzatto writes of two rewards: dynamic reward and static reward. Dynamic reward is the "satisfaction the soul derives from having overcome the enticements of the *yetzer hara* [evil inclination] as well as the difficulties encountered in life." Static reward, on the other hand, "is the feeling of tranquillity and enjoyment which the soul derives from being in a state of spiritual perfection. This is when the soul will achieve complete mastery over the body and cause it to attain constantly higher levels of perfection and bliss." From here on in we work on letting God guide us by receiving and following Divine impulses.

Ascending the Tree of Life, as we reach *Binah* and *Chokhmah* consciousnesses we are getting as close to God consciousness as we can possibly reach without seeing God's face and succumbing to total oneness with God. In Exodus 19 it is stated that the Lord came to Moses in a thick cloud (which kabbalists interpret as wind and breath), telling him to instruct the Israelites not to come near, to create a barrier in fear that the Lord should break out against them because no mortal man may see God's face and live; "whoever toucheth the mount shall be surely put to death." And the Bible goes on to say, "He shall surely be stoned, or shot through," which kabbalists often interpret as people going crazy.

Going up the Tree of Life, *Binah* consciousness is the level of preparation and incubation for the Divine revelation that comes with *Chokhmah* consciousness. It must be done with caution.

RUNNING OF THE HEART

According to the *Sefer Yetzirah, Binah* is considered the spiritual heart. It is the king over the soul, the mind that rules the heart. It's in *Binah* and *Chokhmah* consciousnesses that we can be consumed by the fire (*Sefer Yetzirah* 1:8). If *Binah* consciousness is not balanced by *Chokhmah* consciousness or by the *sefirot* below (the body), there can be what is called the "running of the heart." This is the running and returning from *Binah* to *Chokhmah* and back, without the grounding of the *sefirot* below. We can get so carried away with symbolism, either verbal or visual, that we lose touch with our bodies and reality; the soul leaves the body and may never come back.

An example of this is when we get so engrossed in what we're doing, we become obsessed, thinking about it all the time. We may not sleep or eat. Or else we might constantly be bombarded with thoughts and with the dream world. If we stay here too long, we can get into trouble. It's so seductive, we don't want to face reality.

It is taught that if we do get too absorbed in thought or seduced by the realms of spirit, we can do something physical, such as exercise or eating. Sometimes, however, we can get so absorbed in thought and symbolism that we don't realize it and get thrown off balance, carried away. To keep this from happening, we can make an oath to return. This is accomplished by making a covenant with God for the soul to return to the body if it has a "running of the heart."

Covenant with God

A covenant with God is a contract or mutual agreement made between humans and God. In the oath of "running and returning," the mystic agrees to contemplate the *sefirot* through balance, and not just *Binah* alone. In turn, if the mystic should get too carried away and run back immediately, he or she will be accepted back into the body. It's an oath to keep the spiritual and physical realms joined together.

· Meditation: Making an Oath to Return ·

Do a basic relaxation, invoke the God name YHVH (pronounced *Elohim*), and talk to God. Make a mutual agreement with the deep intention that you will return if the mind starts getting absorbed in too much thought, and that in turn your soul will be accepted back into your body.

PATH BETWEEN
BINAH AND *KETER: VAV* ו

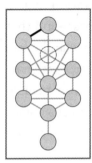

The path between *Binah* (understanding) and *Keter* (oneness/will) is represented by the Hebrew letter *vav,* ו, the letter of thought and truth. *Vav* has a numerical value of 6. It is the third letter in the Tetragrammaton and includes the six *sefirot* following the first three of the Supernal Trinity pertaining to emotions: *Chesed, Gevurah, Tiferet, Netzach, Hod,* and *Yesod.* It also stands for the six days of creation and the six points of direction: up, down, above, below, right, and left. It unites the six directions or six emotive *sefirot* into one.

The letter *vav* can be seen as the spine, which carries the nerve impulses from the brain to the body and back again, incorporating all learning. It is the path of strengthening our intellectual processes, interconnection with people, nature, and the Divine. It's converting our past to goodness by living our Divine purpose. To forward the process of connecting all of life and union with God, meditate on the Hebrew letter *vav,* ו.

FATE AND DESTINY:
RECTIFYING THE PAST

As king over thought, *vav* represents pure thought. Pure thought comes when we totally rectify the past. Kabbalists believe fate is what we bring with us and what we come into in each life, while destiny is what we make of it in each lifetime until we reach our overall Divine destiny.

As we've worked up the Tree of Life, we have worked on letting go of animalistic tendencies, misinterpreted thoughts, and emotional impulses and patterns. At this point, in order to live up to our potential we have even more challenges. The negative side on the path of *vav* is to get "hooked" or attached to something and be unable to move on. Until we understand and release these old charges, we are still ruled by them.

Kabbalists teach that as one generation passes away, the next one comes to replace it. In Exodus 2:5 it says, "The sins of the fathers are remembered even unto the third and fourth generations." Kabbalists interpret this to mean that the third or fourth generation is the same as the first. The *Zohar* states that souls reincarnate in order to correct the "sins of the fathers."

Since we are imbued with DNA and RNA passed down from generation to generation, and every cell has a memory, we are still influenced by our past—and that includes past lives, our ancestors. The path of *vav* represents the spine and nerve impulses carried from the body to the brain and back again. It incorporates the energies, experiences, and memories of the past that are passed down from generation to generation. The brain and mind never forget. Sometimes we unconsciously maintain anger, shame, fear, and resentment from our parents, their parents, and theirs . . . going back to our ancestors many lifetimes ago. It is taught that we carry the parts of their consciousness that have not been perfected. And as we perfect our own souls ourselves, we perfect theirs and rectify the past.

For example, a client who is a writer had a keen interest in a famous historical personality who was snubbed by the public and committed suicide. In college, this client did his master's thesis on this figure. Now in his forties, he is again doing research on him. The client realized he had a tremendous drive to exonerate the man and didn't know where it came from. In doing a past-life regression he remembered some of the places mentioned in the biographical sketches of this historical personality and came to believe he *was* this man in a past life—hence the need to exonerate him.

This work is equally valuable in dealing with our immediate past. The charges we carry from our parents and grandparents may not reflect our own experiences or beliefs, but they are still embedded in our unconscious and still need clearing.

For instance, a client told me that before her mother died, she said she did not want to be put on a respirator or die alone in a hospital. She was very frail, however, and one day she started gagging and couldn't catch her breath. My client's father rushed her to the hospital. Upon admittance and against the family's wishes, the doctors put her on a respirator. One week later she went into a coma. The family stayed by her bedside. Eventually, it became exhausting for my client, who lived two hours away and was staying near the hospital at her brother's home. My client began feeling guilty that she wasn't at home with her husband and children. Finally the nurses had convinced her that her mother's condition was stable and she should go home, which she did.

She received a call at 3:00 A.M. and hurried back to the hospital, where she found her uncle and her father sitting at her mother's bedside. They had been there since six o'clock the previous morning. She was worried about their health and had a deep sense that her father was holding back her mother from moving on. She finally convinced them to leave and get some rest. She accompanied her father home. While her father was sleeping, her mother died.

Ten years later when her father was terminally ill, my client had an obsession to be with him when he passed on. At the beginning of his hospitalization, she stayed with him overnight. The hospital refused to give her a bed or a stretcher, and sleeping in a chair became unbearable. After three totally sleepless nights, her brother convinced her that they should hire a nurse to stay overnight so she could go home to sleep. That night she received a call that her father had passed on.

For more than a year this client felt tremendous guilt for not being there when her father passed on, even though she knew she had done all she could. She worked on releasing the guilt and giving it up to God, but nothing helped. When I asked her one day what this guilt reminded her of, she saw an image of herself convincing her father to go home the evening her mother died. She realized she had picked up her father's guilt for not being there, as well as her own guilt for convincing him to leave. After this awareness, she felt more peaceful with her past.

Some kabbalists believe that the reason some righteous people suffer in this life while some wicked people seem not to is because the righteous in this life may still have sins from past lives that need to be rectified. And the wicked people may not yet experience the effect of their current life's actions, but will surely do so in their next life. It's not until we have corrected all the sins of the past and present that we reap the total spiritual rewards of peace, joy, and abundance.

Kabbalists believe we need to rectify the past through repentance. In practical terms, this comes with releasing all the old instinctive charges, cellular memories, beliefs, and dysfunctional character traits from the past. This includes not only the past in this life but past lifetimes as well.

Furthermore, the sign of *vav* is a nail or peg. It is sometimes seen as a hook and is symbolic of connecting all life: heaven and earth, past and future, male and female, bride and groom.

As part of the path of *vav,* we unite the past with the future.

· Meditation: Past, Present, and Future Lives ·

The Cave of Machpelah is the resting place where Adam and Eve, Abraham and Sarah, Isaac, Jacob, and others are said to be buried. Instilled with mystical properties and energies of the ancients, it is known as the gateway to the Garden of Eden. Many visualizations have been used regarding this cave. Here is a meditation to help rectify and connect the past with the future.

Do a basic relaxation. Picture yourself back in the land of Israel. You are visiting the Cave of Machpelah. As you enter, it is dark and damp. Adjust your eyes to the dim lighting from outside and breathe in the earthy dampness. There are three separate rooms. As you enter the gate to the first room on the left, you get a sense of knowing your personal past. Begin thinking about the past in segments of ten years, pausing to reflect on each segment. Take your time, slowly going all the way back to your teenage years, childhood, infancy, and perhaps even the womb. Take time to reflect.

Now go deeper and deeper into this cave, seeing more than ever before. There's a small bridge of rocks over a stream. Walk over it. On the other side you experience yourself as another person. Look at your feet. What type of shoes are you wearing? You might see a special kind of shoe worn by a soldier, or a sandal that might have been worn in the desert, or a particular style shoe of a certain period. Notice what you are wearing. You are now observing a past life without incurring its feelings; just observe what's going on. Think about what you were doing. Were you fighting a lion in front of a temple, or were you in a Native American sweat lodge? You might have a different ethnic or cultural background or a different financial status.

Think about the people in this life and your relationship to them. Ask what your vocation is. Sometimes an entire life may reel out in front of you like a movie. Other times it might come like snapshots. Notice what comes to you. Ask yourself who in this past life resembles anyone in your life today. Ask what beliefs or impulses you are still carrying from the past that need to be resolved. How can you resolve them? Take as much time as you need. When you are ready to leave this life, walk through the gate back into the center hall of the cave.

Now walk slowly through the gate on the right, the gate of your current life. Here you begin to glimpse your current family's history back three generations to your great-grandparents on both sides. If you have seen pictures of them, or know them or know of them, think about them while you picture them in your mind. Remember what you have heard or know about them: their work ethic, occupations, education, health, family dynamics, hobbies, ethnic and cultural background, tradition, religion, politics, parenting styles, eating patterns, attitudes, financial situations. Also, note their health; particular illnesses; drug, alcohol, or sexual abuses and other addictions; or mental illnesses. Note their overall personalities.

Now think about their children, your grandparents on both sides and their siblings, and how they lived together in their family households. Think about each one individually and consider his or her work habits, attitudes, religious beliefs, parenting styles, and so forth. Think about your mother and father and their siblings and how they lived together in their family of origin. What were their ways of communicating? Who expressed feelings? Who was more intellectual?

Think about the dynamics of your immediate family. What was your role within the family? Notice the timing of events, synchronicities, and connections in marriages, lifestyles, and more. If you recall your parents or grandparents commenting on their rebelliousness or acceptance in their families, make a mental note. Notice what patterns you may have either picked up or rebelled from. Notice any biases or prejudices you may have developed as a result of your background.

Think about the family's work-related interests and hobbies and notice if you have any of them. How do you resemble any part of your family? How are you different? Is there any family member whom you favor? Is there any family member with whom you have unresolved issues? What decisions did you make that turned you into something different from your family as a result of seeing how they lived? How were these decisions beneficial? How were they detrimental? What choices did you make in either defiance or acceptance of your family members? How did you create your life as opposed to others in your family as a result of your decisions and choices? What did you learn from your choices and decisions? Write down where those choices led you.

Think about the repeating themes in your life and the messages they have been giving you. And now think of the emotional charges you may still be carrying around that need to be resolved. As you look around this room, there are many books. Open one up: There's a message for you. Read what it says.

When you have explored this part of the cave sufficiently, return to the center hall. Then walk ahead to the room in front of you. As you pass the gateway, begin to put together your past life with your current life. You see all the pieces of the puzzle. You understand what your past and present lives have been showing you. You are now ready to develop a plan to live your vision without obstacles. You are totally absolved of the past and free to begin to live your future dream. Walk out of this room feeling invigorated with spirit and the motivation to carry out your plan. Imagine yourself doing it free of tension.

As you begin to write your plan, you recognize that it is still your plan for yourself and begin to wonder, *Is this really what God wants from me?* You're still not totally sure. Tell yourself you just need to be patient—for the right time and situation. Walk out of the room, again contemplating God's will for you—but now, since you've experienced yourself already living it, you are confident that it will be given to you. As you leave the cave you are thrust back into your body. You feel energized and motivated. Write down your experiences.

· TWELVE ·

Chokhmah: Wisdom
Prophecy and Revelation

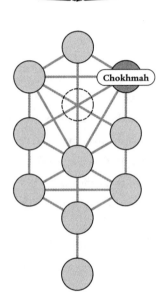

Divine Name: Yah (Short for YHVH)—Eternal Being of God

The *Zohar* describes *Chokhmah* as "a stream sprouting wisdom." The Divine name for *Chokhmah* is Yah, which means "the Eternal Being of God." Yah represents the first half of the name YHVH. *Chokhmah* is the source of energy flow before separation into the lower world represented by *Binah* and the *vav* and *Malkhut* and the final *heh* in YHVH. If we add up the numerical value of the word *Yah* (*yud* = 10, *vav* = 6, *dalet* = 4), we get 26, the numerical value of the entire name YHVH. It is the source of all. The Divine attribute is wisdom.

Archangel: Raziel

Archangel Raziel, "the secret of God," is one of the regents of the thrones. The thrones are known as the wheels of the holy carriage. They inhabit the third or fourth heaven. Raziel

225

is known to be the author of the Book of Raziel, a book on how to live life. Steve Savedow, translator of *Sepher Rezial Hemelach: The Book of the Angel Rezial* [sic], says this book was given to Adam in the Garden of Eden to help him better understand the lessons of life. After Adam was exiled from the Garden, the book was stolen. Adam apparently was lost without the life instructions and prayed for God's mercy. Because Adam served God in prayer, the book was retrieved from the ocean and returned to him. It next went to Enoch, then Noah, and, after Noah, King Solomon. It was from this book that Noah was given instructions to build the Ark and Solomon was given knowledge of magic.

Patriarch: Adam

The patriarch representing *Chokhmah* is Adam. Adam came into being on the sixth day of creation when God said, "Let us make [a] man in our own image." Adam represents the first human being, the father figure of humankind. Due to the sin of eating from the fruit of the Tree of Knowledge, as mentioned in Genesis 3:23–24, "The Lord God banished him from the Garden of Eden to work the ground from which he had been taken. After he drove the man out, God placed on the east side of the Garden of Eden cherubim and a flaming sword flashing back and forth to guard the way to the tree of life." Adam exemplifies the struggle of free will and obedience to God. Adam as the first male represents the seed that impregnates the woman—the seed of creativity.

Personal Attributes: Divine Purpose, Revelation, Prophecy

In *Chokhmah* consciousness we are in the flow of ideas and Divine light. We are open to revelations and wisdom. While waiting for our calling, we prepare for it by identifying who we are and how we can benefit others the most. We pray. We meditate. We let go of thinking in order to receive revelation. We work on developing wisdom and wait for the "aha" experience, the spark of Divine creativity in which we receive the lessons, the tradition, books like the Torah, Prophets, or Book of Raziel, and learn what we are called on to do.

Chokhmah consciousness is the feeling of being in the flow. To emulate this attribute, meditate on *Chokhmah* and any of the representations above or else meditate on the essence of wisdom. At the end, state the affirmation: *I am in the image of the eternal being of God and receive wisdom through revelations and prophecy.*

CHOKHMAH: WISDOM

The English translation of *Chokhmah* is "wisdom." It is the realm through which pure thought flows. In *Chokhmah* consciousness we receive truth through prophecy or revelation. *Chokhmah* consciousness is openness to something beyond this world—to pure undifferentiated thought, original revelation. It comes from beyond our own experiences and knowing. It is right-brain genius. Kabbalists call *Chokhmah* "the hidden brain," often considered to be a person's creative potential.

Chokhmah consciousness is revelation that comes to us in spurts of peak or mystical experiences, often in the form of symbols, spontaneous insights, images, and dreams. *Chokhmah,* being right-brain genius, can be accessed in many ways and for many reasons. Sometimes revelations can be the big ones of cosmic proportions—say, Moses leading the people out of Egypt and receiving the Torah. They can also mean saving one person's soul, or can be an idea of how we can be a better person, such as listening when we would normally speak.

Chokhmah consciousness is the height of creativity that can come through poetry, art, music, drama, solving problems, creating businesses, creating wonderful relationships, creating our lives. It's when all the pieces of a puzzle come together in an "aha" experience. An example might be Einstein pondering different concepts of the relationships of light, energy, and mass in his mind for many years and then suddenly, in a flash of illumination: his theory of relativity. Or it can be a writer taking notes, writing short stories over a period of years. Then suddenly an idea pops into her mind and it all comes together into a book. It can be finding the right livelihood or the right person for a mate, and when it happens, you just know it's right. It can also be answers to questions we've been asking about mundane things such as finding the right house, buying the right dress for that special occasion, or even ordering a special meal at a restaurant that "feels" right.

Once we reach this level of prophecy, the wisdom can be continuous and work in all parts of our lives. Artists, writers, and musicians often say that when they are in the process of creating, it feels as if they are being guided by the hand of God, or the work is being created by God and they are only the channels. It's the openness of the mind to hear God, and to be open to learning and taking action through sharing. When we get into this level of wisdom, we experience both ecstasy and humility: the ecstasy of creativity and being in the flow, and the humility of knowing it's being channeled through us and we are only the vessels. This is the state of channeling God's light. It's living our lives through flow, through God, through the goodness and light of the Divine.

PATH BETWEEN
TIFERET AND *CHOKHMAH: TET* ט

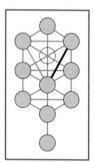

The path between *Tiferet* and *Chokhmah* is represented by the Hebrew letter *tet,* ט. *Tet* correlates to the constellation of Leo and the Hebrew month of *Av* (July–August). This month is ruled by the sun. It involves very high energy, which can be healing or destructive. The sign of this month is a lion. The numeric value of *tet* is 9, which represents the nine months of pregnancy. *Tet* is the first letter of the Hebrew words *tiyul,* travel, and *tov,* good. To strengthen the experience of true goodness, experience spiritual and creative inspiration, and travel to higher spiritual places to receive God's words and plan for us, meditate on the letter *tet,* ט.

DIFFERENT STAGES OF PREPARATION
FOR PROPHECY

The sign and shape of the letter *tet,* ט, is like that of a coiled serpent whose tail wraps around into itself. And just as a serpent sheds its skin, this path represents shedding physical self-consciousness and opening to spiritual consciousness. The numerical value of *tet,* 9, is symbolic of new life growing within the womb of the mind—perhaps an idea or project percolating before manifesting in creative and spiritual potential. It is the spark of inspiration before new creation. It's the planted seed being nurtured, watered, and protected before sprouting and displaying itself. It's the gestation period for a prophetic experience—when God makes himself known to us. That's usually through inspiration and revelation in meditation, but can also be through Divine Providence.

Revelation is sometimes considered an advanced state of intuition. Many kabbalists think of intuition as interpretation of thoughts through our senses—receiving information through sound waves or light, which is then interpreted by the brain and experienced in the body. Revelation, on the other hand, is thought channeled from the Divine directly to the mind without being processed through the brain and sensory perception.

When we receive revelation, there is absolute certainty that what we receive is truth. It resonates within every part of our being. There is no questioning as to whether it feels right, or if it leads us to where we want to go. It's unchanging. It's definitive. It's knowing. It's pure consciousness.

According to Moshe Chaim Luzzatto in *The Pathways to the Way of God,* there are three conditions that apply in order for a prophet to know that a certain vision is actually a prophecy:

1. Clear perception

2. Full knowledge

3. Absolute certainty

This would equate to Moses receiving the revelations at Mount Sinai or Buddha receiving his revelations under the bodhi tree. It's a knowing of truth that comes directly from the Absolute and leaves no question or doubt. Furthermore, when this happens there is an inner knowing that the prophecy will be realized. And although we can't bring on revelation, we can prepare for it.

Kabbalists believe inspiration and revelations come in stages: initiation, incubation, action, and manifestation of the spiritual experience. These are the same stages we have been working on while ascending the Tree of Life. The first stage, initiation, is the first call to leave our birthplace—*Lech lecha,* go unto yourself, and, as God promised Abraham, "I will make your name great, and you shall be a blessing." We strive for greatness and pleasure.

The second stage is the incubation period all patriarchs experienced, that of cleansing and purifying. We work on cleansing our bodies and environment and purifying our thoughts and speech.

The third stage is the challenging work of taking action. We follow our truth and express our uniqueness. This is the preparation for what is to come next.

The fourth stage is the manifestation of the mystical/spiritual experience. It's what we are called on to do, our Divine mission. It's when we are told our Divine purpose.

Moses, after many years of preparation, went into isolation to display his devotion to God and pray for guidance on leading his people out of Egypt. His cries were answered in a mystical experience when he was shown the dynamics of Purgatory and Paradise and the various degrees of cause and effect. He was given the Ten Commandments carved in stone, and an explanation of all creation and how to live life according to the Torah, which was channeled through him.

The mystical experience usually takes place after years of preparation—opening to true goodness and cleaving to the Divine with prayers, meditations, and pronouncing certain holy names. Sometimes mystical experiences happen spontaneously and often through trauma. The prophet is often unaware of what is happening and tries to figure it out afterward. For Jacob, several revelations came spontaneously during times of trauma. His vision of the ladder ascending to heaven came while he was alone in the desert and apparently feeling forlorn. Another, wrestling with an angel, came with the fear of fighting his brother, Esau.

Many people during the Years of Prophecy had prophetic experiences. When this period ended, such a level of revelation ended. Since those years, revelations and prophecies have been veiled; they have not been as prevalent or as clearly defined. Instead, they are revealed through Divine Providence. Occasionally, however, and only to those select few who prepare themselves, prophecies may still occur internally through meditation as a mystical experience. They come on many different levels, however, depending on the prophet and level of preparation and interpretation. Sometimes revelations are on a grand scale of saving a community or nation; sometimes they come on the smaller scale of saving a soul, or just an insight or answer to a question.

The best way to describe a personal prophetic experience is to share in more detail an experience I mentioned in Chapter One and that I had more than twenty years ago, when I still considered myself an atheist. It was during the extreme turmoil of divorce. I began asking the big questions. *What is the meaning of life? Why are we here? What is the purpose of existence?* Answers to these questions started coming in the middle of the night. Becoming obsessed with thought, I stopped eating, stopped sleeping, and ignored feelings. I went into a very high state of ESP, mental telepathy, and I was getting theories on creativity, unconditional love, and God. Suddenly one day while dusting furniture, feeling overwhelmed with nonstop thought and overcome with exhaustion, I started crying. I ran into my bedroom. As I reached my bed my knees spontaneously went to the floor and my arms rested on the bed in prophetic prayerlike fashion. I automatically screamed, "God help me." The crying turned into trembling, shaking, and sobbing. Deep, guttural animal sounds spewed from my mouth. I was crying from the depths of my being. It seemed as if it lasted hours, but in reality it was probably only a few minutes. It felt as if every bit of my being left my body. Totally drained, I lay down on my bed. Then suddenly I was engulfed in an aura of light and love. It was a warm, peaceful silence that I had never experienced before. My entire body began tingling, like soft pins and needles. I remembered thinking, *This is the feeling of love without having someone to love. This is true, unconditional love.* Then I heard a voice sounding like a soft echo through a megaphone that said, "You are a messiah."

I was sure I was hallucinating. I screamed internally, "I'm not a messiah. I can't save the world. A messiah knows all. What do I know?"

The voice answered, "There is all knowing from within. What you know will manifest in poetry."

I was sure I was going crazy. I never wrote poetry. I never even read poetry. In school it would take me three hours to write three lines. I wrote the whole thing off as a hallucinatory experience. I said no to writing poems but remembered automatically thinking I would write at least two books and do research. On what, I had no idea.

Although I said no to the poems, two weeks later I awoke in the middle of the night and spontaneously wrote the first of approximately a thousand poems. These poems were answers to my questions about life, love, God, relationships, and commitment. They came like little ditties, not great literary prose, just my own words, but the insights were profound—as if coming from a higher level of consciousness. During that time I felt very alive, aware, and creative. It was an exhilirating experience.

Afterward, in reflecting on my mystical experience, I interpreted it as being touched by the hand of God. The message was clear, visceral knowing at a cellular level. And the prophecy manifested in the writing of poems. During that time I knew I had reached a higher level of consciousness, but in a very unhealthy way. I wasn't eating, sleeping, or feeling. I was not in touch with my body or reality. I was close to a nervous breakdown. Needing to understand how the experience happened, what I did to elicit it, and how this state could be reached in a healthy way, I started reviewing my journal, reading, researching, meditating, praying, and coming up with answers.

Prior to the experience I had gone to a therapist who was helping me work through my emotional issues, co-dependency, personality flaws, and financial struggles. Unknowingly, I was preparing for the mystical experience. When I cried out to God with heart-wrenching sobs, I released the physical tension and all emotional charges and sensations. I let go of my ego. In the silence God answered in essence and words. In Kabbalah this is known as the *Ruach Hakodesh* experience, the Holy Spirit experience. It is an enlightenment that is bestowed upon us.

Over a period of years trying to understand the "messiah message," I realized that to me it meant that we are each our own messiah. By taking responsibility for our own thoughts, feelings, speech, and actions, and tempering them, we can reach a state of peace within ourselves. By responding in ways that are beneficial to others, we can help others reach a state of peace within themselves. If we all reach a state of peace within ourselves and respond from that peace, we will have peace in the world, and therefore the Messiah will flourish. Transforming our ego and opening to the Divine to experience peace and wholeness is the foundation for the coming of the Messiah and the ultimate kabbalistic goal.

I further realized that by asking the big questions about the meaning of life while not being balanced by proper nutrition, sleep, emotions, and focus, too much came in too fast. It was overwhelming to the point of near breakdown. Although I didn't know it then, I had a "running of the heart," mentioned in the chapter on *Binah*. After the experience I started taking care of myself physically and was more in touch with my feelings. I then began narrowing down the questioning to the meaning and purpose of my own life. Over the next twenty years I was shown through Divine Providence in baby steps.

TRAVELING AND PRACTICING SILENCE

Tet is the first letter of the Hebrew word *tiyul*, travel, in this case, traveling to high spiritual places. Many kabbalists consider themselves "travelers." To kabbalists traveling means journeying out of the physical to higher places to see God and receive God's word; to receive revelations, prophecies, and purpose.

There are specific meditative steps to achieve revelation through internal means. They are: meditation/silence, concentration on God, listening, and interpreting.

Kabbalists believe that in order for us to receive perfection of Divine revelation, our soul must be freed from the body and attached to the will of God. The phrase "freed from the body" refers to going beyond sensory awareness. During times of revelation prophets were not aware of their surroundings, themselves, or anything else. They were freed of sensory awareness—in total silence.

To experience silence ancient kabbalists used many tools, some of which we have been practicing already. Here are some more advanced techniques used by ancient mystics. All involve deep concentration and devotion.

Praying in the Prophetic Position

The prophetic position is placing your head between your knees with your hands outstretched in front. It is taught that bending the two knees, representing *Hod* and *Netzach,* the *sefirot* of prophecy, helps nullify sensory perception and therefore opens you up to channel prophetic energy. Some ancient kabbalists recommended fasting for a number of days, then getting into the prophetic position and chanting, humming, and praying. It is taught that when we do this we can enter into the seven chambers or Gates, an extremely advanced state of consciousness.

Practice Humming the Hebrew Letters *Mem* and *Shin*

Humming the sounds of the letters *mem* and *shin* while in the prophetic state is another way to attain silence. According to Aryeh Kaplan in his translation of the *Sefer Yetzirah,* "the Kabbalists say that the 'fine still voice' (1 Kings 19:12), heard by Elijah, was actually a 'fine humming sound.' This humming sound is used to attain such a state of consciousness, and as such, it is experienced when one is in a prophetic state."

The letter *shin*, שׁ, represents fire. The letter *mem*, מ, represents water. The Talmud explains that the two sounds are experienced in the Hebrew word *chash-mal*, which according to kabbalists represents the physical and spiritual worlds. It is said in the Talmud that the word *chashmal* is the combination of *Binah* and *Chokhmah* consciousness. It represents both speech and the speaking silence. Moving between the two sounds not only brings on the higher energies but also balances the running and returning between *Chokhmah* and *Binah*.

The letter *shin* has a hissing sound of *sh*. The letter *mem* has a humming sound of *m*. By oscillating between the two sounds—*shhh*, then *mmm*—we bring on silence. Hum the two letters and let the sound vibrate in your body. Just experience the sound and don't worry about any meanings.

According to Aryeh Kaplan, a more advanced meditation on the letters *shin* and *mem* is to pronounce them with the five primary Hebrew vowels: o, a, e, i, u. For example:

ShoMo, ShoMa, ShoMe, ShoMi, ShoMu.
ShaMo, ShaMa, ShaMe, ShaMi, ShaMu.
SheMo, SheMa, SheMe, SheMi, SheMu.
ShiMo, ShiMa, ShiMe, ShiMi, ShiMu.
ShuMo, ShuMa, ShuMe, ShuMi, ShuMu.

Concentration on Nothingness

Another technique for silence is to picture nothing in your mind; see blackness, as if you're looking inward behind your head to nothing. Just stay with the nothingness—the dark silence.

Concentration on God

The next meditative step toward receiving prophecy after reaching silence is to concentrate with total focus on God. To help facilitate this we can recite the

Divine names in Hebrew, permute the letters of the God names, or use the dreams and visualizations of God taken from the Torah. For now, another advanced visualization is meditating on Ezekiel's vision.

· Merkavah Meditation: Ezekiel's Vision ·

The Merkavah mystics used the vision of Ezekiel as a vision of reaching the heavenly realms and maintaining higher states of consciousness. Meditating on the images can help keep us close to God. Below is a description of Ezekiel's dream, taken from the first chapter of Ezekiel.

In the thirtieth year, in the fourth month, on the fifth day of the month, as I was among the exiles by the river Chebar, the heavens were opened, and I saw visions of God. . . .

As I looked, behold, a stormy wind came out of the north, and a great cloud, with brightness round about it, and fire flashing forth continually, and in the midst of the fire, as it were gleaming bronze. And from the midst of it came the likeness of four living creatures.

And this was their appearance: they had the form of men, but each had four faces, and each of them had four wings. Their legs were straight, and the soles of their feet were like the sole of a calf's foot, and they sparkled like burnished bronze. Under their wings on their four sides they had human hands. . . .

As for the likeness of their faces, each had the face of a man in front; the four had the face of a lion on the right side, the four had the face of an ox on the left side, and the four had the face of an eagle at the back. . . . And their wings were spread out above; each creature had two wings, each of which touched the wing of another, while two covered their bodies. And each went straight forward; wherever the spirit would go, they went, without turning as they went. . . .

Now as I looked at the living creatures, I saw a wheel upon the earth beside the living creatures, one for each of the four of them. As for the appearance of the wheels and their construction: their appearance was like the gleaming of a chrysolite; and the four had the same likeness, their construction being as it were a wheel within a wheel. When they went, they went in any of the four directions without turning as they went. The four wheels had rims and they had spokes; and their rims were full of eyes round about. . . .

. . . Over the head of the living creatures there was the likeness of a firmament, shining like crystal, spread out above their heads. And when they went, I heard the sound of their wings like the sound of many waters, like the thunder of the Almighty, a sound of tumult like the sound of a host; they stood still, they let down their wings. And there came a voice from above the firmament over their heads; when they stood still, they let down their wings.

And above the firmament over their heads was the likeness of a throne, in appearance like sapphire; and seated above the likeness of a throne was a likeness as it were of a human form. And upward from what had the appearance of his loins I saw as it were gleaming bronze, like the appearance of fire enclosed round about; and downward from what had the appearance of his loins I saw as it were the appearance of fire, and there was brightness round about him.

Like the appearance of the bow that is in the cloud on the day of rain, so was the appearance of the brightness round about. Such was the appearance of the likeness of the glory of the Lord. And when I saw it, I fell upon my face, and I heard the voice of one speaking. And he said to me, "Son of man, stand upon your feet, and I will speak with you."

—Ezekiel 1:1–28

PATH BETWEEN
CHOKHMAH AND *KETER: HEH* ה

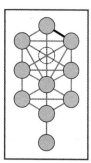

The path between *Chokhmah* and *Keter* is represented by the Hebrew letter *heh*. It correlates to the constellation of Aries and the Hebrew month of *Nissan* (March–April). The sign of the Hebrew letter *heh* is a window, which is often interpreted as the opening to the expression and manifestation of the Divine. The *heh* stands for *hineh*, which means "lo" or "behold." The numerical value of *heh* is 5. Five represents the five fingers of the hand and five toes on each foot. It represents an open hand that gives. The letter *heh* begins the Hebrew word *hineini*, which means "I am here." For being open to the Divine, experiencing Divine prophecy, and creative self-expression, meditate on the Hebrew letter *heh*, ה.

LISTENING INTERNALLY

The sound of the letter *heh* is the closest to the exhalation of breath—almost silent—and is the closest to God. It comes from *Keter*, the nothingness beyond thought that manifests in *Chokhmah*, the origination or the first spark of thought, the "aha."

In this third step toward receiving prophecy or revelation during meditation, after reaching silence and then concentrating on God, we now listen. The path of *heh* is listening—listening to that still small voice within. Here we need to be keenly aware of every nuance, inkling, image, vision, vibration, and voice that is in our mind and body.

Since our receiving and transmitting abilities are not capable of receiving Divine revelation or prophecy directly, as Moses did, most often it comes through intervening forces by God's messengers such as archangels, angels, spirit guides, or dreams. It helps to recognize how these energies differ from one another.

· Exercise: Internal Listening ·

Think about how much you have fine-tuned your internal listening:

- Can you distinguish the different types of impulses and energies in your body?

- Do you see internal images, words, feelings, lights, colors, angels, spirit guides?

Revelations Through Dreams

Revelations also come through dreams. Some are the dreams that help us work through daily emotions, thoughts, experiences, or events and tell us something about ourselves that we need to change or correct. Other dreams are the "big" dreams of revelation and prophecy. Kabbalists believe it's important to pay attention to all dreams. It's beneficial to write out dreams and decipher the messages they are giving us. Dream interpretation is subjective and of course can vary. There are several books on dream interpretations. One in particular addresses 850 kabbalistic symbols: *Divining Your Dreams* by Jonathan Sharp, with an introduction by Dr. Edward Hoffman. This might be a good way to start your dream interpretations.

Interpretating Revelations

The next step toward prophecy is interpreting vague feelings, dreams, revelations, and insights. In analyzing my own dreams, I realized that some were a progression of events leading toward insights into the mystical. In one, for instance, I died, and men in black capes with top hats came to take me away. In another, I went through a black tunnel and at the end experienced three pangs and a big blast of stars. When I opened my eyes I saw a book on the end table, *Born to Win*. I later learned that these dreams were considered to represent the death of the ego and a rebirth into spirit.

The way dreams are interpreted is based on each prophet's way of taking in information. The reason kabbalists believe Moses was the only one who channeled the messages verbally without needing to interpret them is that at one point God actually spoke *through* Moses. He was channeling God's words directly. That's why his revelation of the Torah is considered to be "the word of God." As God said, "I speak to [Moses] mouth to mouth, manifestly and not in allegory" (Numbers 12:8). Others had to interpret their experiences at their own level of understanding, symbols, speech, and language.

Exodus 20:25 notes that at Mount Sinai, three million people who witnessed Moses talking to God "saw the sounds." This is known as synesthesia: interpreting one sense into another, or translating a sensory perception into symbols. There were seventy different languages spoken among the people at Mount Sinai. Rabbi Akiva, remarking on Exodus 20:15—"And all the people saw the voices"—said that they saw the sounds and heard visions. They sensed the "sounds of God," each in his or her own way, which the prophet then had to interpret in images based on his own language, culture, and background to be understood. In Ezekiel's vision, he sees the "speaking silence." Here he is experiencing the visual, verbal, and nonverbal parts of his mind at the same time and translating one sense into another.

To fine-tune our interpretation of internal experiences to a greater capacity, it helps to interpret one sense in terms of another. Furthermore, the more senses we use, the deeper the understanding.

Here are ways to practice interpreting one sense in terms of another:

- "Read" a psalm.
- "Feel" the meaning of a song.
- "See" the music of any song by formulating an abstract design.
- "Hear" the sounds in a picture.
- "Experience" a verbal gesture.

Hearing Our Mission

Heh is the first letter of the Hebrew word *hineini*. When God asked Abraham and Moses where they were, they said *hineini*: "I am here," "I am present," "I am ready to receive." As I've mentioned many times previously, in order to experience the Divine we must be fully alive, ready, and in the present moment.

· Meditation: Unleashing Our Mission ·

When we are ready to receive wisdom and pray, if we are prepared we may be given our mission, a revelation, a *Ruach Hakadosh* experience. Below is a visualization meditation to help facilitate unleashing our Divine mission.

Do a basic relaxation. You are going on a long adventure. Begin to walk on a path traversing a mountain. The foliage as you start is dense and very green. There is wildlife all around: eagles, doves, deer, squirrels, rabbits. As you walk, you enjoy seeing the movement of wildlife around the trees. Your footsteps are part of this movement, and you realize they affect the rest of life as you see the squirrels and birds scamper away when they hear your footsteps.

After a few hours of walking you come to a plateau. Look below: You are gazing down at the trees. You can't see beneath them because the foliage is too thick. It feels as if you've broken through the first level of existence. You like being in the middle of the mountain. There's foliage when you look down as well as up, but each looks different because of the different perspectives. You can see both sides now. Yet you still want to go higher.

When you feel rested enough, get up and start to walk again. Traverse the mountain several times, getting higher and higher. The foliage is becoming more sparse. You find yourself breathing more heavily. And the air is beginning to thin. Take another rest. Sitting at the edge of a cliff, you look down again. This time you can see two layers because of the sparseness of the trees of the second layer. You have now broken through the second level of existence.

When fully rested you again resume your climb. As you get higher and higher, the foliage begins to disappear. There is only rock under your feet. You are totally in the clouds, experiencing the moisture around you. The air is very thin, and you begin to labor for breath. Look ahead: The archangel Raziel is standing in front of the holy carriage. He guides you beyond existence to the realm of pure thought.

Images pass through your mind, one after the other. You realize that these impressions are responses to internal questions you've been asking yourself all your life. Your primary thought now is, *What is my Divine purpose?* Radiant light surrounds and engulfs you like never before. It is quiet, serene, blissful. Raziel brings you up to the gate in front of the Holy of Holies. You begin pondering the first of three questions. *Who am I?*

As you look up on the top of the gate, you realize that there is a message for you. Notice what it says. As you walk to the front door of this celestial abode you are pondering the second question, *Why am I here?* There is a sign above the door. Notice what it says. Walk into a magnificent sanctuary. You're in awe. And as you look above the pulpit there is a scroll flying around. You realize you are pondering the next question, *What is my purpose?* Suddenly the scroll stops in front of you. Read what it says.

Then Raziel brings you up to the pulpit where there is a large throne. You are in the presence of God. In this awe you are speechless, yet internally you call to God with every part of your being, crying, pleading, "How can I fulfill my Divine purpose?"

Suddenly you hear a voice, almost like an echo. You are given your mission for helping others and the ability to do it. Experience it clearly. It may be a big mission or a small one. See it now, feel it, experience doing it so it is carved and engraved on your mind. Take as long as you need to absorb the lesson. Make a commitment to fulfill it. Thank God for the revelation.

As you turn around, you can still experience the radiance within you and around you. You bring it back with you as you come back down the mountain. You maintain the composure of godly existence. You are filled with light and love and everyone around you feels God's presence. You are a channel for God's light. You are prepared to shed light on all.

REVELATIONS COME THROUGH DIVINE PROVIDENCE

If we don't receive our mission internally during meditation, it can show up in daily living. Sometimes revelations appear in the writing of poetry, listening to ourselves speaking, listening to music, singing, dancing, relaxing, playing. . . . Embrace this type of "folly." It's in the release that insights often come. It leads to wisdom.

Revelations Channeled Through Others

God also uses other people in our lives as messengers: friends, acquaintances, and even strangers can be our human angels. They channel information and messages from God for us. For example, the idea for a book may come from a friend who is an editor. He or she asks you to write a proposal for a book on your area of expertise. You get goose bumps and immediately realize how right the task is for you. It fits into everything you have been doing, plus it would challenge you. You have the expertise for it and wonder, *Why didn't I think of it myself?* The revelation was channeled through another person to you. And you know it is truth because it resonates within your being. It feels right. You are excited, energized, and enticed by the challenge. You set out doing it immediately without any thought about your ability, skills, habits, or even possible past failures. It feels right.

1. Who are my human "angels" or messengers in life?

2. What messages have they given me?

3. How have I followed up on the messages?

Revelations Can Come Through Signs or Symbols

People often ask God for signs to show them their purpose or to confirm that they are on the right path. However, they don't know what signs to look for—or how to notice them when they come. We can tell God what sign could be given in order for us to understand it when it comes. For example, when Abraham sent his servant, Eliezer, to find a wife for Isaac, Eliezer prayed to God to show him the right woman and told God how he would know she was the right one. He said to God, "Let it be that the maiden to whom I say, 'Please, tip over your jug so I may drink,' and who replies, 'Drink, and I will also water your camels,' let that be the one You have designated for Isaac." Almost immediately Rebecca, appearing at the well, verbalized exactly those words.

When we resolve what the sign will be, we can recognize it when it comes. An example of this is when I was working on identifying the area I wanted to specialize in. As I described in Chapter One, I decided to offer four different types of workshops one year at a local college and resolved that the one that drew the most people would be my area of focus. That year I offered workshops on Developing Charisma, Tapping Creativity, Pursuit of Happiness, and Kabbalah. The Kabbalah presentation was a lecture/workshop during a lunch-and-learn program for senior citizens at the same college as the other programs. The staff running the program expected approximately twenty people. More than a hundred showed up. That was a pretty clear sign!

1. What signs have I had that I may have ignored?

2. What signs can I give God for God to show me the way?

WISDOM IN TEACHING

If we haven't received our calling through internal means, we can still ascertain the best way of making a difference in the world. Teaching is very important to kabbalists. This can mean leading, sharing, or being a role model for others in some fashion or another. The greatest teachers—people such as Moses, Jesus, Buddha, Muhammad—are those who inspire others to reach their highest potential, to be in the light. They are channels for God's wisdom. In order to teach, we truly need to understand the information we are teaching. Having to explain something actually clarifies the concept for ourselves. Sharing concepts with others makes it real. Teaching helps us constantly stay open to wisdom and Divine creativity. It keeps us in the flow. It's important to have a direction in what we want to teach. Here it helps to make up a mission statement.

Mission Statement

The mission statement states what we do, how others will benefit from it, and how we do it. For instance, my mission statement is to help people connect with the Divine, discover their purpose, and live and love the life they "will" for themselves. I do this by writing, lecturing, counseling, and teaching Kabbalah and the Tree of Life through philosophical exploration, meditation, prayers, experiential exercises, communication techniques, and practical steps.

Here are some other examples of people's missions:

- A female executive of a Fortune 500 company had a dream of helping women to feel secure in a male-dominated corporate world and reach the top more easily and effortlessly. Her mission was helping women build self-confidence and self-worth in the corporate world by helping them retain strong feminine qualities of using intuition and emotional intelligence and finding the language that the corporate mentality could relate to. She started by offering workshops and then developed a school, helping women to succeed in business.

- Another client, trained in the martial arts, had a dream to write a book and offer workshops on martial arts. His mission was to help people use their bodies in ways that would help them regain and maintain vitality, health, and energy by incorporating techniques of tai chi, chi gong, yoga, and polarity therapies.

- Yet another mission might involve leaving a legacy or historical recording to descendants. If we record our own history in stories, tape recordings, or pictures, we give our children a bit of their own history. This can help them know themselves. If we write about or discuss what we learned from our experiences, we offer a lesson in how to live life—or at least the way *we* learned to live life. This is a great gift to give to future generations and becomes a part of our eternal destiny.

WRITE OUT YOUR MISSION STATEMENT

In writing out your mission statement, remember to include answers to the following questions:

1. What do I do that I can teach to others?

2. How will what I do benefit others?

3. How will I do it in the most beneficial way?

· THIRTEEN ·

Keter: Crown

Oneness, Will, Humility, and Selflessness

———◆———

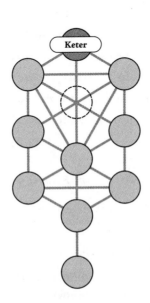

Divine Name: *Ehyeh Asher Ehyeh—*I Am That I Am

Keter is the last gate to enter as we ascend the Tree of Life. It is also the first gate for descending the Tree of Life. It is both the ending and the beginning. The Divine name for *Keter* is *Ehyeh Asher Ehyeh,* I am that I am, or I am that I am becoming, or I am that I will become. It is everything that was, is, and will be—the past, present, and future.

245

Archangel: Metatron

Metatron is considered the greatest of all angels and chief of the ministering angels, or Celestial Academy. He sits next to God on the Throne of Glory and is often identified as the glory of God. His twin brother is Sandalphon, the ruling angel of the earth, who represents *Malkhut*. Metatron is believed to be the transformed Enoch, who is mentioned in the Merkavah literature and the Hebrew book of Enoch. He was the son of Jarod, was wise in the ways of God, and became the archangel Metatron when Enoch reached heaven alive and became an angel. It is believed that the transmission of the Divine spark of light went first to Adam. When Adam sinned, it went to Enoch. When Enoch was transported to heaven, the light went with him as he transformed into Metatron. It is also believed that it was Metatron who accompanied Moses on his journey through heaven and hell, Paradise and Purgatory. Metatron is known as the angel who guided the Israelites across the desert as they left Egypt. He acts as a minister of wisdom and helps sustain humankind.

Patriarch: *Adam Kadmon*—Crown

Some see the *sefirah* of *Keter* as being too high to be represented by anyone. Others use a crown, like the headpiece of a king, on the head of the primordial *Adam Kadmon* as a symbolic representation of *Keter*. *Adam Kadmon* is the blueprint God had of humankind, the epitome of what we can reach. As the androgynous human being, *Adam Kadmon* represents total harmony where male and female energies are in perfect balance. *Adam Kadmon* is not the biblical figure Adam.

Attributes: Intention, Will, Humility, Enlightenment

In *Keter* consciousness we are all one. We live with humility and equanimity. We are in a state of peace and we radiate light, love, and joy. We are also filled with passion and the will to live our Divine purpose and radiate light, love, and wisdom to all. To experience the essence of *Keter*, meditate on it. At the end of the meditation, state the affirmation: *I am that I am, and embrace the Divine light, love, and will to live my Divine purpose.*

KETER: CROWN (ONENESS, WILL)

Keter is known as the crown. It represents the crown on the head of *Adam Kadmon,* the primordial Adam, God's blueprint of humankind before creation. The crown is the symbol of things that are beyond the mind's ability to comprehend. It is experienced as the aura, the halo around the head, and represents Divine essence. In personal terms, it represents oneness and will and manifests in feelings of humility, peace, love, and inner joy.

TRANSCENDENT ASPECTS OF THE SOUL: CHAYAH AND YECHIDAH

At the *Keter* level of consciousness, Lurianic kabbalists include two more aspects of the soul: *chayah* and *yechidah*. They consider the *nefesh, ruach,* and *neshamah* levels of the soul as internal, or within the body, while *chayah* and *yechidah* are transcendent, or out of body. The soul levels of *chayah* and *yechidah* are such high levels of consciousness that they are almost impossible to reach. In the *chayah* level of the soul we experience unconditional Divine love—one that allows us great love for others without our own dependent needs or attachments. It is a selfless love that takes place when we are evolved into the collective soul. In the soul level of *yechidah* we truly identify with the oneness of us all. We identify with the universal soul. We experience everything and everyone as ourselves—all one in the universe.

DEATH

Reaching *Keter* can also represent the ending of life here on earth. However, we are not considered to be dead, either. We will have returned to the collective oneness of the Divine Universal Soul from which we originally came. In Buddhism it is known as the *bardo* state. In Kabbalah it is the *tohu v'vohu*, the formlessness and void. It is the transition between death and birth. Kabbalists believe if we've learned all our spiritual lessons, we can choose whether we want to experience complete union with God and work on the spiritual planes, or return to help others here on earth.

Life Between Life: Heaven and Hell

Many kabbalists believe that heaven, Paradise, Purgatory, and hell are all allegories of states of being that are experienced in life, not death. In addition, kabbalists believe that on a soul level there is no death, but only a transformation from one lifetime to another. The Talmud describes the soul leaving the body as a gentle, painless experience, "like taking a hair out of milk."

Kabbalists believe that at the time of physical death, the *nefesh* stays with the body until the body decomposes. The *ruach*, the emotional level of soul, begins its life review, which starts when the physical body begins to separate from the psychological body. As mentioned in the chapter on *Yesod*, a life review is when we see our life almost like an action movie replayed in reverse, allowing us to experience the impact of our actions on others. This often involves intense pain and pleasure as we relive our lives in detail—every repressed emotion, self-defeating thought or belief, demeaning attitude, harmful behavior, and in general all the evil we may have inflicted on others or ourselves. We also experience the pleasure of every positive thought, feeling, word, or deed—the joys in life. In the *Zohar* it states, "At the hour of man's departure from the world, his father and his relatives gather round him, and he sees them and recognizes them, and likewise all with whom he associated in this world, and they accompany his soul to the place where it is to abide." It is reported by some that Adam greets us at the time of death. Sometimes we also have a vision of the Angel of Death. Often the archangel Gabriel intervenes, however, preventing harm. Furthermore, some speculate that we are also given a brief glimpse of a vision of the *Shekhinah*, who usually comes with three ministering angels.

The next phase is Purgatory. In the world of *Yetzirah*, the *ruach* level of soul involves cleansing all the imperfections and imbalances incurred during life. How long or how difficult this may be is determined by our transgressions or merits. Depending on the amount of cleansing or purification needed, we can rise into Paradise, which is considered heaven or the state of mind of *Beriah;* we can come back into life by descending into the flesh; or we can go down into hell, known in Hebrew as *gehinnom*.

Different Levels of Hell

As pointed out in *Jewish Views of the Afterlife* by Simcha Paull Raphael, kabbalists perceive that there are seven levels of hell—called "fires of hell"—divided into upper and lower hells. Some kabbalists compare the seven levels of hell to the dark side of each *sefirah*. Others depict them as designated categories of sinners for which specific punishments prevail, such as "evildoers, worthless ones, sinners, the wicked, corrupters, mockers, and arrogant ones."

Upper hell, known as the "palace of filth," is for those who constantly commit crimes. These might be criminals who, although they repeatedly do wrong, eventually realize it isn't getting them anywhere and decide to repent. They must go through punishment but can still be rescued.

Lower hell is called *gehinnom.* The type of person who goes here might be the sociopath or criminally insane, who think only of themselves and will do anything to fulfill their own desires with no thought of consequences. These are people who are truly damned. The only one who can release them is God, who gives them a cosmic cycle to repent. If this is accomplished, then they can return to work through their punishments, learn their lessons, and fulfill their destiny. If there is no repentance, these souls are released to what is called "Jubilee of the *Shemittah* at the End of Days." Declared dead or damned, this is considered to be "the pit."

Seven Heavens

After going through Purgatory, the soul begins to enter the regions of "Gan Eden," the Garden of Eden, often referred to as the orchard, Paradise, or heaven. There are seven levels of heaven according to the *Zohar,* and each one requires going through a guarded gate. As we enter one of the seven gates, we are privy to more information, such as knowing the future, knowing who will die, be made poor or rich; seeing all the secret deeds of humans; knowing sorcery; and so forth. When we pass through these gates, we enter into the Merkavah. This is where we get into extremely high levels of energy, and if we are not careful this can lead to destruction. It requires a great deal of concentration, spiritual mastery, and study. To use this energy safely, vigilant self-care and self-purification are absolute requirements. All spiritual masters have teachers they look to for guidance and wisdom.

The seven heavens are divided into lower and upper Gan Eden. The lower is where we still have more purifying to do before moving into the upper heavenly Gan Eden, often known as the Celestial Academy. This is the level of perfume scents and celestial music, where the purified and righteous dwell. It is speculated that after their stay in Gan Eden, souls enter another level called a "storehouse of souls." As mentioned in the chapter on *Binah,* this is where souls who have completed their journey are given their mission and wait to return to a new body and rebirth.

Reincarnation

Kabbalists believe that we can elevate the soul through different lifetimes. Reincarnation comes after dying, going through the purifying and cleansing process, and then waiting until conditions in the physical world suit each soul's lesson plan. We face what is known as *gilgulim,* the "wheels" or the "revolutions"— waiting until the right situation (family, parents, and so forth) comes along—to help us learn the lessons we need in order to evolve spiritually. It is speculated that when we incarnate, we do so with other souls from the same group at a similar time. Each soul, however, can be separated from the others by many miles or even countries. These souls will recognize one another if they meet.

· Exercise: Questions to Ponder About Death ·

In our society, people generally don't talk about death or dying. Yet this is a critical subject that should not be overlooked. It often affects the way we live life and the way we die. At this point it might be beneficial to find out what you believe about death and how these beliefs affect you in everyday living.

1. When was the first time you thought about death or dying?

2. What was your reaction to it?

3. When was the first time you had someone close die?

4. What was your reaction to it?

5. How did you resolve the loss?

6. How did/does your family react to death?

7. What messages did your parents give you about death?

8. What are your beliefs about life after death?

9. Do you believe in reincarnation? If so, what experiences have you had, if any, that have led to your belief in reincarnation?

10. Are you afraid of dying? If so, how does it affect the way you live your life?

11. If you are not afraid of dying, how do your beliefs about death affect your life today?

12. Are you comfortable with your beliefs about dying, or are you still searching?

13. If you are still searching, what is it you hope to find?

REACHING THE GARDEN OF EDEN HERE AND NOW

Rather than waiting for the end of life and death, kabbalists believe we can reach *Keter* conciousness and the Garden of Eden here and now by becoming conscious, bonding with God, and committing to helping others—by bringing heaven down to earth and living our Divine purpose.

Oneness

At the level of *Keter* consciousness we identify totally with the Universal Soul—the Ultimate Being. This equates with the essence of being before Adam and Eve were exiled from the Garden of Eden. It's pure consciousness and oneness, the cosmic energy and light of the Divine, the source of energy and light in the universe. In the *Sefer Yetzirah* it is said that *Keter* is filled with "the spirit of God"—filled with goodness and oneness. It represents the wholeness and unity of all existence. We all have the potential to be aware that we resonate with this level of existence because we all have the same spark of Divine light and love within us. We are all one.

In personal terms it's reaching the Divine spirit within us that manifests in a state of peace, serenity, and inner joy. When we open ourselves up to Divine love, light, and the oneness of us all, we can transmit and receive light and love and wisdom to and from others. We vibrate at a high frequency that includes infinite energies of wisdom, understanding, and knowledge.

Kabbalists teach that to maintain this sense of oneness, we need to live a life of selflessness.

Selflessness

On the path of *dalet,* passing from *Tiferet* through *Daat* to *Keter*—as explained in detail in the chapter on *Daat*—we come to a state of no-thing, only being, essence. As the all or no-thing, regarding people, *Keter* is associated with humility, or selflessness. It's dissolving the "I" into the Thou. There is no "I."

Martin Buber in *The Way of Man* says in answer to the question, *What am I to choose my particular way for?* "Not for my own sake . . . to begin with oneself, but not to end with oneself; to start from oneself, but not to aim at oneself; to comprehend oneself, but not to be preoccupied with oneself." The goal is to take good care of ourselves, know ourselves, but not be consumed by ourselves. We no longer do things for our own sake.

Up until now we have been working on ourselves; developing ourselves to know who we are and become the best that we can be. We've learned to become masters of ourselves, and our work. Now we give it all up. We become selfless. Whatever we do from here on in is for the good of all. All classes we take are with the intention to learn in order to teach or share. Whatever we ask to receive, we receive to give. We begin with ourselves and then forget ourselves. That's becoming selfless. In general, we accomplish selflessness through humility.

Humility

Lao-tzu said, "Lowliness is the foundation of loftiness." To become selfless—or no-thing—we need to live with humility. Moses Cordovero cited eight ways to develop humility. Notice which ones you adhere to.

CORDOVERO'S EIGHT WAYS TO DEVELOP HUMILITY

1. With your head, imitate God by being humble and good to all. "The proud man lifts his head upward." But we should look upon and help everyone in need of our goodness, no matter what their past sins or misdeeds.

2. With your mind, think the thoughts of God. Contemplate God's majesty, the Torah, and how to do good. Do not let negative thoughts enter your mind.

3. With your forehead, imitate the quality of God that accepts everyone and is pleasant to everyone. Your forehead should "have no hardness whatsoever." Even if others provoke you, "appease them and quiet them with good will." If you are harsh to others, you will not succeed in soothing them.

4. Let your ears be open to hear good and useful things but be shut to rumors, gossip, ugly reports, or things that incite your anger.

5. With your eyes, be alert to the suffering of others and avoid gazing at evil. When you see the poor suffer, "give as much thought to their predicament as lies in [your] power, and awaken the pity of heaven and of humans upon them."

6. Your nose should never bespeak anger. (The Hebrew word for "anger" translates literally as "snorting with the nose.") Always be willing to forgive. Be patient with everyone, revive those who suffer, and desire to fulfill the requests of others (as long as they are in accordance with God's laws).

7. Let your face shine constantly. Welcome everyone with joy and a friendly countenance.

8. With your mouth, speak well of everyone. Your words should always engender goodness and blessing. Never allow an ugly comment, a curse, anger, or frivolous talk to escape from your mouth.

Accomplishing these eight steps really means being a good, kind person. It happens when we let go of our ego. We empty ourselves of impure or irrational thoughts, emotional charges, tendencies from cellular memory (memories passed down from generation to generation through the DNA and RNA), and past conditioning. We remain free of all judgments, criticisms, expectations, attachments to outcomes, or internal and external tensions and live in a state of equanimity. In equanimity we see and accept everything and everyone as they are, as truth. When we come from truth and equanimity, we resonate with the essence of the universe, the essence of godliness. In touch with the essence, we have the ability to receive and channel Divine light, love, wisdom, healing, and peace to others.

To understand Cordovero's eight steps in practical terms, we might interpret them as follows:

1. Be with people with an open heart void of judgments, criticisms, expectations, or assumptions. Empathize, understand, and be willing to help in any way without regard to what someone may have done in the past.

2. Always cleave to the Divine in goodness and love. If negative or irrational thoughts come in, elevate them by seeing things from "above it all" through the eyes of God.

3. Have tolerance and patience with people by accepting them for who they are. Give feedback by responding to what is experienced rather than criticizing or telling someone what to do or not to do. And if someone is confrontational, remain calm and maintain equanimity despite what is being said or done, and let go of the attachment to the outcome. Look at people with soft eyes and compassion; come from peace and love.

4. Offer an ear and listen with the intention to hear only truth. Avoid gossiping, listening to gossip, or slandering. Control the evil tongue.

5. Put yourself in another's shoes and ask how you would want to be treated in this situation. Rather than having sympathy for others, bless those who are less fortunate physically, mentally, or financially by praying for them. It brings Divine blessings to help them know themselves.

6. To avoid anger, practice the discipline of constantly releasing your instinctive physical sensations and emotional charges; be open to Divine creative impulses and respond rationally. Be empathetic. Be willing to forgive, make amends, and do what's right.

7. If you constantly cleave to the Divine and remain in equanimity and truth, you receive the radiance of Divine light and love and can radiate it out to others. Welcome others joyfully with an open heart.

8. Compliment others. Be inspirationally proactive and respond rationally rather than being emotionally reactive. Achieve this state by cleaving to the Divine and asking for guidance. When we are an open channel and cleave to the Divine, the right words come out at the right time without an attitude. The truth is heard and, therefore, we are automatically inspirational.

DIVINE WILL

Keter also stands for will. It was God's will to see himself and become the Creator of the universe. If we are in the image of God, it is our job to see ourselves and create. We do this through will. If we have the will to manifest the small part we play in the total scheme of wholeness and intend to use it for the benefit of humankind, by sharing, it elevates us all toward oneness. This is our return to the Garden of Eden.

The *Sefer Yetzirah* tells us that will is the highest faculty in man. Will is pure intention. Achievement starts with will—the deep desire and intention to do or have something that brings light, love, goodness, and joy to the world.

With will, intention, and focus, we weed out everything in order to focus on the one thing that we intend. In *The Essential Kabbalah* Daniel Matt writes, "Whatever one implants firmly in the mind becomes the essential thing." If we constantly implant that we are in Divine radiance and light, we are constantly radiating light in whatever we do and outward toward whomever we come in contact with. This is bringing heaven down to earth and living in the image of God.

Furthermore, if we set an intention—align our will to accomplish something while cleaving to the Divine—we remain in flow and begin to attract what we want easily and effortlessly. The Divine works with us.

To simplify the process of creation, I like to explain a poem I wrote:

> The process of creation is like using a camera
> Snap the picture
> Release the pressure
> And take it all in stride
> See what develops
> And develop what we see
> To make it come alive

1. Call on Divine light and love.

2. Snap the picture by stating your will or intention (prayer). See it, think it, and feel it—as if you have it already.

3. Release the pressure by letting go of the impression, discharging it to the Divine.

4. Take it all in stride by remaining tension-free and living totally in the present.

5. See what develops by observing and accepting what comes without judgment, expectations, or attachment to outcome.

6. Develop what is seen by taking compassionate action with others and/or devoting focused concentration on the work you want to accomplish.

7. Make it come alive—see your intention and will manifest in creation and come to fruition.

Being Born at Every Moment

As long as we are alive and have our mind, we have the ability to create. Creating is what keeps us young. As long as we create, there is something to do, something to think about, something to keep us active, something to keep us alive.

Kabbalists believe that since we are created in the image of God, and God is the Creator, it is our responsibility to constantly create. Even if we are terminally ill, we can still create. We can come to forgiveness and equanimity with the people in our lives and die peacefully, which is creating peace.

In *Keter* there is always optimism. Being in touch with the oneness and being open to ideas, there is always a chance for change. Kabbalists believe that when we cleave to the Divine, there are always new ideas, new opportunities, new challenges to learn.

As Erich Fromm, in *Zen Buddhism and Psychoanalysis,* says, "Living is being born at every moment."

Remember, no matter what age we are, our soul strives to evolve, learn, and grow. We may be a hundred years old and still have many lessons ahead of us, in either this lifetime or those to come. We're never too old to start learning right now. So let us be born every moment. Let us remain open to the spirit. Let us radiate light, love, goodness, and joy. Let us be Godlike in the way we live our lives by bringing Divine light and love within us and around us and radiate it out to others in order to make this world a better place in which to live and love.

· Meditation: Light and Love ·

Do a basic relaxation. Take an inventory of your body. Notice if there is tension in any area. If so, breathe into that area. Keep focusing on that area with normal breathing. When you feel totally calm, call on the Divine by picturing an incredibly brilliant light above your head—like the sun. Think of this light radiating sparks of light around your entire body and engulfing you like a blanket of warmth. Notice what you feel. Take your time. Sometimes there may be a tingly sensation like pins and needles, or a change of temperature. Notice the sensations.

Now think of that radiating light above your head sending a channel of light into your head. Take as much time as you need. Notice what you're experiencing. Then think of this light expanding farther down into your heart. Notice if your heart is filling with light. If not, you may have charges or sensations that need to be released. Pray to release them and see your-self opening your heart to feel the light. Take your time.

Next, think of this light expanding down into your stomach. Notice if it is moving down or whether you still have some blockages in that area. If it's not expanding, you may still have charges that need to be released. Pray to release them and think of opening to the light. Take your time.

Now think of this light expanding all the way down to your feet. Again, take your time. Notice what you are experiencing internally and in partic-ular around your heart. Some people experience it as a vibration, as if energy were bouncing off the inner walls of the body. Others see lights or colors like waves moving in and out. And still others experience overall warmth or expansion. Just notice what you are experiencing. This is the essence of receiving Divine light and love: Divine radiance. If you hold on to it, it may be too strong. So while maintaining a receptive state, you can direct it by focusing on sending it out to others. Think of other people in your life to whom you would like to send light, love, healing, and Divine radiance. Think of sending it to them by focusing on them through thoughts, feelings, or images, ideally using all the senses. Take whatever time you need. Now notice how you feel in the receiving and sharing of Divine light, love, and healing. To show gratitude to the source of Divine light and love, thank God for bestowing this radiance within and around you and for the ability to connect and direct Divine radiance in this way. Take all the time you need. When you are ready, open your eyes. Write about your experience.

GRATITUDE

Completion and Celebration

To show gratitude to the Divine, kabbalists pray and party. In Kabbalah, cele-brations are important. They are called *simchahs*. Whenever we reach a life mile-stone or accomplish a goal, we feel good about ourselves. We feel joyful and want to share the joy with others.

We also know that our forces of creativity and empowerment come from a source greater than ourselves, a source of wisdom, love, understanding, and peace. We acknowledge our gratitude to the Divine. In celebrating milestones and creativity, we are celebrating the spark of God that dwells within us. We are celebrating the life force of flow, ideas, and Divine blessings. We are celebrating being in the grace of God and experiencing enjoyment of life. Take the time to celebrate and serve the Divine in joy. That's truly what the personal kabbalistic goal is: to live in joy and enjoy life.

In the Beginning Is the Ending and in the Ending Is the Beginning

Each journey on the Tree of Life is a new lesson. The more peaceful and fulfilled we are in ourselves, the more we have to give others. The ultimate goal is to work for world peace.

As I come to the end of this book, I thank God for the challenges, lessons, and grace the writing opened me to. I also thank my readers for the opportunity to share these lessons. I sincerely hope you will reap the rewards of walking, connecting, and co-partnering with the Divine, that you will fulfill your Divine mission, living and loving the life you "will" for yourself and helping to make a difference in the world. May we all work toward peace, prosperity, and joy in our own lives as well as peace, prosperity, and joy in the world—a new beginning.

Many Blessings,
Penny Cohen

· APPENDIX ·

History and Schools of Kabbalah

Many people have found the study of Kabbalah confusing. That's because it is taught from many different perspectives and from many different schools even within the same perspective. This brief historical background will help explain the different points of view.

KABBALAH FROM THE BEGINNING

Kabbalah started as an oral tradition handed down through the centuries. The story goes that Adam was the first to receive the secrets of the universe at the time of creation. God, however, withdrew or "veiled" the secrets during the periods of Cain and Abel, the Flood, and the Tower of Babel because of all the corruption, immorality, and evil of those times. Abraham, the first patriarch, was the next recipient of the secrets. He passed them down to his son Isaac, who in turn handed them down to his son Jacob. Jacob passed them to his favorite son, Joseph. It is believed that Joseph died without handing down the knowledge to his children, and therefore the mysteries were lost again until Moses, who received the secrets directly from God. Three months after the Exodus from Egypt, Moses started writing down detailed transmissions from God giving the account of creation. These dictations became known as the Five Books of Moses, and also as the first five books of the Bible—the Torah or Pentateuch. Aside from these written laws it is said that Moses had information that he didn't record in writing, information that was too complex for the layperson; he shared it only with a select few.

King David was the next to receive instructions from God, for building a temple to specific design. Every room had a specific layout and meaning. One such room housed the Ten Commandments. Known as the Holy of Holies, it was said to be the place where God dwelled. The inner temple was constructed to represent the three worlds of physical, psychological, and spiritual planes of existence. Divine Unity, the fourth world, was symbolized in the outer structure. King David passed these instructions on to his son King Solomon.

Prophecy Period: 1312–312 B.C.E.

The prophecy period, during which Moses and other leaders communed with the Divine, lasted approximately a thousand years. Each generation had its prophets who could foretell the future and help in times of crisis. The prophets were called upon for instructions they might receive while journeying to the spirit world.

Merkavah Mysticism: First Century B.C.E.–Tenth Century C.E.

In the sixth century B.C.E. King Nebuchadnezzar of Babylonia conquered Jerusalem. Thousands of Jews were exiled to Babylonia, leading to the decline of the Years of Prophecy. The prophet Ezekiel, a respected priest, was one of the exiles. Ezekiel had many dreams of reaching the Divine. He was the first to record them in detail. Others who sought mystical union with God followed Ezekiel's example. They formed what became known as Merkavah mysticism, which lasted from the first century B.C.E. through the tenth century C.E.

The Hebrew root of the word *merkavah* is *rakhav*, which means "to ride" or "travel." Merkavah mystics would leave their homes, their natural states of consciousness, and travel inward to attain mystical experiences, hear voices, and see visions of God.

They contemplated and meditated on angels, demonic forces, and other universal forces to reach varying realms of heaven. Detailing the upper world, some reported going through seven palaces (seven firmaments or heavens), seeing hosts of angels guarding the gates to each palace, and describing rivers of fire in front of the Chariot of God. Some reported seeing a vision of the Chariot-Throne and visions of God as "a likeness as the appearance of a man upon it." These mystics met in private because they feared their practices would get into the wrong hands.

Essenes: 200 B.C.E.–100 C.E.

The Essenes were another exclusive group of mystics who met in private between the years 200 B.C.E. and 100 C.E. Little was written and known of this puritanical Jewish brotherhood until the discovery of the Dead Sea Scrolls in 1947. Some people think that it is likely that the Essenes were the select few to whom Moses imparted the esoteric knowledge he received on Mount Sinai; he gave the Ten Commandments to all the people. Some speculate that at one point one of its leaders, the "True Teacher" or "Teacher of Righteousness," may have been Jesus, who studied Kabbalah and was a member of the group.

The Essenes were all rabbis who thought that asceticism and strict discipline would bring them closer to the Divine. Following the Essene Book of Moses, which differed somewhat from the Five Books of Moses, they used the language of "heavenly" father and "earthly" mother as forces of heaven and earth with seven heavenly forces above and seven earthly forces below. These forces correlated with the body energy systems as well as the seven mornings and seven evenings of the week and with a paradigm they called the Tree of Life.

This Tree is described as having seven branches reaching to the heavens and seven roots embedded deep in the earth. By tuning in to these cosmic forces, the Essenes believed they could achieve fulfillment. When in an open state, they could communicate by receiving and transmitting through thoughts, emotions, and actions.

To keep the energy centers of the body open, they did daily meditations and yoga exercises in the morning and evening. They believed blocks in the body created conflict within.

Sefer Yetzirah, the Book of Creation (Written Between the Third and Sixth Centuries)

The *Sefer Yetzirah,* or Book of Creation, is the oldest and most obscure of all metaphysical teachings stemming from the Merkavah tradition. Some people speculate that it was written down in Palestine between the third and sixth centuries. Others credit the work to the patriarch Abraham, who was known to be a great astrologer and metaphysician and who received the teachings directly from God. It is said that he wrote a three-page document called *Sefer Yetzirah* or Book of Creation. It revealed ways to reach physical and metaphysical energies of the universe as well as ways to feel peaceful from the inside out.

Abraham, who is known as the father of all religions, passed down this information not only to his son Isaac, but also to Ishmael, the son of his concubine Hagar, who was sent into the desert and ultimately made a home in what is now India. If Abraham was the author of the *Sefer Yetzirah,* the book would actually date back to the eighteenth century B.C.E., the same time as the Vedic scriptures. Kabbalah may predate all the major religions.

The *Sefer Yetzerah* describes how God created the world by means of the ten *sefirot,* which are known as the ten points of light, and the twenty-two letters of the Hebrew alphabet. These thirty-two sources are known as the thirty-two paths to consciousness or wisdom. The book deals with numerology, astrology, and *gematria,* a numerical system in which each letter equates to a number; if the numerical value of one word equates to the numerical value of another, they can be compared for their relationship. The *Sefer Yetzirah* also compares the *sefirot* to the signs of the zodiac and to various body parts in humans. It sets out a method of meditating on the names of God to reach telepathic states of mind and spiritual powers. It has been said that this technique can be so powerful, it can create new worlds, and so intense, it can drive people mad. This is one reason why sixth- through tenth-century kabbalists restricted their teaching to small groups that met in private.

Bahir, the Book of Brilliance: 1176

Around 1176 in Provence a group of rabbis edited the first official book on Kabbalah, the *Bahir,* or Book of Brilliance. The book sets out the basic scheme of heavenly realms and angelic forces, and supports concepts of life after death and reincarnation. The *sefirot* here also appear as lights, powers, and attributes that represent stages of God's inner life. During this period meditation practices involved interchanging (permutating) the letters of the Divine names, the Hebrew alphabet, the ten *sefirot,* and a variety of meditations on colors, breathing exercises, and bodily gestures.

Maimonides: 1135–1204

Maimonides was a distinguished rabbi and physician. His work had a tremendous impact on Kabbalah. Maimonides wrote *The Guide for the Perplexed.* In it he stated that the keys to health were diet, exercise, and a balanced mental outlook. He declared that with proper care, we could awaken our higher mental capabilities. By cultivating our imagination, he taught, we could reach higher consciousness. He recommended song and dance for people with depression or anxiety. His work influenced Abraham Abulafia.

The *Zohar:* Kabbalah in Spain: 1280

During the thirteenth century Kabbalah spread over the Pyrenees, Catalonia, and Castile. It was there that the primary text on Kabbalah, the *Zohar,* also known as the Book of Splendor, was published in 1280. Moses de Leon is said to have been the author, though he denied it and said he was only a scribe putting together the works of Rabbi Shimon Bar Yochai, who lived during the first century. Rabbi Shimon Bar Yochai was sentenced to death by the Romans for denouncing them. He hid in a cave with his son for thirteen years. There he practiced meditation, which culminated in the prophet Elijah teaching him the deepest mysteries of the universe. Rabbi Shimon Bar Yochai and his son had many conversations regarding the structure and function of the universe and man's relationship to it. The *Zohar* is a written version of Rabbi Shimon Bar Yochai's visions and his conversations with his son, as well as later conversations with other mystics.

The *Zohar* is a blend of metaphysics, myth, and esoteric psychology. It crystallizes the secrets in the Torah and focuses on the interplay of the ten *sefirot,* which depict the process of creation, or the ladder of descent and ascent from the Creator to creation and back again. In the words of Azriel of Gerona, "They constitute the process by which all things come into being and pass away." The primary theme of the *Zohar* is that everything is connected.

The *sefirot* in the *Zohar* depict different qualities and essences of God and replicate God's feelings, responses, and actions. By meditating on each of the *sefirot,* we can gain insight into our own existence.

Ecstatic or Prophetic Kabbalah: Thirteenth Century

Ecstatic Kabbalah emerged in Spain with the teachings of Abraham Abulafia (1240–1292), who studied Maimonides' philosophy and taught classes on the *The Guide for the Perplexed.* Like Maimonides, Abulafia believed that any person could develop paranormal abilities. Abulafia's *Ecstatic Kabbalah* was based on specific body postures, contemplation, and altered forms of breathing. While other kabbalists taught knowledge of God through light and visions, Abulafia was concerned with Divine speech, linguistics, and sound. He taught that manipulating the letters of the Divine names of God in Hebrew and reciting them out loud could bring about states of ecstasy. His goal was a direct experience with the *Ein Sof,* the infinite, which he considered more important than a visionary experience. He believed that the soul was part of the stream of cosmic life. Our awareness, though, is limited by sensory perceptions and our cluttered minds. The goal is to "untie the knots" that bind the soul. Abulafia traveled extensively, in particular to Italy and Greece. After trying to convert Pope Nicholas III to Judaism, he was condemned by both Jewish and Christian authorities.

Rabbi Joseph ben Abraham Gikatilla: Thirteenth Century

Rabbi Joseph Gikatilla, a contemporary of Abulafia, moved from the use of language and sound and concentrated more on the mysticism and understanding of the Divine manifestations. His book *Sha'are Orah* (Gates of Light) provides the first comprehensive interpretation of the mystical names of God and the *sefirot* and the essences they represent. It explains how light is dispersed through each *sefirah* and how to reach it.

Kabbalah in Safed: Sixteenth Century

With the expulsion of Jews from Spain, kabbalists traveled through North Africa, Italy, and the eastern Mediterranean. Some journeyed to Palestine and the village of Safed. Rabbi Moses Cordovero (1522–1570), known as the Ramak, is a primary figure here. He systematized the teachings of the *Zohar* as well as other teachings of the ancient kabbalists. He omitted myth from his work and showed how to imitate God by emulating the qualities of the *sefirot*. In his book *Pardes Rimonim* (Orchard of Pomegranates) he outlined the thirteen "gateways" to higher consciousness. *Tomer Devorah* (The Palm Tree of Devorah) is an ethical thesis on how to imitate God. Doing good deeds was a major theme in all his writings.

Rabbi Isaac Luria's Kabbalah (1534–1572)

Rabbi Isaac Luria, later known as "the Ari," was a student of Cordovero and adept in occult powers. As a child he studied the Talmud and as a young man he began an eight-year study of the *Zohar*. He became an ascetic and studied and prayed in seclusion continuously. At one point it is said he was initiated into the teachings by a visit from Elijah.

Although some kabbalists credit Luria as the originator of the concept of *tzimtzum*, contraction and expansion, Aryeh Kaplan in his translation of the *Bahir* explains that Luria gives a clear statement of the concept, which was actually developed much earlier in the *Bahir*. Luria explained that if *Ein Sof*, the infinite, pervaded everything, there would be no room for anything else. He concluded that a vacuum or void was needed in order to have space to create something new. He conceptualized that the first Divine act was withdrawal. Then in the void a ray of light, "a dimensionless point of light," appeared. Since the light was so bright and pervaded all, a constriction was created. Two more expansions and contractions created what we now know of as the Tree of Life, with force, form, and equilibrium.

Luria loved all of creation and avoided harming anything—including worms and insects. He believed that real prayer could be attained only when people were pure in body, mind, and heart and became nothing before God.

Hasidism: Eighteenth Century

Lurianic Kabbalah influenced Hasidism, the eighteenth-century revivalist movement in Eastern Europe, founded by Israel ben Eliezer, more commonly known as Baal Shem Tov (1700–1760). Followers of Hasidism believe that the Divine animates all material existence. They concentrate on one's individual relationship to God. They teach that observing the most ordinary activities can act as an opportunity to discover God. Abraham Isaac Kook (1865–1935), the chief rabbi of Palestine, taught that all existence is the body of God. Emphasis is on ethical principles and doing good deeds as a path toward union with God and holiness. The joy of living comes with purity of heart, intention, love of God, and love of other human beings. As the "way of the heart," they concentrate on emotional aspects of human behavior. Their method is through study of the Torah, storytelling, music, dance, ritual, and psychology.

Chabad Hasidism: Nineteenth Century

Schneur Zalman of Liadi (1745–1812), a follower of Hasidism, wrote the book called the *Tanya*. This was his interpretation of the Torah, *Zohar,* and other scriptural writings. This formed the basis of what is called Chabad Hasidism. *Chabad* is an acronym that combines the first three *sefirot* on the Tree of Life, *Chokhmah*, *Binah*, and *Daat:* wisdom, understanding, and knowledge. Chabad followers focus on the philosophical and behavioral aspects and teach the importance of using the intellect and Divine Mind to conquer the desires of the heart and body.

Lithuanian Mussar Movement: Nineteenth Century

In the mid-1880s Rabbi Salanter founded the Mussar movement, focusing on personal righteousness and ethical behavior. The emphasis in Mussar is to improve ourselves by focusing on our flaws and shortcomings. Concentration was on reading aloud ethically oriented inspirational literature and discussing it in groups. Exercises often focused on deflating self-centeredness and becoming more humble. Such exercises might include taking a train without having a ticket or money and then monitoring your own reactions and feelings (which might include shame and humiliation) when the conductor asked for your ticket or train fare.

CHRISTIAN AND WESTERN MYSTERY SCHOOLS BASED ON KABBALAH

Christian Kabbalah and Western mystery schools have adopted the Tree of Life and its cosmology without the Jewish rituals or deep spiritual heritage. The secular versions concentrate more on meditation and on manipulating the Hebrew letters and their numerical value to get into higher states of consciousness or for their magical benefits. To explain magic, Aleister Crowley, a well-known magician of the twentieth century, defined it as "the Science and Art of causing change to occur in conformity with Will."

Italian Renaissance: Fifteenth Century

During the Italian Renaissance, Giovanni Pico della Mirandola (1463–1494) published *Conclusiones Philosophicae, Cabalisticae et Theologicae,* in which he attempted to prove that Kabbalah was the key to Christian mysteries. He also translated many works on Kabbalah into Latin, claiming "no science can better convince us of the divinity of Jesus Christ than magic and the Kabbalah." Because of this, he was declared a heretic by the church and condemned for using "magic."

Johannes Reuchlin (1455–1522) produced the first systematic work of Christian Kabbalah, known as *De Arte Cabalistica* (The Bible of the Christian Cabala). He believed, as did Pico della Mirandola, that Kabbalah was the key to Christian mysteries.

Nostradamus: Sixteenth Century

It has been said that the French astrologer and physician Michael Nostradamus (1503–1566), Seer of Salon, was taught Hebrew, Greek, Latin, astrology, and medicine by his Jewish grandfathers, which is how he learned the practices of Kabbalah and cultivated the talent for prophecy.

Rosicrucians: Seventeenth Century

Christian Rosenkreutz founded an occult fraternity that studied in secret for more than 120 years after his death. Three pamphlets were circulated in the seventeenth century throughout Europe bearing the fraternity name. They emphasized dedication to the overthrow of the papacy and promoted occult philosophy. These pamphlets were full of kabbalistic influences: *Fama Fraternitatis: The Declaration of the Worthy Order of the Rosy Cross,* the *Confessio Fraternitatis RC,* and *The Chymical Wedding of Christian Rosenkreutz.*

Tarot: Eighteenth Century

In 1781 Court de Gebelin, a Protestant pastor, connected the Tarot, which originated in the fifteenth century, with the twenty-two letters of the Hebrew alphabet. The Tarot is a deck of cards consisting of symbolic pictures. It describes the journey of life and a journey into yourself. In the nineteenth century the French occultist Eliphas Levi also related the Tarot to the Kabbalah.

Hermetic Order of the Golden Dawn: 1888–1900

The Hermetic Order of the Golden Dawn, an esoteric school in England, developed an occult system that influenced the work of most Western esoteric groups today. Their system included a new interpretation and integration of the Kabbalah, the Tarot, astrology, and ritual magic. The Golden Dawn was founded by Dr. William Wescott. He and S. L. MacGregor Mathers decoded manuscripts found in an antiquarian bookstall containing secrets of practical magic. Their emphasis was on unlocking the key to magical talents of the mind by the use of imagination.

The Hermetic Order of the Golden Dawn connected the Tarot with the Tree of Life in pictorial form. The Tarot has twenty-two major trumps; the Hebrew alphabet, of course, has twenty-two letters. The Tarot has ten numbered cards in each suit, while the Tree of Life consists of ten *sefirot.* The Tarot has four suits that represent the four elements; the Tree of Life consists of the four elements—fire, air, water, earth. The Golden Dawn became known for its use of magical techniques to control the external world. Among its famous members were W. B. Yeats and Aleister Crowley, whose books centered on magic and the occult.

The Fraternity of Inner Light: Nineteenth and Twentieth Centuries

Dion Fortune (1890–1946), who wrote *The Mystical Qabalah* and was also a member of the Golden Dawn, criticized the Golden Dawn for dabbling in magic and rituals that overshadowed esoteric thought. She saw Kabbalah as "a living system of spiritual development, that did not need to be bound by tradition." She taught that if you meditate upon a symbol with which ideas have been associated by people in ancient times, and by generation after generation of those who followed, you will gain access to those ideas. She wrote: "The thirty-two Mystical Paths of the Concealed Glory are ways of life, and those who want to unravel their secrets must tread them." Her practices combined Kabbalah, Christian mythology, and Egyptian archetypes.

Twentieth- and Twenty-First-Century Kabbalah Revival

There has been a resurgence of interest in Kabbalah since contemporary kabbalists started teaching it to the general public in the 1960s. The books of Gershom Scholem, Martin Buber, and many others have been making the study of Kabbalah more accessible to the public. Since it is often said that Jesus studied Kabbalah at a mystery school, many more Christians and other non-Jews today have become interested in it. It is also becoming popularized by such entertainers as Madonna, Roseanne Barr, Donna Karan, Gwyneth Paltrow, and many more.

· GLOSSARY ·

Adam Kadmon: Primordial human, the blueprint for the creation of the universe and humankind.

Asiyah: The fourth world; the physical world of action or materialization.

Atzilut: The world of emanation; the first and highest of the four worlds created by God.

Baal Shem Tov: Rabbi Israel ben Eliezer, the founder of modern eighteenth-century Hasidism.

Bahir: A text known as the Book of Brilliance, describing the structure of the *sefirot.*

Beriah: The second highest of the four worlds; the world of creation.

Binah: The *sefirah* representing understanding.

Bohu: The void preceding the existence of our universe.

Book of Raziel: A book given to Adam, revealing the secrets of the universe.

Chayah: The manifestation of the human soul that is known as the "living essence," the life force of the Divine that remains connected to the Divine. It is still in the realm of God and can only be known in the world to come.

Chayot: "Living creatures" in Eziekel's vision; angelic beings with animal faces.

Chesed: The *sefirah* of loving-kindness or mercy.

Chokhmah: The *sefirah* of wisdom and inspiration.

Daat: The non-*sefirah,* usually appearing as a dotted circle, represents knowledge and inner knowing. It is part of the Tree of Life but is not an actual *sefirah.*

Deveikut: Clinging. A mystical state leading to deep connection to God.

Ein Sof: God. The "endless" from which the ten *sefirot* were created.

Ein Sof Or: "Endless" light, the original light that emanated from *Ein Sof* in the creation of the universe.

Elohim: One of the ten biblical names of God.

Gevurah: The *sefirah* of strength and judgment.

Gilgul (pl. gilgulim): Transformation of the soul through its journey of many lifetimes toward complete enlightenment.

Hasidism: A branch of Orthodox Judaism that arose in the late eighteenth century to bring more spirituality into prayer and worship and that included mystical contemplation of the Torah.

Hod: The *sefirah* of splendor.

Kavanah: Concentrated intent necessary for reaching a high state of devotion and mental concentration.

Keter: Crown. The highest of the *sefirot*.

Lamed vav: Thirty-six. The number of hidden righteous men in every generation.

Malkhut: Kingship or kingdom. The lowest, or tenth, *sefirah*, expressing the physical world. (Also regarded as the final manifestation of Divine will.)

Mantra: Sanskrit—a word or phrase that is recited repetitively to achieve higher consciousness.

Ma'aseh Merkavah: "The Act of the Divine Chariot." The mystical teachings associated with the prophet Ezekiel's vision as told in the Bible.

Mashiach: Anointed One or Messiah, who will bring world redemption upon his arrival.

Mayim: Water. In Kabbalah, the substance that preceded matter in creation.

Mezuzah (pl. mezuzot): A small case affixed on doorposts of a Jewish home, containing a small piece of parchment with the prayer *Shema Yisrael*.

Middah (pl. middot): Literally, "measure"; measured flows of energy through the lower six "emotive" *sefirot* on the Tree of Life.

Midrash (pl. midrashim): A collection of inspirational stories dating from about the third to eighth centuries C.E.

Mikvah: Ritual bath.

Mishnah: Oral Law and tradition; this predates codified Jewish law.

Mitzvah (pl. mitzvot): A Divine commandment or good deed. According to the Bible, there are 613 *mitzvot*.

Nefesh: The physical level of the human soul that dissolves upon death.

Neshamah: That portion of the soul that continues after the death of the physical body.

Netzach: Victory. The *sefirah* expressing perseverance and motion.

Ofanim: Wheels, as seen in Ezekiel's vision of the Chariot.

Pirkei Avot: The Ethics of the Fathers. A collection of aphorisms, ethics, and conduct found in the Talmud.

Ruach: The portion of the human soul intermediate between *nefesh* and the *neshamah* and equated with emotions.

Ruach Hakadosh: Holy Spirit; the mystical experience of Divine revelation.

Satan: A servant of the Divine who offers evil as an option of free will.

Sefer Yetzirah: Book of Creation. Earliest known Hebrew mystical text.

Sefirah (pl. sefirot): Ten Divine energy essences (or vessels) on the Tree of Life.

Seraphim: Described by the prophet Isaiah as glowing angelic beings.

Tallis: A four-cornered prayer shawl with fringes, worn by Jewish men during prayer.

Talmud: Commentaries on the Oral Law, including the codified record of it.

Tanya: It Has Been Taught. A work by Rabbi Schneur Zalman of Liadi.

Tefillin: Phylacteries worn during morning prayers by observant Jewish men and boys over the age of thirteen.

Teshuvah: Repentance and return to Divine source of origin.

Tetragrammaton: The four Hebrew letters that represent the name of God: YHVH.

Tiferet: Beauty, the *sefirah* of the heart.

Tikkun (pl. tikkunim): Divine repairing or redemption of the universe.

Tohu: Confusion and chaos.

Torah: Also known as Pentateuch; the Five Books of Moses or first five books of the Bible.

Tree of Life: Main symbol of Kabbalah, the ten *sefirot* and twenty-two paths.

Tzadik (pl. tzadikim): Righteous one.

Tzimtzum: Contraction. The first act of creation, allowing the universe to emerge.

Yechidah: This represents *Adam Kadmon,* the primordial being, the "unique essence," or the idea of creation. It is the highest level of soul. Like the level of soul of *chayah,* this is only experienced in the world to come.

Yesod: Foundation or formation. One of the ten *sefirot.*

Yetzer hara: Evil inclination.

Yetzer tov: Good inclination.

Yetzirah: Third of the four universes denoting the world of emotions.

Zohar: Book of Splendor. A classical mystical text upon which much of Kabbalah is based.

· INDEX ·

PENNY COHEN, LCSW, has been counseling, lecturing, and conducting workshops nationally at professional conferences, universities, and organizations on personal, career, and spiritual development and on Kabbalah for the past fifteen years. She holds a Master's degree in social work from Columbia University, is a licensed psychotherapist, certified hypnotherapist, EMDR practitioner, and Life Coach. Twenty years ago, as a result of a personal mystical experience, she became interested in spiritual and peak experiences, higher states of consciousness, and finding purpose. She became a student of esoteric philosophy, Hinduism, Buddhism, Shamanism, and then, finally, Kabbalah, when she began studying with Hassidic rabbis and secular Kabbalah teachers. Discovering that the other philosophies fit into the universal paradigm of the kabbalistic Tree of Life, she became engrossed with it as a universal map offering a step-by-step progression for higher consciousness, purpose, and fulfillment. She integrates spirituality with psychotherapy in her private practice in Westchester County, New York, and works with individuals in person and by telephone and with groups. She also facilitates study groups. To learn more about Penny, please visit her website, www.PennyCohen.com, or contact her at Penny@PennyCohen.com.